Simon Fenwick is an aut[...] worked on the papers of b[...] Wordsworth, as well as for various country houses, private individuals and charities. He has also written for *The Times*, *Telegraph*, *Independent* and *Guardian* as well as for a number of magazines.

Praise for *The Crichel Boys*

'Fascinating' Laura Freeman, *The Times*

'Very entertaining . . . the preservation of old houses, a cause with which many of the leading characters were involved one way or another, is skilfully used as a running theme in a book that, with a fine balance between nostalgia and clear-sightedness, commemorates a privileged world long since vanished' Peter Parker, *Spectator*

'Highly evocative . . . a portrait of an enchanted world' Ysenda Maxtone Graham, *Daily Mail*

'The Crichel boys . . . left behind merely a memory of charm, kindness and generosity, to which Fenwick pays a tender tribute' *Financial Times*

'A rich, luscious account of a postwar Britain that often gets lost' *Mail on Sunday*

'Fenwick, it must be said, is very much at home in this somewhat rarefied milieu, writes perceptively about the quartet's achievements and is sensitive to some of the problems caused by having four neurotic personalities intermittently at large under a single roof' D. J. Taylor, *Literary Review*

'Absorbing new history' Alexander Larman, *Observer*

'Fenwick gives us some fascinating vignettes of the often downplayed cultural life of post-war Britain' *The Lady*

The Crichel Boys

Scenes from England's Last Literary Salon

Simon Fenwick

CONSTABLE

CONSTABLE

First published in Great Britain in 2021 by Constable
This paperback edition published in 2022 by Constable

1 3 5 7 9 10 8 6 4 2

Copyright © Simon Fenwick, 2021

The moral right of the author has been asserted.

A CIP catalogue record for this book
is available from the British Library.

ISBN: 978-1-47213-248-2

Typeset in Garamond Pro by SX Composing DTP, Rayleigh, Essex
Printed and bound in Great Britain by Clays Ltd, Elcograf, S.p.A.

Papers used by Constable are from well-managed forests
and other responsible sources.

Constable
An imprint of
Little, Brown Book Group
Carmelite House
50 Victoria Embankment
London EC4Y 0DZ

An Hachette UK Company

www.hachette.co.uk

www.littlebrown.co.uk

Contents

Principal Characters

ALINGTON, NAPIER. Napier Alington succeeded to his title as the third Lord Alington and inherited the Crichel estate on the death of his brother in 1918. Indulged by his mother, he led a tumultuous life. Cecil Beaton wrote of his considerable charm but 'however much pitch he wallowed in it never stuck.'[1]

BOWEN, ELIZABETH. An Anglo-Irish novelist, Elizabeth Bowen's books bear the mark of her troubled childhood. She inherited Bowen's Court in County Cork from her father but the house was sold in 1960 and subsequently demolished. Her wartime affair with Charles Ritchie, a Canadian diplomat, was probably the happiest relationship of her life.

GRANT, DUNCAN. A member of the 'Bloomsbury Group', Duncan Grant was also involved with the Crichel Boys. Together with Vanessa Bell he decorated Raymond Mortimer's flat at 6 Gordon Place. In 1926 he had an affair with Eddy Sackville-West. He also designed fabrics for Long Crichel and painted pictures of both Eardley Knollys and Desmond Shawe-Taylor. In later years he lodged in the basement of Patrick Trevor-Roper's London house.

HILL, DEREK. The last of the Crichel Boys, Derek Hill came to Long Crichel after giving his house in Ireland to the Irish state. He only paid rent and never had a financial share in the property. After an eventful youth, Hill made a career as an artist. Despite being a portrait painter to the establishment, he always resented his lack of greater recognition. A friend of the Prince of Wales.

JEBB, JULIAN. The grandson of Hilaire Belloc, Julian Jebb was brought up in an atmosphere of intense Catholicism, but later lost his faith. A natural enthusiast, he was an affectionate – if over-emotional – friend to many people. He worked principally for the BBC, but really wanted an artistic career of his own. Eventually drink and drugs caused his life to fall apart.

KNOLLYS, EARDLEY. Eardley Knollys had a background in estate management and, together with Desmond Shawe-Taylor, discovered Long Crichel House. A partner in the Storran Gallery with Frank Coombs until it closed on the outbreak of war, he subsequently worked for the National Trust. He owned a flat in West Halkin Street close to Frances Partridge.

LEES-MILNE, JAMES. Apart from a short time before and during the war, 'Jim' Lees-Milne worked for the National Trust from 1936 until his retirement. He was chiefly responsible for directing the Trust towards the rescue of historic houses. As well as writing a number of books relating to architecture and history, he was one of the twentieth century's great diarists. Lees-Milne's wife Alvilde and he had a stormy relationship.

LEHMANN, ROSAMOND. Rosamond Lehmann came from a gifted family. Her great-grandfather, Robert Chambers, was co-founder of the publishing firm Chambers. Lehmann's novels deal with the role of women and matters like abortion and homosexuality.

She married twice and lived with the poet Cecil Day-Lewis. Traumatised by the death of her daughter Sally, Lehmann turned to spiritualism and became vice-president of the College of Psychic Studies.

MACAULAY, ROSE. A stalwart of the London literary scene, Rose Macaulay published poetry, novels and literary criticism. In 1932 the literary critic Queenie Leavis described her books as upper middle-brow bestsellers, 'to be found on the shelves of dons, the superior kind of schoolmaster, and in the average well-to-do home.'[2]

MARTEN, MARY ANNA. The only child of Napier Alington, Mary Anna inherited the extensive Crichel estate as an eleven-year-old. In 1949 she married Toby Marten, a naval officer, who instigated the inquiry which became known as the Crichel Down affair.

MITFORD, NANCY. A novelist and the oldest of the Mitford Girls, the daughters of Lord and Lady Redesdale. Raymond Mortimer and Evelyn Waugh were Nancy Mitford's principal literary advisors. Eddy Sackville-West was the model for the hypochondriac 'Uncle Davey' in her novels *The Pursuit of Love* and *Love in a Cold Climate*.

MONTAGU, EDWARD. Inherited the title of 3rd Baron Montagu and the Montagu estate at Beaulieu in Hampshire as a child. In 1954 he was prosecuted together with Peter Wildeblood and Michael Pitt-Rivers for conspiring to incite acts of gross indecency with two RAF servicemen and spent eight months in gaol. The case subsequently led to the Wolfenden Committee report. He also founded the Montagu Motor Museum and the Beaulieu Jazz Festival.

MORTIMER, RAYMOND. A protégé of the Bloomsbury group, Raymond bought a share in Long Crichel House several years after Eardley, Eddy and Desmond, and was the oldest of the four Crichel

Boys. He wrote for both the *New Statesman* and the *Sunday Times*. As well as Long Crichel, he also shared houses near Henley in Oxfordshire and in Canonbury Square in Islington with the architect Paul Hyslop.

NICOLSON, HAROLD and SACKVILLE-WEST, VITA. Harold Nicolson was a diplomat, a politician, and a writer and diarist; Vita Sackville-West was both a writer and garden designer. Both had relationships with partners of their own sex, yet their marriage remained loving and strong. Vita was Eddy's cousin. She resented the fact that he was heir to Knole which made the relationship between the two difficult.

ORWELL, SONIA. Born in India, Sonia Orwell (née Brownwell) came to England in 1927. After schooling in Switzerland, she came to England and worked as a model for the Euston School of Painting and Drawing. Through her lover, the painter William Coldstream, she encountered Cyril Connolly and Stephen Spender and the literary world including George Orwell whom she married. He died three months later. Subsequently she had a disastrous marriage to Michael Pitt-Rivers on his release from gaol.

PARTRIDGE, FRANCES. 'Fanny' Partridge came from a Lake District family. After Cambridge she worked in the Bloomsbury bookshop of Birrell and Garnett where she came to know, among others, Leonard and Virginia Woolf, John Maynard Keynes, Lytton Strachey, and Ralph Partridge with whom she fell in love and married. A diarist of Bloomsbury and Long Crichel and the longest lived of the original Bloomsbury generation.

RADEV, MATTEI. A refugee from Bulgaria who arrived in England in 1950. In 1957 Radev met Eardley Knollys and Eddy Sackville-West, an encounter which, unintentionally, disrupted the arrangements at Long Crichel. He also had an intense relationship with E. M. Forster.

RYLANDS, GEORGE 'DADIE'. Rylands was always called 'Dadie' because he could not pronounce 'baby' as an infant. After Eton he went to Kings College, Cambridge and spent the rest of his life there. Taken up by the Bloomsbury Group because of his intellect, good looks and 'pussy cat smile'. He also became an influential theatre director.

SACKVILLE-WEST, EDWARD 'EDDY'. One of the original three owners of Long Crichel House. Previously he had lived in the gate house at Knole in Kent. A novelist and a music critic, he worked for the BBC during World War II. In 1955 he bought Cooleville, a house in County Tipperary and afterwards he divided his life between Cooleville and Long Crichel.

SHAWE-TAYLOR, DESMOND. The youngest of the original three Crichel Boys who bought Long Crichel House in 1945. Desmond was Anglo-Irish and he wrote on music, principally for both the *New Statesman* and the *Sunday Times*.

TREVOR-ROPER, PATRICK 'PAT'. The younger brother of the historian Hugh Trevor-Roper, Pat was an internationally famous ophthalmologist. A keen traveller, he was a campaigner for many causes including gay rights and the conservation of old buildings.

WALKER, SEBASTIAN. Frances Partridge called Sebastian Walker 'a gossip hound and social climber.'[3] He had a stellar career in publishing and founded Walker Books which published books for children. Died of AIDS in 1991.

Introduction

By the end of the war large areas of the English countryside were looking forlorn. A green and pleasant land had been turned into a land of Nissen huts, barbed wire and aerodromes. The Home Guard had removed or painted over all the signposts, milestones and railway-station signs in order to confuse the battalions of German parachutists who had been expected to descend from the sky but never arrived. Without signposts, not only the enemy but all outsiders, however benign, were likely to get hopelessly lost when deep in unfamiliar countryside and with no one to ask the way. A small, secluded village like Long Crichel in Dorset must have seemed more remote than ever.

Long Crichel was the village which, in the spring of 1945, two men set out to find. They were coming to inspect a house for sale. Desmond Shawe-Taylor was a captain in military intelligence waiting to be demobbed. Eardley Knollys, his companion, was Assistant Secretary to the National Trust and his job entitled him to the use of a car and a petrol allowance. He particularly wanted a house which was within reasonable distance of Bath, where his widowed mother lived. The house also had to accommodate a third friend, Eddy Sackville-West, who was to join him in buying somewhere as a holiday home and week-end retreat. During the war Sackville-West had been a BBC producer.

Long Crichel House was an old rectory built in the time of Queen Anne. It had six acres of garden and the parish church was directly beside it. There was no electricity. Dark and full of shadows inside, the house was lit only by gas-lamps and candles, and the water supply was inadequate. They were informed by the surveyor that an outbreak of typhoid in a neighbouring town had been traced to the effluent water from the septic tank of a mansion owned by one of his clients nearby. They decided however that this was the house they were looking for; although Eddy Sackville-West did not go to see it for himself, he agreed to buy a third share anyway.

Despite all its apparent drawbacks by the end of the year Long Crichel House had become warm and welcoming. There was always good food on the table, generous quantities of drink and excellent conversation. In the warmer months there was croquet on the lawn. But everything that took place happened in the aftermath of war – two men from the village had been killed during the fighting, and the RAF had dropped practice bombs on land close by. Even so, this was where, in such an improbable place, the last literary salon in England began.

The salon was the product of a leisured society, and it has had a long history. In London during the inter-war years hostesses like Sybil Colefax and Emerald Cunard held court in their drawing rooms, and, insofar as they were able, they continued to do so even after the war had started. Both social devotees and scalp-hunters, they delighted in bringing their guests together as if they were cocktails mixed with improbable ingredients. After her house was bombed Emerald Cunard found rooms on the seventh floor of the Dorchester Hotel and carried on as before. With the war all around, banging and crashing above and below, even in the most deafening moments she paid no attention. 'War is so vulgar,' she said.

Long Crichel was always much quieter and less formal. Hosts and guests were not expected to dress for dinner. The architectural historian Jim Lees-Milne, who loved the house and its residents, deplored their lack of fastidiousness. The owners generally wore woolly jumpers. Raymond Mortimer, who very soon joined the other three in this nest of bachelors, was forever covered in cigarette ash. Patrick Trevor-Roper, a later co-owner, used to sit around in his vest. When Desmond's young nephews came to visit they were given a little table of their own beside the main one. Long Crichel was post-war literary salon as communal living – and probably not quite of the standard which Lady Cunard would have had in mind for the Dorchester.

However, she would have approved of, even envied, the Crichel Boys' friendships and connections. The visitors' books reveal a kind of *Who's Who* of the arts, particularly from the worlds of literature and music, in post-war Britain: Nancy Mitford, Benjamin Britten, Laurie Lee, Cyril Connolly, Graham Sutherland, Somerset Maugham, Elisabeth Schumann, Lennox Berkeley, E.M. Forster, Greta Garbo, Cecil Beaton, Vita Sackville-West and Harold Nicolson, and very many more. After a visit Rosamond Lehmann wrote a letter of thanks saying she looked on Long Crichel as one of her 'treats and pleasures'. More than this, Long Crichel became known as a 'prose factory'. Not only did its denizens find it a conducive place to work, but so did its visitors. Patrick Leigh Fermor came to the house intending to write. Lees-Milne and Frances Partridge, two of the twentieth century's finest diarists, were guests at Long Crichel so often they practically lived there, and they wrote about the house and its residents frequently.

Yet there was to be more to the story of the house than what a critic called a group of 'hyphenated gentleman-aesthetes', men who delighted in one another's company in an era of battery radios, shellac records, long letters and diaries. In the years that followed, the village saw a national scandal at government level which filled the papers for days on end. A local sex scandal filled the very same newspapers, as did the Wolfenden Report which followed in its wake, and the AIDS crisis resonated here years later. The story of Long Crichel is also part of the development of the National Trust and other conservation movements. The spring morning on which Desmond Shawe-Taylor and Eardley Knollys set out to look for a house in a remote Dorset village they found themselves not only on the threshold of an old rectory but also on the threshold of the history of more than fifty years of British society.

It was January the first time I went to Long Crichel. Having travelled down from London I was collected at Salisbury station and driven along narrow twisting high-hedged lanes into unfamiliar countryside. The day was damp and grey and sunless but the house, when we arrived half an hour later, could not have seemed more welcoming. Rose and Jamie Campbell, the owners, showed me around, going up and down staircases, into bedrooms and the attics in the roof. There were stacks of paintings, piles of books and, among Long Crichel's prized possessions, a luggage label which had once belonged to Henry James. I wandered round the kitchen garden and looked at visitors' books and photograph albums in front of the drawing room fire. By the time I left it was evening and, in the twilight, the patches of snowdrops in the garden and the churchyard and the lichen glistening on the church walls looked like snow.

The late Janetta Parladé, Rose Campbell's mother, suggested I write this book. She died the summer after I first visited Long Crichel. I am deeply grateful to her and can only hope that she would have been pleased with what I have written. I thank Rose and Jamie for their hospitality and for their assistance and stories. I also thank Michael Bloch; Joey Casey; Laura Cecil; Norman Coates; David Fenwick; Lady Selina Hastings; Harley Mitford; Lord Sackville; Chris Sandford; Desmond Shawe-Taylor; John Shawe-Taylor; Maurice Sheppard; Richard Shone; Father Julian Shurgold; Julianne Simpson; Damaris Stewart; Olivia Stewart; Nick Tatham; Jochen Voigt. I am also grateful to my agent Michael Alcock of Johnson and Alcock, and my editor Andreas Campomar and his colleagues at Little, Brown.

I am grateful too for access and archival help from Patricia McGuire and Peter Montieth at King's College, Cambridge; Adrian Glew at Tate Gallery Archives; Kirsty McHugh, National Library of

Scotland; Michael Rush and Dolores Colon at the Beinicke Library, Yale University, New Haven, Connecticut; Isabel Planton at the Lilly Library, Indiana University; Squirrel Walsh at Princeton University Library, Princeton, New Jersey. I also owe much to the staff and resources of the London Library.

The extract from *In Tearing Haste: Letters Between Deborah Devonshire and Patrick Leigh Fermor* is published courtesy of the Literary Executors of Patrick Leigh Fermor. Letters of James Lees-Milne © Michael Bloch. Letters of Frances Partridge © Sophie Partridge and Gill Coleridge, RCW Literary Agency.

Extracts from letters appear with the permission of the Provost and Scholars of King's College, Cambridge.

This book is dedicated to Ian Maxwell, my oldest friend. Much of the research for *The Crichel Boys* was done in Cambridge and discussed over lunch with him. I am grateful for his advice and opinions and a lifetime of conversation.

London and Long Crichel, August 2020

1

Two Houses

Sometime in the 1970s or 1980s (the letter is dated 18 December but no year is given) an elderly lady sent a packet of photographs to a man whose name she did not know and had never met before. She addressed the envelope to an anonymous 'The Owner, the Old Rectory, Long Crichel, Dorset'. Doubtless she hoped for a reply and some appreciation for her unexpected gift.

The rather frail writer was a rector's daughter called St Barbe Hill. The unusual Christian name is unexplained. At the time the ownership of the rectory was shared by three men, but the man who wrote back to St Barbe was a doctor called Patrick Trevor-Roper. The aspect of medicine in which Trevor-Roper specialised was ophthalmology: he was an authority on the structure, functions and diseases of the eye, and in this field he was internationally famous. Old houses and their preservation were another passion. Pat, as he was generally known, was also an ardent and very active supporter of gay rights. So far as we know, Pat and St Barbe never met. She lived in Surrey, and she rarely left her house. She told him she suffered from Menière's disease, which would have given her dizzy spells and made her unsteady on her feet. However, they corresponded about the rectory and its history. The photographs, or 'snaps' as she called them, were pictures of Long Crichel rectory as it had been at the end of the First World War. Pat copied the photographs and sent them back to St Barbe, but she returned them again: 'not because I do not like them, but no one else is interested in the house, never having known it, and I am ancient now and would not like them to be cast away in the future'.

St Barbe told Pat how her father, the Reverend Mr H.B. M'Neil-Smith, had once been the rector of Long Crichel. After the departure of his predecessor Mr Emlyn James in October 1917 M'Neil-Smith arrived in the parish with his wife and family. St Barbe was nine at the time. In the photographs her parents and other members of the family and friends sit in deckchairs or stand on the rectory's croquet lawn. In one of the pictures she is identified as a dark-haired girl in a frock who is standing with one hand on her pony's head. There is another girl on the pony's back, and there is a little French boy in the same photograph. St Barbe seems tall for her age. Her father is a tall man in a dog collar at the edge of the group.

She also wrote down some of her random recollections. There was a big stable block with six stalls and a hayloft, a coach house and a backyard outside the kitchen door with clothes lines. The house was bitterly cold in winter and the plumbing was still primitive – there were earth-closets in the stables, and the water was never more than lukewarm. The drive continued around the back of the house; later it was moved to the other side when it became the front entrance. The windows were also enlarged. Both St Barbe and her father used to get around the village on bicycles. She went by pony and trap to Blandford Forum to catch the train to Bournemouth when she went to school. She once played Peaseblossom in *A Midsummer Night's Dream* at Gussage All Saints, a village rather larger than Long Crichel nearby.

And then in 1919 a number of people including M'Neil-Smith's wife and the cook fell ill. St Barbe was not allowed to come home, so she stayed at her school in Bournemouth. Both the cook and Mrs M'Neil-Smith recovered, but the rector's wife's heart was weakened and soon afterwards she died. She was buried in the churchyard at the end of the garden. Her husband could not bear to stay in a house so close to her grave, and so he exchanged his parish with the Rev Mr

H.B. Harris, a vicar in Wiltshire. M'Neil-Smith, St Barbe and her two brothers moved to Wiltshire, where they lived in a Georgian vicarage, and eventually the rector married again. (Pat used to claim gleefully that according to village gossip Mrs M'Neil-Smith had been murdered by her husband.) Mr Harris moved into the rectory at Long Crichel and lived there for more than a decade.

The former rectory at Long Crichel is separated from the church at the back of the churchyard by a fence and a gate which leads into the garden. There are also just over six acres of kitchen garden, which was formerly the rector's glebe. The house is large, rambling and architecturally untidy. It was built in the time of Queen Anne as a dower house for the widow of a former member of the local landowning family, the Sturts, but over the course of time there have been various alterations and accretions. This very untidiness gives the house its character. On the outside of the west-facing wall, between two Victorian windows, there is a large square plaque with a Latin inscription:

> This house was repaired, enlarged, and extended for the use of the rectors, and the churches of both Crichels consolidated and endowed in perpetuity with the lands adjacent to this dwelling, at the instance and personal expense of Sir Humphrey Sturt the true and undoubted patron, who, amid larger endeavours, was carried off by the unforeseen force of death on XIII calends November AD1786.*

In 1930 Mr Harris placed an advertisement in the 'Cars for Sale' column: '4-seater all-weather "Vulcan", leather upholstered, good condition, £30, Rector, Long Crichel'. He was leaving and wanted a new car. His replacement as rector, with an income of £460 a year, was the Reverend Mr Tom Floyd. Perhaps it was the remoteness of

---

* i.e. 20 October 1786.

the parish which had caused Mr Floyd to apply for the position. For nearly twenty years he had lived in South Africa in the midst of a large, sprawling, railway hub in the suburbs of Cape Town called Maitland. Long Crichel could scarcely have been more different. His correspondence with the local estate includes letters relating to the Church of England School, the almshouses, the tithes and rectory, and three farms – Higher, Middle and Lower – in the village and Holly Grove Farm immediately to the east.

Between the wars Long Crichel was, as it remains, little more than several cottages, the church and rectory, and a few farms scattered around the village. There was neither a pub nor a shop, although there was a small school and a cabin which sold cigarettes and sweets. The station five miles away at Blandford Forum was on a line which connected Bath to Bournemouth and several of the small towns in between. Long Crichel was mentioned in the local newspapers in the columns which advertised for kitchen maids or dairymen. Sometimes there was trouble from trespassers or poachers out for game and rabbits, and there were reports of rowdy motorcyclists and of damage caused by gypsies. But, as is recorded by the *Western Gazette* in the summer of 1930, sometimes there was also violence. The case involved Lower Farm, which is beside the parish church. Bertie Cutler the farmer wanted to evict a dairyman called Harris from his cottage and replace him with a new worker:

A lively scene, with a fight between a dairyman and a farmer was described to the Wimborne Bench on Friday during the hearing of assault preferred by Bertie Cutler, of Lower Farm, Long Crichel, against his former dairyman, Berkeley William Harris . . . Asked to leave the premises, defendant rushed at [Cutler] again, grabbed him and tried to pull him down, tripped him up on some boards, and still pressed and grabbed at his throat with both hands, remarking with an oath, 'I will do you in,' and tried to strangle him. Harris almost hooked his left eye out with his thumb and bashed his right eye with his fist. Mr Miller came up and told Harris to get off him, and his (Cutler's) wife asked him to leave. Defendant said with an oath he would punch her. Whilst witness was on the ground Harris told Miller that he would catch Miller alone and use his boots on him. Miller eventually got defendant off the premises, and witness was helped upstairs to bed by his wife. He threw up a pint of blood, had two ribs broken, and was bruised.[1]

The dairyman pleaded not guilty, but the magistrate fined him ten shillings and costs.

Long Crichel and its twin village Moor Crichel, a mile or so away, are on Cranborne Chase in the north-east of Dorset. They are sited in the midst of narrow, twisting country lanes with high hedgerows which have probably grown there for centuries. This is an ancient landscape – traces of prehistoric settlements are plentiful. Twenty-four round barrows are contained within the parish limits, and the old Roman road from Dorchester to London crosses the Sturt family estate at Moor Crichel. In 1930 most of the land in the area was owned by the Sturts. Their estate covered some 18,000 acres, both in Dorset and in the East End of London. There were 354 people in the parish: most of the men worked on farms; most of the women were in domestic service.

There are two churches. St Mary's at Long Crichel has a late medieval tower which is attached to a mid-Victorian nave, transepts and apse. Inside on the north wall there is a plaque commemorating the five villagers killed in the Great War: William George Frampton, Ernest George Rendall, Arthur John Maidment, Harry Bennett, Charles Bennett. Beneath their names the legend reads: 'They are in Peace'. There is a Noah's Ark made from carved stone in a niche by the communion rail in the chancel; animals look out on the congregation, and the figurehead at the prow is the head of a camel.

The second church is at Moor Crichel, a village of only a handful of widely dispersed houses and farms which is even smaller than its neighbour. The Victorian church is also dedicated to the Virgin. It sits on the lawn immediately in front of Crichel House, the eighteenth-century Sturt family mansion. Inside the church the family pews have high doors, which were upholstered in crimson velvet with comfortably padded seats. Both house and village were rebuilt when Sir Humphrey Sturt inherited the estate in 1765. He decided to landscape the grounds to his new house in the manner of Capability Brown, and to do so he drowned the original medieval village, which now lies under a lake in front of the house. In May 1925 *Country Life* published three long articles dedicated to Crichel House, its architecture and its gardens. The photographs accompanying the articles show sparsely furnished rooms with double-height ceilings decorated with plaster mouldings, shaped into coves and cornices with scrolls as delicate and fanciful as the sugar-icing piped on wedding cakes.*

The Sturts had the right to appoint the rector to the living. When Tom Floyd arrived at Long Crichel the estate's owner was Napier – 'Naps' – Sturt, the third Lord Alington, a descendant of the Humphrey Sturt who had rebuilt the rectory. Napier's father had been a Conservative MP, a striking figure known in Parliament both for his nickname 'Trotters' and for the gorgeousness of the scarlet carnation he always wore in his buttonhole. On his farm everything – cattle, dogs, poultry – was entirely white. Trotters and his wife, Féodorovna, or 'Féo', were friends of Edward VII, who was a regular visitor to Crichel House.

Féo, 'a permanently recumbent Brünhilde', had two boys, Gerard and Napier. They were very unalike: Napier's actual father was probably Prince Marcantonio Colonna, the assistant to the Pontifical Throne, the highest lay dignitary in the Catholic Church. After war was declared in 1914, Gerard, the elder son, became a lieutenant in

---

* Photographers were in the habit of choreographing the furniture so that rooms looked completely different from how they were actually lived in.

the Coldstream Guards. He had been engaged to be married, but after having been wounded early in the war he was confined to a wheelchair, and he broke off his engagement. On Armistice Day 1918 he died in the arms of his valet. When Napier heard that his brother Gerard was dead he went into the woods and shot off the fourth finger of his left hand. Later he made this less obvious by keeping the next two fingers together in a sort of point and by wearing a ring with a blue stone on his little finger. Napier's father died the following year, and Napier succeeded to his title and the estate's vast property and wealth.

Napier was born in 1896. After Eton he was supposed to study at Christ Church, Oxford. But when he arrived in Oxford he joined up immediately. He probably did not stay long enough to unpack before he returned home. His name is not even recorded on the Christ Church First World War roll of honour, which includes the names of those men who survived as well as those who gave their lives. He spent the war in the Royal Flying Corps, watching out for enemy aircraft on the south coast of England.

In January 1921, at the age of twenty-four, Napier went to learn about banking. Mrs Cornelius Vanderbilt had arranged a job for him at the Guaranty Trust Company, a huge financial institution in downtown New York. Lord Amherst, an Eton contemporary working as a journalist on the *New York Morning World*, claimed that Napier seldom got to bed before two or three in the morning and would struggle into the subway in a dazed condition to get to his office just before opening time. Amherst once asked him what he did there: 'But he was not too sure – something to do with mailing lists he thought.'

While Mrs Vanderbilt took her duties as the queen of New York society seriously, her visitor was more interested in tasting the pleasures of the Jazz Age, which was by then in full flower. One evening she threw a huge dinner party in his honour only for Napier at the last moment to beg to be excused on account of a splitting headache. The following morning Mrs Vanderbilt came across the most handsome of her footmen half asleep in the doorway. On demanding an explanation, he told her he had spent the night roaming Harlem with her aristocratic guest. The Polish composer Karol Szymanowski was so taken with Napier that he dedicated his 'Songs of an Infatuated Muezzin' to him.

Napier's many lovers were of both sexes, and they included the actress Tallulah Bankhead.[2] They first met at an impromptu party in Greenwich Village when he turned up wearing a coat over his pyjamas and carrying a bottle of bootleg gin in his pocket. 'We were together constantly in the winter of '21–22,' she wrote in her autobiography. 'Though thirty years have elapsed I vividly recall breakfasts – eggs benedict at the Brevoort on early Sunday afternoons, dancing with him in the early hours of the morning at Reisenweber's, a gay place which flourished in the Columbus Circle. Here we'd be accompanied by a frustrated young Englishman, then living on herbs and berries – Noel Coward.'[3] She said that he offered to marry her, but she turned him down because she wanted to concentrate on her career. As a lover he was an impossible conundrum: sometimes loving and generous; sometimes the very opposite. Alington was the love of Bankhead's tumultuous life: 'Sporadically, I was in love with him for years. But my love was mixed with resentment. He was a riddle I couldn't solve, which made him all the more attractive, all the more desirable, he was unpredictable, irresponsible. He rarely kept appointments, always had the most disarming excuses.'[4]

At one of the Count Etienne de Beaumont's celebrated masked balls in Paris he arrived dressed as the Sun King, his skin painted soft gold. By the time he left he had lost his Louis XIV facemask, his golden stockings, his underwear and his filigree figleaf. He departed completely naked.

In November 1928 Napier married Lady Mary Ashley-Cooper, the daughter of his Dorset neighbour, the 9th Earl of Shaftesbury, at St Margaret's in Westminster. In the society columns Lady Mary was described as tall and strong and the best swimmer in Mayfair. At her wedding she carried a sheaf of lilies and wore a large aquamarine pendant which was a gift of the groom. The newly married couple received almost a thousand wedding gifts – including large pieces of furniture and 'a platoon of wastepaper baskets in mass formation'. Napier was interested in contemporary art and gave £500 on loan towards the setting up of the Redfern Gallery in Bond Street. Dora Carrington met him at Fryern Court, Augustus John's studio near Fordingbridge in Hampshire, when his wife was heavily pregnant. In a letter to Lytton Strachey she wrote:

> In half an hour another car, Naps Alington, his cousin Philip Yorke, both half naked in vests and a ravishing female beauty a cousin of Nap's wife (who is bulging with child so didn't come). They had been swimming at Kimmeridge. They lingered for [an] hour, carrying on a most extraordinary patois between themselves . . . We got back at half past 10 to Fryern, at 11 o'ck Naps and his cousin Yorke came reeling in, Naps looking marvellous in a complete evening dress of black velvet. He is a very odd character, looks Jewish and Russian. He gave strange accounts of freaks at fairs. He has a passion for them. They stayed till 2 o'ck, getting drunker and drunker. Naps has an appalling cough. I do not think he will live long. But I thought for pure S[ex] A[ppeal] he had more than almost any man I have met . . . I worked all Thursday at my painting. And in the afternoon came over here for tea. Lady Mary is here. So beautiful that I can do nothing, but gaze with rapture.[5]

Mary Anna Sturt, the only child of the Alingtons' marriage, was born in September 1929. The Wall Street Crash at the New York Stock Exchange took place the following month and, in the words of F. Scott Fitzgerald, the Jazz Age leaped to a spectacular death. The Crash was followed by the Great Depression, the effects of which were felt all over the world. In 1933, in an attempt to alleviate the suffering on his own estates, Alington offered to feed, house and train in agricultural work on his property in Dorset twenty-five of the unemployed from the slums of Hoxton and Shoreditch which they also owned.* When the plans were made public, they were besieged by applications from all over London. The Mayor of Shoreditch promised to provide each man with a pair of suitable boots. There were also offers of blankets and bedding, and arrangements for recreation were made for the men at Wimborne Minster a few miles away. Each individual was fed and received five shillings pocket money at the beginning of each week. On their arrival it was reported that the men were 'unaccustomed at first to the vivid contrast even in their drab existence of life "far from the madding crowd" with dark lanes, unprotected ditches and the monotony of rural surroundings' but the locals, who had been suspicious at first, accepted the newcomers in their midst. The Lloyds gave them lantern lectures about their years in Africa, and Lord Alington gave a talk on Dorset. After having taken part in forestry, carpentry, painting and work on the Crichel golf links the men returned to London for Christmas. The Mayor of Shoreditch stated that the men were changed physically, and that they were eager to resume the healthy life they had been leading for the last three months. However paternalistic it might seem, this life was doubtless better than the East End dole queue.

Napier meanwhile decided that Crichel House was too expensive to run. In an attempt to economise he thought it would be a good idea to move into a much smaller house close by. At the last moment he decided it should be slightly enlarged. It was a hopelessly false economy. Years later he was still fussing and changing things – and doubtless making life difficult for Paul Hyslop,† his architect.

In May 1935 the young, would-be writer Paddy Leigh Fermor met

---

* There is still a Sturt Street in Hoxton.

† Charles Geddes Clarkson 'Paul' Hyslop (1900–1988). Hyslop was fashionable among the British upper classes. His work was notable for its sensitivity to detail and an exquisite sense of colour. Vanessa Bell referred to him as 'Curly Lips'.

Napier Alington in Athens. On his walk across Europe from Rotterdam to Constantinople Leigh Fermor had met Balasha Cantacuzene, a Romanian princess with whom he was having an affair. Alington was a friend of Balasha, and he became a friend of Leigh Fermor, who, more than sixty years later, recalled some of his memories in a letter to Deborah, the Duchess of Devonshire. Napier had 'a slightly *lifted* tone of voice, the sort that Douglas Byng, the cabaret star and female impersonator, used to imitate or aspired to, and was unbelievably funny and warm. He was a mixture of *grand seigneur* and, in a way, of clown, in the sense of seeing comedy whoever it was and helping contribute to it.' In a palazzo in Rome Alington was tricked into entering a lift shaft because his host thought he was having an affair with his wife, and he fell thirty feet but recovered. The story was in the papers but not the reason why it came about. 'You would have loved him,' Paddy told Debo.

In 1937, as war began to seem a possibility, the Air Ministry started to look for new sites for bombing practice. After having examined five areas of land in Dorset they decided that a site at Long Crichel – Crichel Down – would be the most suitable. Local villagers were taken to Porton Down in Wiltshire to see a bombing-practice site already in use. The Long Crichel farmers, protesting that their livelihoods would be affected by the bombing, wanted an alternative site to be found near Blandford Forum, but Blandford Town Council objected that the range would prevent people from coming to the neighbourhood. A *Times* correspondent reported that 'someone from Crichel maintained that more houses would be near to the range if it were at Crichel. This was disputed by a Blandford visitor who said that anyway the real grievance at Crichel was that it would interfere with the partridge shooting. So the discussion went on in a somewhat parochial strain. On the whole, however, a disinterested observer gained the impression the Crichel site would be more suitable for the proposed bombing range.'

In August 1938 Hitler mobilised his troops and three quarters of a million men were sent to the Czech borders under the pretence that they were just on army manoeuvres. The BBC began broadcasting public-service messages about gas masks and evacuation plans for children. Neville Chamberlain, the Prime Minister, and Edouard Daladier, the Prime Minister of France, met in London on 18 September in order to coerce the Czechs into agreeing to the surrender of the Sudetenland (those areas of the Czech lands historically inhabited by Sudeten Germans). Capitulation took place over a good lunch, where claret (Château Margaux) and an 1865 cognac were served. 'In international diplomacy the darkest hour is generally before lunch,' said Chamberlain. On 28 September the MP and journalist Harold Nicolson recorded in his diary that Chamberlain had announced that Herr Hitler had agreed to a conference with Signor Mussolini and Monsieur Daladier in Munich. The House of Commons was ecstatic. He added later, 'I remained seated. Liddall* behind me, hissed out, "Stand up, you brute!"' The following day, 29 September, Nicolson wrote:

> The papers are ecstatic about Chamberlain. Raymond [Mortimer] rings me up and says, 'Isn't this ghastly?' Eddy rings me up and says 'Isn't this hell?' Margot Oxford† rings me up and says 'Now Harold you must agree that he is a great man?' I say 'Not at all.' 'You are as bad as Violet [Bonham Carter],'‡ she snaps, 'He is the greatest Englishman that ever lived.'
>
> It seems that my refusal to stand up yesterday when all the rest of the House went hysterical has made an impression. Everybody has heard of it. I was ashamed of the House yesterday; it was a Welsh revivalist meeting.[6]

---

* Walter Liddall, Conservative MP for Lincoln 1931–1945.

† Emma Margaret Asquith, Countess of Oxford and Asquith, second wife of H.H. Asquith PM until his death in 1928.

‡ Violet Bonham Carter, daughter of H.H. Asquith by his first wife.

Raymond Mortimer was Literary Editor of the *New Statesman* and an intimate friend of Nicolson. Paul Hyslop and he shared a cottage called The Bothy at Culham Court near Henley. Eddy Sackville-West was a cousin of Vita Sackville-West, Harold Nicolson's wife.

On 3 September 1939 Britain and France declared war on Germany, two days after Hitler's invasion of Poland. At the end of the month *Country Life* published an item, 'Country Houses Today':

> Readers of *Country Life* until a year ago were only too familiar with the appeals that we made from time to time to save this or that country house threatened with the pickaxe. In the last twelve months the situation has so completely changed that the most unmanageable white elephant of a mansion is now securely harnessed to the war-time machine. Indeed the more wings and outhouses a residence possesses the more desirable it has seemed. As emergency offices, storehouses, dormitories for evacuees, the interiors of these houses, still to outward appearance dreaming unconcernedly in their parks, present a spectacle that would have astonished their builders. A large number have been offered as hospitals, a great many more as schools. Donnington Hall again opens its hospitable doors to prisoners of war in place of racing motorists. Blenheim, Bowood and Corsham, Crichel, Attingham, Lillieshall Abbey and Finchcocks are among those into which evacuated schools, public and private have been transferred.

With the arrival of the boys from Dumpton House Preparatory School from Broadstairs in Kent, and its most precious treasures put into storage, Crichel House was turned into a school for the foreseeable future. Paddy Leigh Fermor's last weekend in England before he went abroad as a member of the Special Operations Executive (SOE) was spent at Crichel. Elsewhere in the house three young girls were staying in the same room – Napier's daughter Mary Anna, a cousin and a friend, all about ten years old. Napier thought it would be fun to haunt them, and he and Paddy crept into their room with loud moans and sheets over their heads. The girls adored it, and sat and shrieked with their arms clasped around their knees.

Wanting to relive his youth again, Naps Alington told Jeffrey Amherst that he intended to join the Royal Air Force. Given his age and health he appreciated that this would not be in a flying capacity; instead, he expected he would be a very junior officer and put to work in headquarters at some lowly desk job until his abilities were assessed. His much younger colleagues would be qualified in commercial or engineering skills. No doubt they would be completely mystified as to what this peer of the realm twenty years older than they were thought he was up to by being there at all. Nevertheless, as reckless as Naps might seem, he also possessed an extraordinary charm – a charm which had always got him safely around awkward corners. He pulled strings and got himself commissioned into the Administrative and Special Duties Branch of the Royal Air Force Volunteer Reserve, service number 83058. He was posted to Cairo. In Egypt he was popular with the younger men, and always ready for fun even if the habits of a lifetime made it impossible for him to give up late nights. He was no more able to get up in the mornings in time to be at his desk at 8.30 a.m. than he had been in New York twenty years earlier. 'One of the most charming and fascinating people who ever existed,' said Peter Coats, Lord Wavell's ADC, when he met him in a Cairo hotel bar: 'He is clearly here to spread charm.' But Napier was also disastrously self-destructive. One day the crew of a bomber invited him to join them in a personal capacity to go on a reconnaissance mission over Benghazi. Despite the fact that over 10,000 feet the temperature falls very low, he had not listened to warnings to put on thick flying clothes. When he landed after the mission he soon developed pneumonia. He was looked after by the daughter of an American financier called Momo Kahn at her parents' home on Zamalek Island. He died peacefully, more or less on active service and in uniform, which was what he would have wanted. Captain Napier Sturt, 3rd Baron Alington, was buried in the New Protestant Cemetery on the outskirts of Cairo next to a railway line. As he had no male heir, the title became extinct on his death.

On a damp depressing day in late September Cecil Beaton attended Napier's memorial service. He wrote in his diary:

Now that the inevitable has happened, one wonders why the impossible should not have continued: It is perhaps more shocking when someone near extinction for so long suddenly disappears . . .

The service in the chapel was a travesty. The arrangements were in the hands of a housekeeper–secretary whom Napier disliked, and the date had been peremptorily fixed without asking advice from relations or friends with the result that, war conditions being as they are, few intimates were able to be present. The vicar who gave the address assumed that Napier had been a conventional young peer, and obviously knew nothing of his audacity or courage, his sophisticated taste, bubbling fun, naughtiness and kindness. Napier would have chuckled at the description of himself but would have been pleased at the way his favourite extract from St Paul to the Corinthians – on charity – was read by old Lord Shaftesbury.

At the macabre tea-party which took place afterwards, I managed to escape to Napier's small sitting room. It is a room replete with so much personal charm and relics of his epoch, showing its owner as a dilettante in the arts. He was in no sense a connoisseur but had an avid interest in, and tremendous appreciation for, Chippendale furniture, Chinese jades and porcelain, jewels, English and French literature, the stage, the Russian ballet – almost every form of aesthetic manifestation . . .

Napier died at forty-three, a boy. A tired boy in appearance, but essentially young, with the willowy figure of a bantam-weight champion, a neat head covered with a cap of silken hair, pale far-seeing eyes and full negroid lips.

He made life seem almost bearable to a large number of people, many of whom will be hard put to continue without him.[7]

It rained on the day of the memorial service. The service, which Beaton so disliked, was conducted by the Reverend Emlyn James. In April 1939 the Reverend James had returned to the parish of Long with Moor Crichel from North Yorkshire. He had been rector here thirty years earlier as a much younger man from 1906 to 1917, before the arrival of Mr M'Neil-Smith and his wife and children, including his daughter St Barbe.

The rectory had already been sold by then and Mr James lived elsewhere. In 1937 the house was bought by a Miss Duncan from the Church Commissioners. Wellesley and Wills, one of the most fashionable architectural firms of the time, was asked to modernise it. The work was carried out by Gerald Wellesley, the future 7th Duke of Wellington, a practising architect and, together with Trenwith Wills, a partner in the firm. In effect he turned the building around. A new door was opened up and a new flight of stairs inserted. Individual sinks were built into the bedrooms and the plumbing improved. In 1939, however, the house stood empty until in November that year it was advertised as one of four properties for sale to a 'Discreet Buyer' for a total of £35,000 by Messrs Rawlence and Squarey of Salisbury.

2

Love and Melancholy:
The National Trust and War

Born in November 1901, Edward Charles Sackville-West was five years younger than Napier Alington. Like Napier, he too became heir to a barony and to a large country house. In his case the house was Knole in Kent. Henry VIII had liked Knole so much that in 1538 he forced Thomas Cranmer, his Archbishop of Canterbury, to give the house to him. In 1603 Thomas Sackville, 1st Earl of Dorset and Lord Treasurer to Elizabeth I, took possession of Knole, embellishing and extending it. Knole was transformed into one of the largest houses in the country and had remained in the hands of the Sackville family ever since.

Eddy – as he was always known – was the only son of Major-General Charles Sackville-West. His father had enjoyed a distinguished military career in the South African Wars. After the First World War, during which he saw active service in France, he became the British military representative on the war council, and from 1920 to 1924 he was in Paris as a military attaché. He also had a reputation as a ladies' man. Eddy was completely different: homosexual, an aesthete to his fingertips and not remotely militaristic. His mother died when he was only nineteen, and although there was mutual affection, relations with his father were often strained.

Because of his father's career his early life was itinerant. He lived out of suitcases, either staying in hotels or with relations or travelling abroad. He felt most at home in Bourne Park in Kent, which belonged to his mother's family. Knole was a house he scarcely knew and never greatly cared for. When he was young it was lived in by his reclusive great-uncle, the second Lord Sackville, who suffered from what Eddy called 'the temperamental melancholy which dogs all Sackvilles and has driven many of them to end their lives in blackest solitude'.

After a preparatory school in Enfield, Eddy attended Eton College. One of his teachers was Aldous Huxley. Eddy told Sybille Bedford, Huxley's biographer, that he must have been one of the most incompetent schoolmasters who ever faced a class. The boys in the back row but one turned their backs on the rest of the form and made up a bridge four with boys in the back row: 'The majority simply conversed in loud voices. It was useless in that pandemonium . . . From time to time Aldous would pause, look up, and say in an imploring tone, "Oh! Do be quiet!" No one took the slightest notice.'[1] Despite having Aldous Huxley as a teacher, Eddy thrived academically. He was also an outstanding pianist and his performances were highly praised in the school magazines. In 1918 he was awarded the school music prize. Eddy was short and slim, and from the Sackvilles he inherited the heavy lids which accentuated his own air of 'temperamental melancholy'. Like his sister Diana he had also inherited from their mother telangiectasia, an abnormal dilation of the blood capillaries which caused profuse and unexpected nosebleeds. The disease was debilitating and caused him a great deal of unhappiness. Despite his frailty Eddy was physically active. He played badminton and he skied, and there are photographs of him rock-climbing.

Eddy arrived at Christ Church, Oxford for the Michaelmas term of 1920. He passed 'Mods' in Scripture, his first set of exams in Hilary term 1921, then he read Modern History for a year and switched to Modern Languages in his final year, but he left without taking a degree because of his ill health. However, what mattered more than exams was his social life and the friends he made. On his first day he met Eardley Knollys, who had come up from Winchester College to read English. Harold Nicolson described Eardley to Vita as 'that Hellenic vision with scented amber curls'. Eardley was Captain of Tennis, and Eddy and he were both members of the Uffizi Society, which was started by Anthony Eden for fellow students with artistic interests. They also had an affair of sorts. A friend called Kyrle Leng wrote to Eddy, 'As for EEK [Eardley Knollys] I suppose in time you would gain your end but whether this would be a success or not is doubtful.' In fact, the affair was very brief but they remained close.

Eddy's sexual affairs at Oxford always ended unhappily. In 1924, in order to seek a cure for his inclinations – and their unsatisfactory outcomes – he went to Freiburg in Germany. On the recommendation of the society hostess Lady Ottoline Morrell he spent a couple of months in the clinic of a Dr Marten. Marten was a medical doctor, but he also dabbled in psychoanalysis at a time when analysis was all the rage. Lady Ottoline had attended the clinic herself. However, both Marten's theories and his therapies were wholly bogus. He told Eddy that his indigestion was mainly due to a maternity complex. He also started Eddy on a course of aversion therapy as treatment for his sexuality. Eddy recorded in his journal that Marten pumped him full of a substance which, at the end of his dinner, 'had a sudden effect on the seminal glands and I spent 3 1/2 hours of intolerable agony. Martin [*sic*] said my subconscious was prepared for pain just there. God! what agony it was! I thought the pain flowed in and out like a lamp in the wind swaying to and fro in gusts of agony.'[2]

Three years later, having given up looking for a cure, Eddy was back in Germany. He went to Dresden and Berlin for both the music and to perfect his German, but he also returned for boys and bars, the more unruly pleasures of the new Weimar Republic. As Christopher Isherwood discovered, as well as its thriving culture – for these were the years of *The Threepenny Opera*, *The Cabinet of Dr Caligari*, *The Magic Mountain*, the Bauhaus and Marlene Dietrich

– Weimar Germany also represented sexual liberation and experiment. For the seeker of thrills the tourist trail included the Institut für Sexualwissenschaft, the Institute for Sexual Research, which sought to educate the public with lectures on every aspect of sex. Its headquarters were in a building once owned by the great violinist and friend of Brahms, Joseph Joachim. Isherwood described the museum within the Institute:

Here were whips and chains and torture instruments designed for the practitioners of pleasure-pain; high-heeled, intricately decorated boots for the fetishists; lacy female undies which had been worn by ferociously masculine Prussian officers beneath their uniforms. Here were the lower-halves of trouser legs with elastic bands to hold them in position between knee and ankle. In these and nothing else but an overcoat and a pair of shoes, you could walk the streets and seem fully clothed, giving a camera-quick exposure whenever a suitable viewer appeared.[3]

Eddy told E.M. Forster that he found Berlin:

triumphantly, abominably ugly, – ugly that the mind is left quite free to pursue its own fantasies, unhindered by Beautiful Buildings . . .

The only thing I can liken Berlin to is *Ulysses*. It has all Joyce's power & variousness, & also his chaos & disgust & intelligibility. Much of the life seems really quite meaningless. I was dragged about at night from one homosexual bar to another. The behaviour is perfectly open. There are even large dance places for inverts. And some of the people one sees – huge men with breasts like women & faces like Ottoline, dressed as female Spanish dancers – are really quite unintelligible. One can think of no context in which they could possibly mean anything. They just moan about like great question marks, stopping occasionally at the end of sentences that aren't questions.

I spent a pleasurable & interesting night with a Lithuanian peasant of 20, covered with mother of pearl buttons, very beautiful creature. He was passionately interested in revolvers, one of which he insisted on taking to bed (I did not feel frightened). He even loaded it slowly, all the six chambers; but I could not make out what he did with it. He was very friendly and charming. Another unintelligible figure.[4]

A week after writing to Forster, Eddy wrote to Virginia Woolf likening Berlin to a lunatic asylum.

After Oxford Eddy embarked on a literary career. Between 1926 and 1931 he published four novels. His writing was heavily influenced by Gothic fiction; it was also influenced by *A Rebours*, the most famous book of the French author Joris-Karl Huysmans, the story of a sickly, reclusive aesthete with whom Eddy probably identified. Although the novels have not lasted, *The Ruin*, *Piano Quintet*, *Simpson: A Life* and the bizarrely titled *Mandrake over the Water-carrier* were generally well received at the time. *The Ruin*, originally written at Oxford, was clearly autobiographical. The setting, Vair, a vast country house in Kent, is Knole. Its hero, Marcus Fleming, is all too obviously based on Jack McDougal* an Oxford contemporary and one of the many young men with whom Eddy fell unhappily in love. Despite Eddy's passion, McDougal was not remotely interested: this was to be a recurring pattern in Eddy's life. Marcus Fleming is so insultingly described that the book was almost actionable, but McDougal seemed not to mind – if he read it at all. Eddy's way with words is often eccentric: 'Marcus pointed a look at him'; 'he literally pulled his eyes away and fixed them upon the piece of cake in his hand'; 'his marvellous hair . . . waving this way and that like an

---

* Jack McDougal became a director of the firm Chapman and Hall and published Evelyn Waugh. After the publication of Michael De-la-Noy's biography of ESW, McDougal's daughters sued for breach of copyright. The offending paragraph was removed in subsequent editions.

exuberant chrysanthemum'; '[Denzil's eyes passed] like a knife-blade on to Marcus upon whose face embarrassment had stamped a curious expression: he looked somewhat like a good-looking fish.' Yet when not indulging in Gothic extravagance or turning his emotional disasters into fiction Eddy could write perfectly well. In 1925 Virginia Woolf commissioned a pamphlet eventually called *The Apology for Arthur Rimbaud* which was published by the Hogarth Press two years later. The Hogarth Press also published a translation of Rainer Maria Rilke's *Duino Elegies*, a joint collaboration by Eddy and his cousin Vita in a limited signed edition with illustrations by Eric Gill.

Eddy's biography *A Flame in Sunlight: The Life and Work of Thomas de Quincy*, which was published in 1936, won the James Tait Black Memorial Prize. A year earlier he published his first 'Gramophone Notes' for the *New Statesman*, and for the next twenty years he became one of the most widely read and respected music critics of his time. Frances Partridge, by no means the most generous of judges, found his music criticism 'brilliant, amusing and beautifully written, as were those of literature, backed by wide reading in several languages'.

Lord Sackville shared Knole with his daughter Victoria, who was married to her cousin Lionel. Lionel became the third Lord Sackville in 1908. Lionel and Victoria's only child, Vita Sackville-West, lived with her parents until her marriage to Harold Nicolson in 1913. For Vita, Knole was an obsession. She adored the house, loving it with an almost atavistic passion. She had spent her whole childhood wandering through its 365 rooms, exploring its attics and bedrooms, its corridors and long galleries, its state and domestic rooms, and its cellars, stables and outbuildings until she knew them completely. As a child she had assumed that one day all this would be hers. It was only when Vita reached adulthood that she fully understood that, on account of her sex, she would lose the right to its possession. That Eddy who barely knew Knole could not love the place, and even dreaded having responsibility for its ownership, was agony to her.

In 1926 Lionel gave Eddy an apartment at Knole in the Gatehouse

Tower and West Range. The rooms gave Eddy freedom to exercise his creative imagination. Paul Hyslop, one of his first guests, probably advised on the decoration and fittings and the brightly coloured paintwork throughout. The Gatehouse rooms were accessed from the Green Court via a staircase, which he painted sage green; the colour continued into the dining room and bathroom on the first floor, where there were two guestrooms, one dark blue, one mustard; Eddy's bedroom was white with a blue bookcase, doors, pelmets and windows; there was also a white dressing room, a red bathroom and a blue lavatory; the music-room walls were bright pink. The rooms were furnished from the vast collection in Knole's attics, although Eddy also added some of his own. John Banting, a highly fashionable and rather scandalous painter – Eddy considered him 'congenial, interesting, good + beautiful' – added a corner cupboard, a wardrobe and a four-fold screen featuring large, stylised figures representing the arts. Duncan Grant contributed a fire screen as well as a portrait of Eddy. At the time, Duncan was enamoured by Eddy, even though Eddy was sixteen years his junior. 'By the way I think I ought to tell you I have never received any proper education,' he warned Eddy. 'You may be shocked by my writing, spelling, lack of knowledge, etc, etc.'[5]

Shortly after Eddy moved into the tower, he invited Vita to dinner. However, she was appalled by what she had seen and wrote an account of her visit to Harold, who was serving as a *chargé d'affaires* for the British Diplomatic Service in Tehran:

I dined at Knole, and there was Paul Heslop [*sic*]. Darling, his rooms are rather awful. He has a pale mauve light in his bedroom. Then the three stone turret rooms at the three corners of his sitting room are eingerichtet [furnished] with a sort of ninetyish affectation – a green light in one, a red light in the third; a rapier propped up in the corner, a crucifix on the wall. It made me cross; it was all so decadent, theatrical and cheap. My lovely Knole! And Eddy himself mincing in black velvet. I didn't dislike Paul Heslop, but the whole establishment had a nasty flavour about it. I don't object to homosexuality, but I do hate decadence. And it is a nasty fungoid growth in Knole of all places.

After the death of her father in 1928, when her uncle Charles, or 'Charlie', Eddy's father, inherited Knole and became the fourth Lord Sackville, she visited the house only twice again. When Charles gave Vita a key to the garden she said that it became her most treasured possession. She once made use of it by night. In 1935, Lord Sackville, who was 'very thin, gaunt about the nose and with very gleaming false teeth which he picks, like Eddy', entered into discussions with the National Trust as to how Knole might best be taken over by them. After this the house which Vita adored slipped out of her grasp absolutely and for ever.

In July 1934 at the annual general meeting of the National Trust Philip Kerr, the eleventh Marquis of Lothian, gave a speech in which he advocated that the Trust should guard not only the landscape but extend its protection to the country's historic houses. He saw them as every bit as much a part of the national heritage as the countryside, and now they too were threatened with potential destruction. When he said that the English country house was under sentence of death, and that 'the axe which was destroying them was taxation', the audience cheered. Lord Lothian spoke from his own experience: not only had he inherited his title unexpectedly, he had also gained several houses and some very considerable death duties. His speech included a number of suggestions which were directed at the Treasury and related to death duties and maintenance claims. He now proposed that the National Trust itself should take over a number of furnished historic houses. (Although it already owned houses, only two were substantial country mansions, Barrington Court and Montacute, both of them in Somerset and both of them empty.) The Lothian speech marked the beginning of a campaign, and two years later in 1936 the Treasury put forward a couple of schemes: firstly, the National Trust was invited, together with government officials, to draw up a list of the houses regarded as particularly worthy of preservation which would be relieved from death duties in the event of their owners donating them to the Trust; the second proposed a form of affiliation to the Trust. The National Trust assembled a Country House Committee in order to compile lists of owners who might be interested in taking part.

To help with the work the Trust also decided to appoint an extra member of staff and in March 1936 they appointed James Lees-Milne as its first Secretary at £300 a year. The National Trust at the time was effectively run by amateurs and enthusiasts. Lees-Milne had been told about the job by Harold Nicolson, whom he had first met in 1931 when Nicolson stood unsuccessfully for Sir Oswald Mosley's New Party (Mosley was the son-in-law of Lord Curzon, his former mentor) and Jim Lees-Milne had volunteered his services. Jim was now twenty-eight. He later described himself as 'raw and ignorant' at the start of his career, but he was a natural aesthete. Among his closest friends were John Betjeman, Osbert Lancaster and Robert Byron, all of whom were passionate about architecture. He had been brought up at a house called Wickhamford in Worcestershire, and he liked to give the impression that he came from old Worcestershire gentry. In fact, his father had bought the estate only two years before he was born, and the family money had come from a Lancashire cotton mill. However, this pretence was convincing, and he was helped by his youth, his good looks and his genuine enthusiasm.

For the next three years Jim worked in the National Trust's cramped offices at their headquarters in 7 Buckingham Palace Road, a red-brick house opposite Victoria Station. He spent his time drawing up lists of possible donors, dealing with the correspondence and making site visits. Since the Trust did not own a motor car visits were usually made by travelling by train to the nearest railway station and then on an old bicycle which he brought with him in the guard's van.

Although the outings were not always fruitful, they were invariably interesting. By September 1939, three and a half years after Jim had started work for the National Trust, the Country House Scheme had started to make significant progress. They had already been promised half a dozen properties and another half-dozen were looking hopeful. With the outbreak of war, however, the scheme was abruptly suspended, and Lees-Milne was made redundant.

Having failed to find any other satisfactory employment, in June 1940 Jim joined the Irish Guards Training Battalion at Lingfield in Surrey. He had been advised to join the Irish Guards because he had been told that there were many Roman Catholics among their number, and Jim had converted to Catholicism six years earlier. He was always going to be wholly unsuited for service life, but his time in the army was even briefer and more disastrous than might have been expected. In October, only a few months after he joined, he was returning from a brief period of leave and crossing Hyde Park Square when there was an air raid. He crouched for safety under the portico of the nearest house. The house immediately received a direct hit from a bomb and was nearly demolished with only the portico left standing. He was thrown by the strength of the blast ten yards across the street, as far as the railings of Hyde Park Square. Eventually, he managed to get back to his barracks in Lingfield, but he began to experience fainting fits and blackouts. He was diagnosed as suffering from Jacksonian epilepsy, which manifested itself in involuntary jerks or spasms and mild confusion, a condition he had inherited from his mother. The following ten months were spent in and out of five military hospitals. In July 1941 he wrote from the Queen Elizabeth Hospital to Eddy Sackville-West, who was a friend, albeit one famed for his hypochondria:

> I long to know how you are in health and whether you are any less unhappy. I am still haunted by that army of sinister bottles upon your washstand. Can nothing be done to induce you to leave off

drugs, for I know that ill health can only be mitigated by increasing quantities of them.

I am perhaps not in a position to exhort you to leave them off for I have now begun my own again. I have been in Hospital over a month. My leg became so painful I could barely stand. So long as I rest it seems to be all right but the moment I start exercising myself back comes the pain. Goodness knows when I shall be allowed out. Added to this my old trouble has returned since I have been here and I am obliged to take luminal* tablets again to prevent the fits – which they do thank God – but they, the fits, put some strain upon my leg during convulsions and hence the vicious circle. But so long as this leg can be cured I am certain I shall be all right for I shall never again leave off my luminals.[6]

Eddy replied tetchily:

My own health has improved with the warm weather. Of happiness this is not the time to speak. The row of bottles which gives you so much pain is mostly T. C. P, Dettol, Milk of Magnesia, GlycoThymolin† and the like; but of course Luminal is there & I take it as you know, every night. The alternative is no sleep, raging nervous dyspepsia & general despair. I leave it to you to judge which is best . . .[7]

After a fifth and final stay in hospital Jim was declared unfit for active service and discharged from the army in October 1941. He took medication for the rest of his life, but the fact that so many friends and comrades had hardships and danger to endure while his own war service had finished so soon caused him lasting embarrassment.

---

* Medication used to reduce seizures; also to calm anxiety during periods of sleep.
† Mouthwash.

Shortly after the outbreak of war the National Trust moved out of London into West Wycombe Park in Buckinghamshire and became tenants of Sir John Dashwood and his wife Helen. Not only was it a house the Trust greatly coveted, but it was also very convenient – both within commuting distance and outside the London bombing range. The main house was a Palladian mansion and there was also an estate village and the park, an eighteenth-century garden land-scape. The architecture on the outside was made up of colonnades and porticoes, and inside there were splendidly decorated rooms and painted ceilings. However, the Dashwoods had no money and, for all its grandeur, the house had been decaying since the agricultural depression, which had begun in the 1870s. The silk on the dining-room walls was in tatters, there were holes in the carpets and the leather on the eighteenth-century chairs was disintegrating. When it rained the water poured down the walls. There were nine reception rooms and twenty bedrooms. The National Trust was not the only tenant: the contents of the Wallace Collection had been moved from Manchester Square into the blue drawing room and music salon. A nursing home for mothers and babies occupied the top floor, and a troop of gunners had taken over the service wings, which had been sealed off from the rest of the house for decades and left to rot. The park was used for inflating barrage balloons.

In November 1941, a few weeks after his army discharge, Jim moved to West Wycombe to resume his career at the National Trust. Just over two years had passed since he had been made redundant, and he was now aged thirty-three. The Trust was desperately short-staffed, and his return was more than welcome. On Thursday, 1 January 1942 Jim made the first entry of the new year in his diary and he complained about the cold. He described how the radiators worked only fitfully, and although the house was singularly beautiful, its principal living rooms faced due north, and from January to December the long, double colonnade of the south front induced a double eclipse of the sun. The Trust's offices were in the Brown

Drawing Room and Sir John Dashwood's study beyond it. Donald Matheson, the National Trust Secretary, Florence Paterson, the head of the clerical team, Eardley Knollys, who was Matheson's assistant, and Jim worked in the study, while Miss Ballachey, a typist, and the fifteen-year-old office junior were in the bigger room with all the filing cabinets. Matheson, Eardley or Jim were generally away visiting properties and seldom in the office together. As Jim's boss, Matheson was a bad delegator and not ideal for his post. As Jim put it, 'his previous job as Secretary of the Gas Light & Coke Company had not made him an aesthete'.[8] He was frequently absent on account of his health, and in his absence everything was much more enjoyable. Eardley had a background in estate management, and he had been given the job as an agent on the strength of his rural background. He was practical, and he did as much work as was possible in the circumstances.

Apart from the tenants, the Dashwoods also provided a home at West Wycombe for rather up-market paying guests, most of whom just happened to be the Dashwoods' personal friends. The guests included Eddy Sackville-West and Nancy Mitford. Eddy had left Knole because his father wanted his rooms for a friend who would help him run the house. As Eddy admitted, this was perfectly justifiable because he himself was incapable of doing so himself. Knole was under the flight path of the German bombers, and many of its finest contents had been sent for safekeeping to a slate mine in Wales. 'How dreadful everything is!' Eddy complained before he left. 'I have just spent three days stowing away all the Knole silver (11 cases of it) in banks in the west of England. A very exhausting job.'

While Eddy and Jim were at West Wycombe because they were unfit to serve in the armed forces, Nancy was convalescing after a hysterectomy. In the summer of 1941 she had met a French man with the *nom de guerre* of André Roy (his real name was Roy André Desplats-Pilter), who had come to London in 1940 to join De Gaulle's Free French Forces and was working as a liaison officer at the Quartier

Général. According to Eddy he was 'a very charming French Frog who spoke English remarkably well'.[9] Nancy's marriage to Peter Rodd had been a dismal failure, and she was lonely and unhappy. Roy was charming and amusing, and they had an affair which was never serious but did not end well: so great were André Roy's charms that she had become pregnant. It turned out to be an ectopic pregnancy; the foetus was lodged in the fallopian tube, which had to be removed. Before the operation she begged the gynaecologist to make sure that she could still have children, but when she woke up from the operation she discovered that she had had a full hysterectomy. For Nancy it was a crushing blow. She wrote to her sister Diana:

> I have had a horrible time, so depressing because they had to take out both my tubes & therefore I can now never have a child . . . The Rodds have been wonderfully true to form – my mother in law was told by the surgeon I shld be in danger for 3 days, & not one of them even rang up to enquire let alone sending a bloom or anything. I long to know if they bothered to look under R in the deaths column, very much doubt it however.
>
> I never hear from Peter or he from me it is too depressing like the grave. Also he never gets pay. Muv [her mother] was wonderful, she swam in a haze of bewilderment between me & Debo.* When my symptoms were explained to her she said 'ovaries – I thought one had 700 like caviar!'[10]

The MP and art collector Sir Alfred Beit, who was stationed nearby, and his wife Clementine (a cousin of Nancy) were also at West Wycombe. Sometimes Eddy used to play the Bechstein piano from the music salon, which had been taken into the hall. In the evening everyone sat together reading, gossiping and knitting in the

---

* Nancy Mitford's younger sister Deborah Cavendish (subsequently Deborah Devonshire) had just given birth to a still born baby.

tapestry room in front of the fire – or at least in front of a few green logs in the fireplace. Jim was knitting socks. Clementine Beit suggested, given Jim's professed religion, that what he was actually knitting was 'the true sock', which would, instead of liquefying, unravel 'on St Milne's day' to signify a good harvest. For his part Eddy was knitting an endless khaki scarf. His evening wear was a blue cloak with silver buckles and a red-velvet waistcoat with coachman's gold livery buttons. Eddy and Jim sat side by side on a pair of upright Chippendale chairs before the fire. 'I suppose we were an odd spectacle,' Jim wrote. 'Still, I wish Helen would not call us the old bombed houses.'[11] Meanwhile, Nancy was obsessed with Captain Scott's doomed expedition to the Arctic. Because the upstairs lavatory faced due north and the window was permanently open she called it 'the Beardmore' after the Beardmore Glacier, and in the depths of winter the lavatory floor was under a drift of snow. Helen Dashwood did not find this joke funny. After lunch one day, in Helen's absence, Eddy, Nancy and Jim started to discuss her 'extraordinary unadult character' – how she hated being left out of whatever was going on, her pique when plans went wrong, and her resentment when others were enjoying themselves but felt that she might be missing something.[12] In Helen, however, Nancy had found the perfect character for a future novel.

At the outbreak of the war Eddy volunteered to work in the personnel department of the Red Cross in Grosvenor Crescent. After this proved unsatisfactory, he made strenuous efforts to get posted to Air Ministry but without success. Raymond Mortimer, who was about to start work with the Ministry of Information, suggested that he might like to take his place as a temporary literary editor of the *New Statesman*. Eddy declined the position, pleading ill health. Raymond begged him 'with all the affection I have in my heart' not to surrender to gloom.[13] Instead of going to the *New Statesman* he applied for a commission in the Administrative and Special Duties Branch of the

Royal Air Force Volunteer Reserve. 'I'm interested to hear you're [trying] for the RAF again: the Boys Book of the Royal Air Force once more thumbed with eager fingers!'[14] Desmond Shawe-Taylor wrote archly. But once again Eddy's application was refused. In August 1941 he had a medical inspection. Inevitably the medical board gave him a Grade 4 National Service Card, which ruled out any kind of military service. This was the same card which had been given both to Jim and to George Orwell. Orwell had remarked, 'I have what half the men in this country would give their balls to have, a yellow ticket, but I don't want it.'[15] Eddy's response was somewhat milder: 'So I suppose I shall end up in the B.B.C! I daresay one could do worse.'[16]

In the 1940s radio became a lifeline. Nearly everyone listened. The moments which defined the nation's collective memory of the Second World War – Chamberlain speaking from Downing Street in 1939; Dunkirk; the Blitz and the Battle of Britain; Churchill's fighting speeches on D-Day – were all mediated through the BBC. Orwell, unsentimental and drily sceptical as ever, concluded in 1941 that Britain 'is a land of snobbery and class privilege, ruled largely by the old and silly. But in any calculation about it one has to take into account its emotional unity, the tendency of nearly all its citizens to feel alike and act together in moments of supreme crisis.'[17] And this was a time of supreme crisis. The Battle of Singapore – 'the Gibraltar of the East' – lasted from 8 to 15 February 1942. When it fell, 80,000 British, Indian and Australian troops were taken prisoner. Winston Churchill called it the worst disaster in British military history. In his diary Harold Nicolson wrote that he feared a slump in public opinion would deprive Churchill of his legend: 'His broadcast last night was not liked. The country is too nervous and irritable to be fobbed off with fine phrases. Yet what else could he have said? A weaker man would have kept away from the wireless and allowed someone else to tell us the bad news.'[18]

For a while the BBC broadcast hours of organ music interspersed with news reports from Reuters, but its programming soon improved considerably, using popular entertainment to gain listeners. Assigned a writer and producer to the Features and Drama Department headed by Val Gielgud, the brother of the actor John Gielgud, Eddy turned out to be unexpectedly good at the job he was given – it was as if he had at last found a proper role for himself. Eddy's contributions included a series of talks called 'Studies in Interpretation', which, although 'highbrow', were representative of the high standards the BBC expected of itself. One of the programmes in this series brought a fan letter from Vivien Greene, the wife of Graham Greene. 'Owing to the grace & skill of your three talks,' she wrote, 'I shall be always unceasingly grateful that I have a new glimmer of understanding when confronted with fine musicianship.' He was also popular with his colleagues. Freda Berkeley, the wife of the composer Lennox Berkeley, found Eddy wonderful company: 'He always made you feel you were the only person he wanted to see.' On the other hand, he was a little preoccupied with his health. According to Jim, his favourite topics of conversation were food, regurgitation and wind.

Eddy shared an office with Stephen Potter, who later became famous for *Gamesmanship* (a humorous book about the art of cheating by pretending not to). Potter, who often mentioned Eddy in his diaries, found his company could be both irritating and delightful:

> E. slightly gets on my nerves, because he gets in a pansy flap and agonises over a detail . . . I wanted him to say an Italian line and he said 'Oh no really, I can't' and at the rehearsal comes down three floors to tell me so. I, already irritated by being kept waiting 15 minutes for a circuit, shout at him. A strange high voice comes out of me – 'for God's sake go upstairs and read a line. That's all I want you to do . . .'

Eddy could also be charming. At a weekend when they were both guests in the same house Potter wrote:

Eddy is there and a very good person to have – a) he plays the piano, b) we talk about the job (on a cold walk along the railway line), c) for his complete lack of vanity and his ancient calm wisdom (so entirely belied by his office voice), d) for his lack of self deception and absence of moan about his many bodily weaknesses. He talks about Knole. The 24 weekend guests, with never less than 12 guests in the house. 'If you have 20 servants they eat so much that the guests don't really make any difference.'

Eddy's most significant achievement was a radio play called *The Rescue*, which he wrote during his weekends at West Wycombe. Based on the concluding passages of Homer's *Odyssey* and described by Eddy as a 'Melodrama for Broadcasting', *The Rescue* was first performed in two parts in November 1943. The musical score was provided by Benjamin Britten. Many of the critics thought the music was the best part of the programme, an opinion with which Eddy said he could not quarrel. The play was published two years later with half a dozen colour plates provided by Henry Moore, and after the war the play was translated into French and Italian and several times revived. Val Gielgud assured Eddy that it had become firmly established as a genuine broadcasting classic.

By the end of the war in 1945 nearly every country house of any considerable size – perhaps 2,000 or more – had been requisitioned by compulsory order, or in a sort of by-product of the 'Dunkirk spirit', because the owners voluntarily offered them out of patriotic duty. The Special Operations Executive alone took over so many houses that the initials 'SOE' was said to stand for the Stately 'Omes of England. It was not just the houses but the gardens and grounds around them. In the lead up to D-Day the physical nature of the country was put into a state of mobilisation. Owners found their gardens cut up by mortar ranges and assault courses, while lorries and tanks drove all over them and sentry boxes sprang up at the park gates.

Crichel House got off lightly. For the evacuees of Dumpton House Preparatory School, the house, with its quaint boathouse and swans' nests, its sweet-smelling cedar trees and watercress-filled streams, was a magical experience. There were butterflies everywhere in the grounds: white admirals and hairstreaks, silver-washed, pearl-bordered and dark-green fritillaries, and even the rare high-brown fritillary and the small copper. The boys did PE underneath the portico and ate in a dining room with an enormous chandelier. They ran relay races in the Italian Garden and played tennis on a grass court surrounded by banks of fragrant camomile. Weeping birch trees grew beside the croquet garden. Inside the house there was a long gallery on the top floor and a sumptuously red-carpeted and wide spiral staircase. All this seemed rather wonderful to a seven year old. Because the boys had been told that the Egyptian Room was out of bounds, they believed among themselves that it must be haunted. Even the fantastically beautiful and elaborately decorated lavatories had seats four feet wide. Once a month in Moor Crichel Church the choir sang 'Benedicite Omnia Opera' under the direction of Mr Gilbert, the local organist, and indeed everything seemed truly blessed and dreamlike.

Two elderly ladies, Miss Cotton-Stapleton, who wore a black patch over one eye, and Lady Anna Sturt, also lived in Crichel House in a private wing. Lord Hardinge of Penshurst and his wife, the young Mary Anna Sturt's guardians, were among the residents of the village. In 1943 Lord Hardinge, who had been private secretary to King George V, King Edward VIII and King George VI, had resigned his post following a breakdown caused by overwork and his never-ending duties. In September 1944 the *Tatler* reported that he was making good progress back to normal health. Until the recent death of his father he had been living a very quiet life in the seclusion of his country home at Crichel, where he had been occupying his time with hay-making and other outdoor activities.

In 1940 the old rectory at Long Crichel was bought by a Miss Yorke, who had lost her property in the Netherlands on account of the war. Her main house was in London in Spanish Place, off Manchester Square. Although she added a bathroom and kept four servants at Long Crichel, she only went there for weekends. For a short time in 1941 the rectory was used as a school, but both the lighting and the water supply were inadequate. So, instead of having a school as a tenant, for the duration of the war Miss Yorke let the house to Mrs Seivewright, the wife of a naval captain, and her five children.

By 1945, the fiftieth anniversary of the National Trust, it owned seventeen houses with restrictive covenants over five more, including medieval cloisters, the half-timbered and the neo-classical. All seventeen were open to the public. West Wycombe, which Sir John Dashwood had finally given to the Trust two years earlier, was among the number. Dashwood was delighted to rid himself of the responsibility, and the National Trust became the owners of his eighteenth-century mansion and its grounds on condition that both he and his descendants could go on living there should they want to. Vita Sackville-West, however, never got over the loss of the house she loved. When Knole was bombed in February 1944 Eddy telephoned to tell her. In her distress Vita broke down completely. In his diary Harold wrote: 'It seems that it was a blaster bomb and that it crept round the house and broke windows in every part including that of her old bedroom. She minds terribly and the whole incident opens a sad wound.'[19] In 1946 the Sackville family finally handed over Knole to the National Trust with an endowment towards its maintenance. The family retained possession of the park and many of the contents of the house; they were also granted a 200-year lease on various private apartments.

At the end of 1939, just a few months into the war, Maria Huxley, the wife of Aldous Huxley, sent a Christmas hamper to Eddy and Raymond Mortimer from her home in California. 'If it ever gets there, remember it was sent with love and melancholy,' she wrote. 'Melancholy because it is really impossible to write anything. Yet I think much about you and all the unguessable part of English life becomes like a burden.'[20]

Five years later, the end of the war was in sight. Eddy relinquished his appointment as a producer with the BBC on Christmas Day 1944. Richard Garnett recalled his last, sad, sight of Eddy in the BBC canteen surrounded by scruffy tables and spilt tea, moving about, he said, like some rare animal in a squalid cage at the zoo. Stephen Potter stayed on, and he became the writer and producer chosen for the BBC's main appreciation of Winston Churchill for the day after VE Day.

Jim recorded his impressions of VE night in his diary:

We drank muscat wine and listened to the King's speech at 9. It was perfect, well phrased, well delivered in his rich, resonant voice, expressed with true feeling and tinged with an appropriate emotion for the occasion. Bridget [Parsons]* and I cooked the dinner, she scrambling eggs and I frying bacon in great quantity. This was all we had but it was delicious. We drank some excellent white wine and some very old brandy, sitting till 11.45 at the table. At midnight I insisted on our joining the revels. It was a very warm night. Thousands of searchlights swept the sky. Otherwise there were very few illuminations and no street lights at all. Claridges and the Ritz were lit up. We walked down Bond Street passing small groups singing, not boisterously. Piccadilly however was full of swarming people and littered with paper.

We walked arm in arm into the middle of Piccadilly Circus which was brilliantly illuminated by arc lamps. Here the crowds were singing and yelling and laughing. They were orderly and good-humoured. All the English virtues were on the surface. We watched individuals climb lamp posts, and plant flags on the top

---

* Bridget Parsons was the sister of Desmond Parsons, with whom JLM was in love when they were at Eton together.

amidst tumultuous applause from bystanders. We walked down Piccadilly towards the Ritz. In the Green Park there was a huge bonfire under the trees, and too near, one poor tree caught fire. Bridget made us push through the crowd collected on the pavement to a ring of people round the bonfire. They were very funny, bringing huge posts from nowhere and hurling them on to the fire. Six or seven people were struggling under barricades of wood and whole doorways of wood from air raid shelters which they dragged on the fire . . . Bridget took a flying leap over the pyre in sheer exuberance of spirits. The scene was more Elizabethan than neo-Georgian, a spontaneous peasant game, a dance round the maypole, almost Breugelian, infinitely bucolic. No-one was bullied into joining if they didn't want to, and the spectators enjoyed it as much as the participants. I thought if we could have a V night once a month, and invite the Poles, Germans, even Russians to do what we are doing now, there might never be another war.[21]

3

The Bruderhof

Jim first mentioned Desmond Shawe-Taylor in an entry in his diaries written in February 1945. Desmond, a captain in the intelligence services, and Eddy had joined Jim for lunch at Brooks's. Eddy told them that 'just for fun' he and his father had recently been to the family vault at Withyham in Sussex. Seventeen years after he had died his late uncle Lionel's coffin was still lying on a trestle. Eddy said he had decided that he eventually wanted to lie there as well, entombed amongst the velvet palls and silver coroneted coffins of his eighteenth-century Sackville ancestors.

Eddy and Desmond had known one another for about ten years, having met through their mutual love of music. Eddy had invited Desmond to stay at Knole the night before a journey north to Glasgow to see *The Trojans* by Berlioz, which they both wished to see. It was an opera which was rarely performed and from this acquaintanceship a close friendship followed. Desmond was one of Eddy's last guests at Knole before he left the house – in effect for good. Through Eddy, Desmond also came to know his friends, including Raymond Mortimer, Eardley Knollys and Jim.

Born in Dublin in 1907, Desmond's background was Anglo–Irish and his father a farmer. The playwright and Irish nationalist Lady Gregory was a great-aunt. He remembered William Butler Yeats as a somewhat comical figure, with his talk of fairies, pixies and a Celtic twilight. This happy childhood was cut brutally short when his father, who was both a magistrate and the High Sheriff for County Galway, was murdered – although it was never discovered who by or why. (Desmond received a pension all his life as compensation.) Before Desmond was born, an elder sister, Vera, had also been killed in a riding accident. After her husband's death, the remaining family – Desmond's mother and her two sons – went to England and lived with relations in Shipston-on-Stour in Warwickshire. Over the years Desmond's mother grew more and more eccentric, and he grew increasingly estranged from her. After he left Shrewsbury School, he won a place at Oriel College, Oxford to read English, but on the day he first left for Oxford his mother tried to prevent him from catching the train because she was afraid he was being kidnapped.

After graduating with a First, Desmond was employed briefly at the Royal Geographical Society as Assistant Editor of the *Geographical Journal*. He also began to contribute musical and literary reviews to various London periodicals, including the *New Statesman*. Film reviews were submitted using the pseudonym Peter Galway. In 1936 he published his first book, an appreciation of the Irish novelist George Moore.

During the 1930s Desmond travelled on the Continent, where he could enjoy sunbathing and naturism. In July 1935 he was in Denmark and wrote to his friend the poet Eric Falk:

> There's a great deal that's strange about Denmark, nothing more so than the meal-times, which are 12 and 6.30. I find however that it suits me quite well, and am in radiant health and well on the thorny road to browness [*sic*]: for I go nearly every day to bathe at Herrenbad in Charlottenhund . . . where one wears nothing at all, which I find hugely increases the joy of bathing, besides ensuring that you look your best that you don't have a nasty white patch just where you want to look your best . . .[1]

Four years later Desmond was on holiday in the Dordogne when he was called back to England. He had already joined the Royal Artillery Territorial Unit, but he was two days late getting to their encampment, HAA Battery, on Primrose Hill. He arrived – to cheers – in a Bentley driven by a friend. On 8 September he wrote to Eddy saying it was like the beginning of term. He was on a gun-team working with 'whopping great 4.5 inch guns':

You have no idea how often I have wanted to write to you, but I have been unable to find a moment. We have been working night and day, mostly filling sandbags and trenches, and since the War broke out have not been allowed out of the camp once. The glorious weather is some compensation. I work in nothing but shorts, am getting brown, and feel better than I have for years . . . So far, of course, it has been no war at all, only an extension of the camp-public-school-proletarian atmosphere which I know so well . . .

I simply ache for a little rational conversation and music. I think it was the day before the declaration that I was on a cookhouse fatigue, sitting peeling potatoes (a job I like) in the garden of the house where the Battery were eating. The caretaker's wireless streamed out of the open window, and suddenly it struck up the Bliss Viola Sonata: in those surroundings it seemed extra-ordinary beautiful. But my joy was short-lived: before the first side was finished, there were cries of disgust and exclamations of 'Po-Music'! and atropos descended on the switch. I dared not protest and continued snottily peeling my potatoes . . .

a Bombardier (slightly drunk it is true) tried to seduce me. I doubt if even you or Jack [Rathbone]* would have complied. He is Scotch, moustached, about 45 and wears a German haircut. It was exactly like the House Prefect leading the New Boy astray: 'Come on – come for a walk – come over 'ere – see wot I mean?'

---

* A friend from school and probably sometime lover with whom he lived for many years. Subsequently Rathbone was also solicitor to the National Trust.

He had just had his first bath for a week: 'One gets extraordinarily filthy, and after a bit one scarcely notices it; I have long since reached the stage at which I ought to feel ashamed to reveal the state of my undies.'[2] Despite its drawbacks Desmond admitted that he was enjoying himself immensely. He wrote to Eddy, who was still living at Knole:

> Dear Eddy, the thought of you bouncing about on the Knole sofas and putting Mahler on the [gramophone] and opening letters with an enormous penknife is extraordinarily comforting: please continue to do these things, and don't be totally absorbed in the martial machine, even in the more cultural side of the horrid thing.
>
> This is much more like the Regular Army than the average Territorial Unit; gents only started trickling in during the last year. Pansy jokes are however on the increase with seclusion; and I have great success with the hoariest *queenly* remarks, which are new and daring to them. I honestly don't think, however, that a soul suspects.[3]

Eighteen months later, in February 1941, when Desmond wrote to Eddy again, he was based at Wick in Caithness in the far north of Scotland. It was all very different from Primrose Hill, and there was much more to complain about – not least having to rise at five o'clock in the morning and the constant vile weather:

> I was simply delighted to get your letter, almost my first contact with civilisation for more than a month. Not that I have anything to complain about, for I have not written a single letter myself until now. My reason? The numbing cold, the searing winds, the snow-blocked railway and roads, the feeling that weeks might elapse before one's letters reached destination, above all the never ending busy-ness of gunsite life. In the greater part of the time I have had the sort of responsibility you so much dislike, being left

alone in an isolated position (quite near the Sinclairs'* home at Thurso) in charge of nearly 100 men, in a state of incessant agitation about coal and rations and drainage and privy pits and maintaining discipline and contracting boredom . . . Rarely does the day end before 9 o'clock at night. And then begins the censoring horror, dozens and dozens of letters to be censored from the men. (You will note that even this has been censored – by myself: and remember that your letters too are liable to be opened at Inverness).

Censoring was unremittingly tedious. The same words, sentiments and Americanisms ('Oh boy!' was a favourite) were endlessly repeated; nothing varied in the letters except the degree of literacy. The men – who were all married – thought nothing of war aims but only of getting back to their wives in Sheffield, Manchester or Glasgow. 'More and more I marvel that people have the patience to write and read all those glumly accurate proletarian novels,' he wrote. His own preferred reading included Marcel Proust and Ivy Compton-Burnett. There were also frequent references in his letters to the *New Statesman and Nation*. In 1930 the Fabian-supporting paper was merged with the *Nation & Athenaeum*, a Liberal periodical. Under the editorship of Kingsley Martin, the magazine became the *New Statesman and Nation*. Popularly known as the 'Staggers and Naggers', the magazine was a lifeline to civilisation and the outside world. Desmond told Eddy that he went climbing in the local mountains with an Irishman who read both the *New Statesman* and modern poetry, but otherwise there were very few people in the camp with whom he had anything in common. He had met a couple of officers at the local naval base who were followers of the 'N. S.'. One of them also read the highly mannered novels of Compton-Burnett, which Desmond found almost incredible: 'They wanted to know about you, and seemed to

---

* Sir Archibald Sinclair MP (1890–1970), subsequently Viscount Thurso; leader of the Liberal Party and Secretary of State for Air, 1940–1945.

enjoy your things, though not musical; they even remembered my peacetime contributions. I had quite a nice triumph in the mess.'

Desmond spent the whole of his long months of confinement in the north of Scotland longing for close companionship. 'Without you as the *pièce de resistance* it would make a very flat leave,' he told Eddy about a forthcoming short respite. There were also times when he allowed himself to think optimistically about the future and how, after such dark times, a normal life might be resumed. 'I should very much like to be on the ground floor of your castle in Spain,' Desmond wrote: since Eddy had no great desire to return to Knole, perhaps it might be an idea to try living together with like-minded friends such as Desmond, Eardley and Raymond – maybe in Bath?

Ever the optimist, Desmond replied enthusiastically to Eddy's pipe-dream, however distant it must have seemed. In a letter of August 1941 he compared the project to a *Bruderhof.* Set up to follow a non-violent way of life and follow the teachings of the Sermon on the Mount, *Bruderhofs* flourished in Germany in the 1920s and early 1930s. After the imposition of compulsory conscription, such Christian communities were suppressed and their property seized by Hitler.

Desmond continued:

An attractive plan, and I really think a measure of communal living might prove both necessary and enjoyable after the war. Of course R., who would be a natural centre of fraternity of such a scheme, could not edit the Staggers from Bath; nor do I suppose it would be a very remunerative spot for a picture gallery (but it *might*). And I have rural longings, and pine for a house *outside* Bath, lovely though the city is. But by all means let us toy with the thought of this Bruderhof – at least it makes a pleasant change from slogans and bomb scares.[4]

If Desmond considered Raymond Mortimer 'the natural centre' of the scheme it was because he was the oldest and most experienced of the four. As Literary Editor at the *New Statesman*, he had found work for both Eddy and Desmond as well as for many others within his circle. Born in Knightsbridge in 1895, the son of a prosperous parliamentary solicitor, Raymond was six years older than Eddy, seven years older than Eardley and twelve years older than Desmond. Within the worlds of art and literature he was extremely well connected.

Raymond's mother died when he was young, and he was brought up by an aunt and uncle at Redhill in Surrey. The household was neither intellectual nor aesthetic, but he was able to take pleasure in its old pictures and furniture and especially in the tremendous amount of books. Two educated Swiss girls taught him French, and many of his holidays were spent in France – his appreciation of the country, its language and literature were lifelong. After Malvern School, which he looked back on as philistine and brutal, he went to Balliol College, Oxford to read history. In 1915 he volunteered for military service, but he was rejected as unfit and instead worked in a hospital for French soldiers in Cannes. On his return to England he did not go back to his studies but received a wartime BA and was seconded to work in the Foreign Office as a cipher clerk. Already a friend of Maynard Keynes and George Rylands, he met Leonard and Virginia Woolf, who were their friends, while on holiday in 1923, and this was his entrée to the Bloomsbury circles. The following year he moved to a flat at 6 Gordon Place and employed Duncan Grant and Vanessa Bell to paint and decorate it.

In her diaries Virginia Woolf called Raymond 'all angle & polish . . . half a dandy'.[5] He was not conventionally good-looking, but as a young man he was slim and supple with curly, dark hair. He loved clothes and wore raw silk trousers and distinctive Charvet ties from Paris. Some people found him intimidating, which he did not mind at all. He told Frances Partridge that he found wealth and all that it bought sexually attractive. Raymond first met Harold Nicolson at the end of the First World War during his secondment to the Cypher Department. They met again in 1923, by which time Harold was losing interest in foreign politics, and they had an affair which, for both parties, was more than just a passing attraction. Harold, although discreet, became transfixed: '[you are] at the back of everything & everything is conditioned in its importance by reference to you. And, damn it all, what and who are you to have secured so masterful an obsession?' The obsession lasted for two years before settling into a deep and mutual affection and friendship. Both Harold and Vita frequently had relationships with members of their own sex, but their marriage remained the bedrock of both their lives, and Vita looked on Raymond benignly.

Raymond Mortimer's professional breakthrough came about in 1927 when, at the instigation of Virginia Woolf, he went to work for the *New Statesman*. Martin and his colleagues instinctively brought into words the thoughts and ideals of liberal, middle-class opinion of mid-twentieth-century Britain, and the influence of the new magazine was enormous. As far as Martin was concerned an article might be as challenging as the writer wished so long as it was well-written and had a certain style. This was also true of the literary pages, which, following the departure of Desmond MacCarthy in 1935, were edited by Raymond. Martin said of him that he was the sort of literary editor with whom he scarcely ever wanted to interfere: 'he was more a Liberal and less a Socialist than I was, but he looked out of the wide window and shared my forebodings about the world'.[6] Martin's policy of non-interference allowed Raymond considerable leeway. V.S. Pritchett later identified the 'tone' which Raymond allowed to develop as 'Bloomsbury', a curious mixture of liberalism and ruthless intolerance: literature was for pleasure and intellectual curiosity. University academics were likely to be treated with contempt. By the end of the Second World War the *New Statesman and Nation* had played its part in representing the ideals for which Britain was fighting, and its circulation had risen to 70,000 while doing so.

E.M. Forster's journal entry for 2 June 1940 records Raymond saying 'petulantly', 'We must hate the Germans, or we shall lose, and *hate then hate.*' Eddy, who was with them, echoed his words: 'hate, hate in aggrieved tones'. Pacifist friends like Forster and Ralph and Frances Partridge did not approve of such militaristic and so-called patriotic instincts. In order to work for the Ministry of Information Raymond took leave from the *New Statesman.* He played a large part in the setting up of the French-language radio service Radio Londres, which was operated by the Free French from a BBC studio with the aim of opposing the German propaganda broadcasts from Radio Paris and Radio-Vichy. Its broadcasts famously began, '*Ici Londres! Les Français parlent aux Français . . .*'

On 14 June German tanks took Paris unopposed. Charles de Gaulle, a junior minister and brigadier-general, had escaped to London as the French government prepared to sign an armistice with the invading forces. He was a lone figure at the time, and some members of the British cabinet wanted nothing to do with him, but they were overruled by Churchill, who gave him a platform from which to launch the Resistance. Such was the confidence of the French in Raymond that he was put in charge of their broadcasts, including the transmissions by General de Gaulle. This meant that he was the first person to read the script of *L'appel du 18 juin*, the radio appeal by which De Gaulle, aged fifty, entered history. Although heard by very few people at the time it was printed in *The Times* the following day. Gradually its message filtered through, and the speech came to be regarded as having both signalled the start of the French Resistance to German occupation and saved the honour of a defeated, demoralised nation. However, only a couple of days later the French government signed an armistice treaty with Germany and Raymond broke down in tears.

In November Raymond wrote to Frances Partridge from his cottage near Henley:

I've only slept one night in London during the last week – and then I didn't sleep despite strong barbiturates till 4. AM. The din is indescribable. It's very difficult to know how to arrange one's life – especially if one dislikes basements . . . The other day I drove from Bloomsbury to Victoria, & St James's Park was one great glow, with 30ft flames rising from Carlton House Terrace and Queen Anne's Gate, in all the windows in Buckingham Palace reflecting the flames, pall of smoke overhead, shells bursting, searchlights – really the most fantastic apocalyptic spectacle. When one gets up in the morning, after listening to the bombs whistling round me, it is a surprise to see the familiar buses still opposite . . .[7]

By the end of the year Raymond was ill and exhausted. He resigned from the Ministry of Information and returned to his former job at the *New Statesman*. Radio Londres continued to broadcast until 1944 when France was liberated.

In the spring of 1945, the dying months of the war, Eddy and Eardley visited Raymond and Paul Hyslop at The Bothy. Eardley had also lived with Raymond and Paul for a time, travelling on his motorbike every day to West Wycombe ten miles away. Conversation turned to the idea of some sort of communal living, which Eddy had first suggested five years earlier. If not exactly a *Bruderhof*, it would be something similar, albeit secular and decidedly more sybaritic. Eddy, Eardley and Desmond together decided that while they all needed to live in London during the week, they might also like to find a house in the country which they could share together for weekends and holidays. Eardley's widowed mother had a house in the Circus in Bath. She always wanted to know everything he was doing, and – in her mind at least – wanted him to be as close to her as possible. It was also the area he knew best, and he subsequently became the National Trust representative for the south-west, so a house in the region would give him a local base.

On only their second day of looking, Eardley and Desmond found the old rectory in Long Crichel through a Cheltenham estate agent. When they reported back to Eddy, who had not bothered to accompany them, he agreed to their decision immediately. The house would be large enough for three bachelors – friends who could pursue their individual interests while enjoying a certain amount of privacy from one another. Most importantly, it also seemed to offer opportunities for artistic stimulus. There would be space enough for them to write, listen to gramophone records, and keep their books and paintbrushes (despite having run an art gallery Eardley had only just taken up painting). The old rectory was also large enough to accommodate staff. The three of them agreed to buy the house together with its six acres of land and unkempt garden. The price of £7,500 was fairly expensive for the time. 'I'm sure it's delightful if you say so,' Eddy said, still without going to see it for himself.

No doubt to the considerable relief of Miss Yorke, the owner of Long Crichel, her difficult tenant, Mrs Seivewright, was leaving at last. At the end of February Mrs Seivewright placed an advertisement for the sale of a child's cot, a wooden bed and a Jersey cow which had just had its second calf, 'ideal for private owner'. Eddy and Desmond left it to Eardley, with his experience of estate management, to organise everything. Eardley also corresponded with the Wessex Electricity Company regarding the possibility of providing Long Crichel with an electricity supply. Their district manager told him that because of restrictions imposed during the war to conserve 'the utmost material and labour resources of the war' he would have to wait. Despite these problems the sale went through. Eardley, Eddy and Desmond moved into the house in the first week of August. Eardley told Miss Yorke that they were 'in a fine muddle', and he sent lists of items he wished to buy from the house. They included two satin footstools, two teapots, four chamber pots and a mahogany commode. He said he understood 'there were also some high steps here but they have left the house in the same direction as some other things you wrote about'. In September he had a reply from Miss Yorke that she was still endeavouring to get the stepladder back from 'that awful Mrs Seivewright'.

The new owners employed Mr and Mrs Deverell as a live-in cook–housekeeper and butler. They were Eddy's find. He had met them when they worked for the Earl and Countess De La Warr, relations of Eddy with whom he sometimes stayed in London. When the De La Warrs sold their flat in Chester Square the Deverells were happy to move to Dorset to take up new posts. There were also two charwomen, a gardener-cum-carpenter and Eardley's secretary, whom they had discovered in the village, and together they performed wonders.

Visitors soon began to arrive. After having been shown the church and churchyard, Mrs Watkins, a friend of Desmond, asked him if he intended to be buried there. In November Eddy wrote to Helen Dashwood, his wartime hostess, inviting her to stay, although, he warned her, everything was still chaotic. 'We shall not do too badly, I can't help thinking. Incidentally, "The Old Rectory" is not only wrong but against the law (I don't know why) . . . I doubt if you will care for it: it is the most remote, secluded, peaceful spot I have ever encountered. The house has considerable charm, but has been altered frequently and has no pretentions.'

'We shall not do too badly, I can't help thinking' was one of Eddy's favourite phrases. Lady Dashwood, ever inquisitive, visited nonetheless.

Jim Lees-Milne's name was written on the first page of the Long Crichel visitors' book and many times more. He soon began to spend long periods there: 'All the inmates at Long C., Eddy, Raymond, Desmond and Eardley are angelic to me and this house has become a sort of second home,'[8] and a few weeks later, 'At Long Crichel Eardley, Eddy and Desmond ran around, greeting me like three big, affectionate dogs.'[9] Staying there provided a respite from the world outside. He found the post-war years a depressing experience. During the conflict there was a cause to fight for and an aim in sight. Victory proved hollow. The country was weaker than before and nearly bankrupt: this was just defeat by another name. Rationing continued and even grew worse because of a succession of bitterly cold winters.

So much had been destroyed that housing became hard to find, taxation rose and a new age of austerity followed. The new Labour government – in which so many placed so much hope – appalled him. These barbarians at the gates threatened to destroy the standards of deference, loyalty and class distinction which had bound society together as he understood it and wished it to be. The British Empire rudely came to an end when India and Pakistan gained their independence in 1948; inevitably the remaining colonies would claim their right to self-rule too – causes long espoused by the *New Statesman*, a magazine he personally deplored, despite being very close friends with some of its writers. One June evening in 1947 he visited Brockhampton, a medieval manor house in Herefordshire. 'How beautiful this place is,' he wrote, then added bitterly, 'This evening the whole tragedy of England impressed itself upon me. This small, not very important seat in the heart of our secluded country, is now deprived of its last squire. A whole social system has broken down. What will replace it beyond government by the masses, uncultivated, rancorous, savage, philistine, the enemies of all things beautiful? How I detest democracy. More and more I believe in benevolent autocracy.'[10]

In particular, he feared for the future of great houses and for the National Trust. In the event both Hugh Dalton, the Chancellor of the Exchequer, and Sir Stafford Cripps, his successor in the new Labour government, proved friendly towards the Trust and were ardent members: the idea that the many would now be able to enjoy a privilege formerly enjoyed only by a few was a good socialist principle. In 1946 Dalton created the National Land Fund out of the sale of surplus wargoods as a thanks offering to the nation for victory. This enabled the Treasury to compensate the Inland Revenue for money lost by the transfer of houses to the National Trust in lieu of death duties. Any fears that the Trust might be nationalised proved groundless, for both Dalton and Cripps helped ensure that its inalienable property was scarcely affected by any planning legislation made by socialist governments. In 1948 Sir Ernest Gowers was invited by Cripps to examine the Country House Problem, an initiative which would lead to the establishment of a system of government grants to National Trust and private houses, and the opening up of a number of houses to the public. Harold Nicolson, who had lost his seat in Parliament in the Labour landslide, now sat on the National Trust's executive committee. In 1947, while staying at Long Crichel, he visited their properties in the west and south-west of England. He wrote a supportive article for the *Spectator* trying to explain the purpose of the Trust and its officials as guardians of country houses:

> It is not their purpose or desire to create a series of desiccated museums, a stereotyped succession of period pieces. In some cases, where funds are available and opportunity offers, they will nonetheless be able to convey to future generations some conception at least of how their ancestors lived. The pinnacles of Montacute will continue to cast their shadow across the lawns, and the nymph of Stourhead will sleep oblivious in her cool cascade. For those of us who believe ardently in an ultimate future it is not necessary to become mawkish about the past: it is even more unnecessary for those who hate the past to destroy its lovelier vestiges. And if we are one day to build what will one day be valuable without destroying what has once been valuable, we must accord to the National Trust more informed understanding and more practical support.[11]

The National Trust in those years was almost entirely run by Old Etonians. It could be argued that schemes for the acquisition and upkeep of country houses which might otherwise be demolished could be seen as evidence of the Establishment's ability to reinvent itself. Public access to houses was in some cases for only fifty days a year, and, as the Trust admitted, at hours as far as possible to suit the donor's convenience. In October 1946 Jim was present at a National

Trust meeting in Montacute House to discuss arrangements for its opening. Sir Robert ('Bertie') Abdy also attended. Jim recorded: 'Meeting quite a success, in spite of Bertie's sole comment which electrified the others. He commented that the public could not of course be admitted to the house because they smelt. There was two minutes dead silence, after which Sir Geoffrey [Cox] resumed the discussion as though nothing untoward had happened.'[12]

Jim and Eardley worked closely together at the Trust and, although very different, the two of them became intimate friends. Eardley's views were left-wing and he was an atheist, while Jim was deeply traditionalist and an ardent convert to Catholicism. However, they shared a sense of humour, and the eccentricities of the owners of the houses provided an endless source of amusement. They had no feelings of physical attraction towards one another, but they shared confidences about their infatuations and their love affairs. Much of the work at both Montacute and Stourhead was organised by them from Long Crichel. The two houses were two of the National Trust's great treasures. Montacute, a great Elizabethan mansion, had come into the National Trust's hands in 1931. Although magnificent, it was completely empty, and Eardley and Jim spent a great deal of time finding and furnishing the rooms with furniture and pictures. Stourhead in Wiltshire was near to Montacute. In 1946 the Palladian mansion, the grounds and 3,000 acres of land were made over to the National Trust by Sir Henry Hoare and his wife Alda. Their only son and heir had been shot through the lungs during an attack on the Mughar Ridge in Palestine in 1917 and buried in Alexandria. There were no other close relations left to inherit, and the Hoares – 'they are the dearest old couple' – died within hours of one another in March 1947. Jim's diary entry for Wednesday, 21 May, just two months later, reads:

Motored Eardley to Somerset. We reached Stourhead at 3 o'c. By that time the sun had penetrated the mist, and was gauzy and humid. The air about lake and grounds of a conservatory consistency. Never do I remember such Claude-like, idyllic beauty here. See Stourhead and die . . . We walked leisurely around the lake and amused ourselves in the grot trying to remember Pope's four lines correctly by heart, and forgetting, and running back to memorize. The temples are not in bad order, the Temple of Flora and the Pantheon being particularly well kept. We had tea at Stourton; then walked rapidly round the first floor of the house, reserving our detailed survey for tomorrow. We were staggered by the amount of first-rate furniture and pictures. There is more than enough upstairs to fill the whole *piano nobile*.

That night Jim stayed at Long Crichel. Both Eddy and Desmond were at home and 'full of affection and gaiety. I greatly enjoy being here.'[13] Eardley and Jim were still working at Stourhead in December. They spent three days in the house – Tuesday, Wednesday and Thursday – and Jim stayed at Long Crichel for two more nights:

Stourhead in turmoil. We had to start from scratch, sorting, rejecting, with the minimum of help, carrying heavy furniture and busts together, back-breaking, yet giggling work. We sold a collection of sheer junk for £75 to the local antique dealer in Mere, who took it away on Thursday, for which I hope the Trust will be pleased. We tried to trace all the younger Chippendale's pieces of furniture scattered about the house to put them in those show rooms to which they rightly belong. But we did no sort of arranging. It was the greatest fun, and oh how I enjoy Eardley's companionship. We think we make a splendid team, because we never spare criticism, neither taking offence; on the contrary each relishing outright condemnation of the other's efforts. I know we shall eventually succeed in making the house look splendid, we having picked the brains of all our experts, sifted, endorsed or rejected their several pieces of advice.[14]

The late Alda, Lady Hoare, became a great mythical figure at Long Crichel. Eddy said he was going to write a novel about her. Desmond called Jim and Eardley 'the Despoilers'.

In October 1949 Frances and Ralph Partridge made their first visit to Long Crichel. They too wrote regularly for the *New Statesman*. Frances reviewed children's books under the name Frances Bird, while Ralph's interests were nineteenth-century history and detective stories. At the time of the visit they were making expeditions to Broadmoor, where Ralph was doing research. His book, *Broadmoor: A History of Criminal Lunacy and Its Problems*, was published in 1953.

In an entry in her diary dated 18 October, a few days before they arrived, Frances wrote about Sonia Brownell's recent marriage to George Orwell. Everyone knew that Orwell was bedbound and dying from tuberculosis, but, with a reckless romanticism so typical of Sonia, she had convinced herself that she could keep him alive.* This was as near to not being married at all as it was possible to get, Frances wrote: the marriage was 'neurotic' and 'a drastic limitation to the range of human pleasures . . . but then I'm all for as much variety in human relationships as possible. So hurrah for homosexuality and also for the happy friendships between buggers and women, and vice-versa.' The next entry in the diary was made three days later: 'Somewhat in tune with my last entry, we set off today on our first visit to . . . Long Crichel House.'

Once they arrived they found 'warmth' and 'elegance'. The dinner and wine were delicious, and afterwards they listened to some of Desmond's records. Conversation was 'lively, easy and flowing, and about almost everything except politics'. But, she added:

---

* Sonia made plans to fly George Orwell to a clinic in Switzerland, but he died on 21 January 1950, four days before they were due to go.

I wish I didn't feel absurdly apologetic for my female sex. Looking at the visitors' book I see almost no visitors came in earlier days except mothers and sisters. When marriage is discussed it is generally a marriage of convenience, for some practical reason like companionship, care of each other's orphaned children, rather than love. I am hopelessly outclassed by Raymond's high standards of feminine 'chic', Eddy's *nice* women', and the elegance of bosomy Edwardian beauties in an album lying about. Nor do I think they would agree with me in preferring . . . a touch of androgyny in both sexes. But really! I am ashamed of such idiotic thoughts!

Unfortunately, Frances and her husband were put in separate bedrooms and, over-stimulated by the new environment, she found it difficult to sleep. In the morning, by house convention, guests were left to themselves. While the others worked in their rooms Frances walked with Ralph along the lanes to Crichel House. The walk took them beside a stream running under stone bridges and bordered by a hedge of tall pampas grass, handsomely outlined against dark shrubs. The boys of Dumpton House Preparatory School had departed and the house was now occupied by a girls' school.

Frances and Ralph had lived unorthodox lives. In 1920 Francis Birrell and David Garnett had opened a bookshop in Taviton Street in Bloomsbury. The rest of the house was divided into small flats and bedsitting rooms, one of which was occupied by Ray Marshall, an art student and elder sister of Frances. David Garnett occupied another. David Garnett and Ray Marshall fell in love and married in 1921. In the same year Frances came down from Newnham College, Cambridge and was offered a job as accountant in the bookshop at £3 a week – a job which was in fact made impossible because Birrell was in the habit of paying for personal expenses straight from the till. Despite a sense of chaos the bookshop prospered and became fashionable, and it also filled with interesting people – Edith, Osbert and Sacheverell Sitwell, Arthur Waley, Ottoline Morrell, Clive Bell

– who stood around gossiping, arguing, buying books. In slack periods the books would be read by the staff, then replaced on the shelves, albeit frequently marked with bus tickets, fingerprints and ash from Frankie Birrell's pipe.

In the evening there were parties, where a host of younger people collected. Frances called them 'fringe-Bloomsburies' – some from Oxford, like Raymond and Eddy, or from Cambridge, like Dadie Rylands; musicians such as Constant Lambert; Arthur Waley, the scholar and translator; Stephen 'Tommy' Tomlin the sculptor (with whom Eddy had at one time been in love); and the MacCarthys. People got rather, or very, drunk, and there was casual love-making. There were also hours of passionate dancing to the Blues, the Charleston and the Black Bottom which would go on until three or four o'clock in the morning when everyone reeled home with some new and temporary, or even permanent, partner. It was at such a party in the late summer of 1923 that Frances first got acquainted with Ralph Partridge. They danced, talked and spent most of the evening together. She found Ralph attractive, disturbing and puzzling, and this made her fall silent. The next day she received a letter from him: 'Have I committed an atrocity? I can't go to sleep without some sort of apology. You became so aloof. I'm unhappy about you, not that it matters to you. I don't want you to dislike me if you can help it. You were absolutely charming to me, and I have doubts what I was to you. It was your party for me.'[15] This was the beginning of their relationship, followed, eventually, by their marriage.

Ralph Partridge was handsome, cheerful and broad-shouldered ('an ox's shoulders and a healthy brain' according to Virginia Woolf). An ex-army officer, he had been awarded both the Military Cross and the Croix de Guerre for gallantry during the First World War. In 1921 he married the artist Dora Carrington, despite her own obsessive love for Lytton Strachey; Strachey, however, was homosexual and he in turn was infatuated with Ralph Partridge. In 1923 Strachey bought Ham Spray, a house just outside the village of Ham in

Wiltshire, and all three moved in together, although by then Ralph was falling in love with Frances, which Carrington resented. Strachey died of cancer in January 1932; overcome with grief, Carrington committed suicide a few weeks later – aiming for her heart, she shot herself in the side. (Many years later, Frances recalled that she found the Carrington triangle 'rather wearing. I remember getting rather thin.')[16] She moved into Ham Spray with Ralph – the house was already in Ralph's name – and they married in March 1933. At the time they were working on an unexpurgated edition of the diaries of the nineteenth-century politician Charles Greville, which were eventually published in eight volumes in 1938.

Frances Partridge became, like Jim Lees-Milne, a sort of honorary member of the Long Crichel household. Although they shared many acquaintances and, as in the case of the Crichel Boys, close friendships, Frances never felt intimate with him, and they were always somewhat wary of one another. However, he would have agreed with her when she reflected, decades after she first visited: 'I look back on my first visit to this most hospitable of country-houses with gratitude and affection, nor can I think of any other where I have spent so many happy times, both with Ralph and, in my later, lonelier life, right up to the present day.'[17]

4

Peculiar Friends

Raymond Mortimer was among the early visitors to Long Crichel. He was so impressed that he came back often, and eventually, in 1949, after giving up his tenancy of the Bothy, he bought a fourth share in the household and became a co-resident.* At fifty-five he was its oldest member. In his bedroom he had wide khaki-coloured striped wallpaper and inlaid Boulle furniture. He had more shelves built and filled them with French books, 'jaunes', which he had bought by the yard for decoration: their yellow spines made an attractive display although eventually they became so decrepit that they fell apart in one's hands. There were books all over the house, in all the rooms, hundreds of them, crammed onto shelves, in stacks on the floor, lying around on tables and on any spare piece of furniture.

Raymond had resigned from the *New Statesman* the previous year and gone to work at the *Sunday Times* under Desmond MacCarthy. Not only did the newspaper pay him more money, it also gave him more free time and fewer responsibilities. On MacCarthy's death four years later he succeeded him as chief reviewer. Cyril Connolly, another MacCarthy-trained journalist, soon joined him, and the two writers became the most celebrated critics of their time. Raymond had a particular interest in the visual arts: in 1929 he published

---

* After Raymond moved out Paul Hyslop asked Pat Trevor-Roper to move in, but he found Hyslop bossy and difficult to live with.

The New Interior Decoration with Dorothy Todd; in 1932 *The French Pictures, a Letter to Harriet*, was an exposition of how to look at pictures; and in 1944 he wrote an introduction to Edouard Manet's *Un bar aux Folies-Bergère* and a small monograph on Duncan Grant. He also contributed to several photographic collections, including, in 1936, Bill Brandt's *The English at Home*, in which he used his introduction to protest against the extremes of wealth and poverty which Brandt had witnessed. In his preface to *Channel Packet* – an anthology of writings from several periodicals which was published in 1942 – Raymond claimed that in his passport he had described himself not as an author but as a journalist. Apart from these few short monographs and two collections of his articles, this was effectively true: despite Raymond's very obvious talents he seemed to have no further writing ambitions. Cyril Connolly on the other hand had already edited the enormously influential magazine *Horizon* during the war years and had several books to his name. That Connolly regarded himself as a serious author was not in doubt; this was the difference between the two.

The residents of Long Crichel had various sobriquets and were known as 'the Crichel Boys', 'the Bears' or 'the Bachelors'. Each member – Eddy, Eardley, Desmond and Raymond – added his own singular character to the house. Frances compared them to a string quartet. Raymond, 'certainly not the least dominant', was the cello. Eddy she likened to the first violin, 'at times poetical and mellifluous, at others wailing or strident, always exact and confident'. Eardley was the most practical of the four, 'the one to be relied upon to make decisions about planting trees, or to seize his gun and shoot a pheasant straying on the lawn'. Desmond for his part 'always contributed boundless high spirits, optimism, volatility, and interest in everything that came his way'.[1] Together they set their initials into a mosaic among the stones at the foot of the French window leading from the sitting room into the garden. Eddy's initials – ESW – were the most obvious, since his health required him to have many coloured medicine bottles, which provided him with plenty of glass fragments. Around them Paul Hyslop designed windbreaks to provide shelter for sitting outside to read or talk or sunbathe.

Mr and Mrs Deverell, the butler and the cook, were also very much part of the household. Anne Deverell's devotion to her 'dearest Mr Eddy' and her interest in his personal welfare was rather tiresome, but her cooking was excellent and greatly appreciated. Her portly husband was more of a problem, and visitors were advised not to leave any small change around in the bedrooms where he might find it. Frances described how when Desmond MacCarthy died it was Deverell who had received the phone call and entered the sitting room 'with stately tread' to make an announcement to the weekend party: 'I thought you might like to hear the news.'

Eardley recorded the exchange between Desmond Shawe-Taylor and the butler on a rare occasion when Mrs Deverell had not provided enough to eat. The young art master from Bryanston School was one of six at the table, but there was a very inadequate amount of chicken à la King and Eddy had to replace part of his very small helping:

> Deverell to Desmond who was helping himself last at the sideboard: 'The boy cleared the dish.'
>
> Desmond: 'Quiet, Deverell.'
>
> Deverell: 'The boy cleared the dish. Right up to here.' (Gesture with a knife.) 'He cleared it.'
>
> Desmond: 'Shut up, Deverell.'
>
> Exit Deverell, muttering: 'The boy cleared the dish.'

When Mrs Deverell provided what turned out to be a highly success-ful lunch for Greta Garbo and Cecil Beaton, and her husband asked Eardley whether it might be possible to meet Miss Garbo, Garbo replied abruptly: 'No.' The Deverells also bred pedigree golden

Labrador puppies, which they advertised as ideal Christmas presents. Dogs were always part of the Long Crichel ménage, and over the years there was 'an overlapping series of large, soft and affectionate Labradors rushing to give visitors a gratifyingly enthusiastic welcome before filling the hearth-rug with their outstretched bodies, or looking up with doe-like eyes pleading for a walk'.[2]

Soon after they moved in Eardley, Eddy and Desmond started a book of Crichel anecdotes and stories concerning the house which had amused one of them at the time. The anecdotes, which were written down in a sort of ledger-book, might be snobbish, schoolboyish, silly, witty or eccentric, but these unguarded remarks betrayed the speaker's character. As Julian Jebb, a much later visitor, said in a comment which was also included, 'It's the *timing* I admire about Long Crichel.'

6 April 1947. EK (pensively): I wonder if I stole enough of those vases from Montacute . . .

2 January 1948. ESW: There! You see! Eardley has shrunk off without doing anything about those pictures. How like a man!

14 March 1948. ESW: Oh yes, I could sink into a Slough of Despond; but not in a dressing-gown.

7 January 1949. (Diana Sackville-West [Eddy's sister] finds a chocolate in the sofa) ESW: Well, I'm always puffing out those cushions; it can't have been there long.

13 January 1950. ESW (to R and D): It's very cold in here. I think *I* shall go to bed. (Turns out gas fire, and exits.)

6 October 1951. James Strachey to ESW after dinner: Would everybody hate it if you showed off your instrument to us?

29 June 1952. DST and EK after Sunday-morning drinks [at Crichel House]. The talk there turned on fans. EK (suddenly): My Uncle Gerald left me a fan.

Boxing Day 1955. DST: Is it all right the Pope saying he rather wishes he had died when he was so ill. I mean isn't it heretical – almost equivalent to suicide? ESW: It's quite permissible to argue with God; even to speak sharply to Him. DST: Do *you* ever speak sharply to Him? ESW: I've been known to.

[Undated.] ESW: I've left several things for you on your table. DST: Nice things? ESW (after short pause): Not necessarily.

15 December 1957. Ian McCallum* (giving advice about South America to DST): And then there's a charming man in Bahia. I believe he calls himself Martin now; but I knew him as Eros.

8 December 1958. (Jim Lees-Milne has been recommending the pleasures of always staying in one place). RM: Well you might as well be in the grave. ESW: There is something to be said for getting used to the grave before you are in it.

28 March 1950. (After tea) Godfrey Winn to Cuthbert Worsley†: You can't go yet. You've only just met me.

9 August 1966. Raymond: Did you do any acting when you were young? Morgan [Forster]: No, never. I . . . no, but that wasn't acting . . . I played the triangle once.

---

* Ian McCallum, architectural journalist (1919–1987).

† Godfrey Winn, popular author and journalist (1906–1971); Cuthbert Worsley, television and theatre critic, writer (1907–1977).

There is a photograph of Eddy as a baby in his pram which he said 'showed the enormity of his discontent'. Frances said he had never really changed. While Raymond, Eddy, Eardley and Desmond all regarded their sexuality as normal, Eddy was still able to find it a cause for unhappiness – as Jim recorded in February 1947:

Brilliant fireworks from Desmond who is the gayest, sweetest-tempered, most informative person in the wide world. After dinner a curious discussion which ensued about homosexuality. Eddy showed deliberate unreason, and refused to concede a point. He maintained that born homosexuals could never become hetero-sexuals, whereas I maintained, with no intent to annoy, that this was simply not the case. People are not necessarily born one way or the other; that heterosexuals could become homosexuals, and vice-versa; and that there were people capable of falling equally in love with men and women. Eddy stoutly denied the possibility of persons being ambisexual, and with vehemence quoted himself as the over-riding disproof of this notion, assuming that his case was a precedent the world over. He adopted a highly self-pitying attitude, became furious with Desmond and, after much high-pitched querulous shouting that Desmond 'always' attacked him, left the room. Desmond meant to do nothing of the kind. Afterwards Eardley and Desmond admitted that it was impossible to carry on discussions with Eddy. Indeed they are right. In my hearing Eddy announced that he preferred not to arrive at the truth than to involve himself in controversy, which made him ill. In spite of this I have great affection for Eddy. He told me the next day that he knew he ought to be contented with his lot but his chronic ill-health and difficult temperament prevented him acknowledging his good fortune. Every day, he said, he was pursued by angst. I understand this because in a lesser measure I am too. But not, perhaps, every day.[3]

In 1952 the artist Edward Le Bas exhibited his picture *Interior at Long Crichel* at the Royal Academy. Figures in interiors, as well as still life, were among his favourite subjects, and this Crichel conversation piece – of Eddy, Eardley, Desmond and Raymond gathered in the sitting room – was regarded as particularly successful. In future years the furniture always stayed more or less in the same positions as it was in the painting. Just as there were books everywhere, there were also pictures all around the house. 'Eardley, Desmond and Eddy lead a highly civilised life here,' Jim wrote on one of his first visits. 'Comfortable house, pretty things, good food. All the pictures are Eardley's, and a fine collection of modern art too. After dinner Desmond read John Betjeman's poems aloud, and we all agreed they would live.'[4] Eddy also brought pictures of his own from Knole, including the Banting screen, and later Raymond added to the collection. Eardley, however, had once owned an art gallery, so most of them were his.

Eardley's mother Audrey, who came regularly to Long Crichel to stay with her son, was a source of several entries in the anecdote book. Raymond told Frances that she was 'a marvellously unadulterated Victorian, having led the most sheltered of lives in the most conventional of worlds. I doubt if she has found reason to change any opinion during the last sixty-five years . . . What she makes of her son's friends I shudder to think – "very peculiar" is the most probable verdict though we have been at pains to conduct ourselves with decorum.'[5] Her penchant for serving banana sandwiches as teatime delicacies led to a discussion as to whether the slices should overlap or not. Eardley used to tell a story about his mother and her cook, Mrs Veal, who had been in her service for many years. Getting older and fed up with Mrs Knollys' demands – and wanting to move on – she announced one day that she was handing in her notice. Mrs Knollys replied, 'Nonsense, Veal, get back to the kitchen!' Which she did, and there she stayed for another ten years. Raymond once visited Mrs Knollys at her house in Bath with Paul Hyslop. He wrote to Eardley from his hotel:

Your Mama very kindly asked us to tea, & gave us a very warm welcome as friends of yours. I thought her house delightful; & we had a whopping tea. I was enchanted by a photograph of you as a little boy in a skirt with a little boat! (I specially asked her if she had any photographs of you as a little boy – I wanted one of you at the seductive age of 14 – but did not get that! I hope we didn't make too sinister an impression – your mother said she so much liked to meet your friends! – which I thought faintly alarming. She couldn't have been kinder to us. Your aunt also was very sweet ... Your mother's chocolate cakelets are delicious.[6]

Eardley was born in 1902 in Alresford in Hampshire. His father Cyprian was a land agent and founded the Land Agents Society, and Eardley inherited his love of the countryside. Discouraged at Winchester from taking art classes, he became interested in pictures by living so close to the collection of old master drawings at Christ Church. After graduation he worked briefly in advertising for Lever Brothers and J. Walter Thompson until Anthony Asquith, a friend from school who had already started on his own career in film-making, suggested he go to Los Angeles to try and enter the film world. All that remains as evidence among his papers of this aborted career is twenty-four pages of typescript of a story for a film which Eardley sent to Paramount – as well as a letter gently rejecting his proposal.

Having failed to make a success of his time in Hollywood, Eardley returned to Europe. In France he met Glenway Wescott and Monroe Wheeler, two Americans who were to be friends for the rest of his life. Wescott and Wheeler first met in 1919 at a poetry club and were together – married in everything but name – for sixty-eight years. Wescott was the son of a Wisconsin pig farmer and Wheeler, who was three years older, was the son of a Chicago fish-broker. Wescott intended to be a writer. He said that he 'pretended to be a genius . . .

in order to get on in the world'. Funded by a wealthy Chicago patron, he and Wheeler travelled to Europe, where they said they saw enough to know that they never wanted to be anywhere else again, and they spent most of the 1920s living in France and Germany. In Paris they mixed with other American émigrés like Gertrude Stein and Ernest Hemingway. While Wescott began his career as a writer of novels, essays and stories, Monroe Wheeler and an American railway heiress called Barbara Harrison bought a small printing press to make limited-edition books. They published thirteen in all, two of them by Wescott.

In January 1925 Eardley wrote to Monroe Wheeler, who was in the USA. Eardley was in Stanford Dingley in Berkshire, staying with Bob Gathorne-Hardy and Kyrle Leng, two Oxford friends:

My dearest Monie – How are you and are you coming over – I expect to be a night or two in Paris about Feb 20 & am quite lost there without you. Will you recommend me to one of your best friends there – don't really bother but if you happened to have a nice American boyfriend who happens to be in Paris & and will you tell me if you know of anyone who can tell me about *gymnasiums* in Paris. I bet there are lovely chromium & glass gymnasiums in Paris where chaps go & exercise & I want to see them . . .

I am here for the weekend but this cottage is too ruddy cold in winter – we survive, you I think would die! Julian is 1/2 way through a cure – He has been at a home near London run by a fascinating American doctor called Cullum who reminds me of you. The cure has been to starve for a fortnight & then have milk for 10 days plus jumping on his spine & work outs & fruit juice – He is now ending the hectic season & it appears to have cured him – I hope it has because he was in pain after every meal – Meanwhile all my London friends & the rest of the population of Stanford Dingley have been head over heels in love or in bed with a young

American from Honolulu called Leslie Leo*. If you saw a film called Cleopatra it was him lying on the left of Nero dressed in a bunch of grapes. He is wonderful company & you see the roof of his mouth & a battery of pearly teeth when he laughs. I can't say I've done more than hold his hand but he is there for the kissing for those that like and does not insist on ore deposits although he is admittedly a gold mine by profession – Broken hearts are all over the place & chaps are taking one another to Switzerland to stop chaps throwing themselves from windows . . .

I have that lovely picture of Lloyd [Glenway Wescott's brother] in my heart & photo of him in my bedroom. Is he as nice as ever & still preoccupied with girls. By the way I don't think much of them – one gets so *involved* – & they are so difficult & not much to sleep with . . .[7]

Four years later Eardley was staying at the Hotel Welcome in Villefranche on the French Riviera with his boyfriend at that time, a writer called Jamie Campbell. Eardley, Jamie, Monroe and Wescott had all become part of Jean Cocteau's circle. Cocteau went to the Hotel Welcome because it was where the sailors used to go. The place was often rowdy. Eardley remembered a night when the sailors trashed it. There was complete uproar in the bar with breaking glass and furniture flying everywhere, but the landlord remained imperturbable. 'Les jeunes gens s'amusent,'† he told the residents in an attempt to reassure them – a phrase Eardley continued to use as a comment on any art that he considered destructive but thought would pass in due course. Eardley and Jamie sometimes took Cocteau out for drives into the surrounding hills. They once stopped to admire a view and Cocteau took out a syringe to inject himself with heroin.

---

* Leslie Fullard-Leo (1909–2001) grew up in Hawaii, studied acting in London and appeared in over 30 films.

† The young men are enjoying themselves.

He invited Eardley to follow but he refused – out of cowardice, he said. Cocteau also showed him the typescript of his newly written play *La Voix Humaine*, which Eardley translated into English. In *La Voix Humaine* a woman speaks on a telephone, desperately trying to keep her lover who is on the point of marrying someone else. Sybil Thorndike wanted the part but the play was performed instead at the soirée of a fashionable Mayfair hostess.* As well as his script, Eardley's other relic of Jean Cocteau was his typed copy of *Le Livre Blanc,* a semi-autobiographical 'white paper' on homosexual love. Cocteau decorated it for him with drawings of sailors. At the time Cocteau had been smoking too much opium and was near collapse. Eventually he left for a nursing home in St Cloud for a cure. Eardley by this time knew Cocteau well enough to discover that, in his words, he was 'too intricate' in bed and made an unsatisfactory lover.[8]

Back in England the following year Eardley was appointed private secretary to Viscount Hambledon, the owner of W.H. Smith Ltd. His duties included management of Hambledon's London and country houses. The experience he gained from the post was the preparation he needed for his subsequent work with the National Trust. Hambledon was so impressed by Eardley's abilities that in 1936 he gave him backing when he wanted to become a partner in the small Storran Gallery, which occupied two basement rooms opposite Harrods. It had been founded by a Mrs Cochrane. Eardley described her as, 'One of those English-speaking women, who, with no special talent, feel a need to become involved in the arts.'[9] When the gallery first opened it sold prints and greeting cards, but a year after its foundation she had been joined by an energetic and charming Austrian woman called Ala Story; the names Story plus Cochrane created the portmanteau word 'Storran'. The anxieties of the late 1930s made dealing in art far from easy, but Ala Story's talents were

---

* *La Voix Humaine* was filmed in 1948 by the Italian director Roberto Rossellini with his then wife Anna Magnani as the first part of his film *L'Amore.* In 2020 the play was filmed as *The Human Voice* by Pedro Almodóvar and performed by Tilda Swinton.

such that the gallery proved successful, the exhibitions improved and she began to attract artists who wanted to exhibit their work with her, as well as a public who bought it.

In 1935, after Mrs Cochrane left, Ala Story took on a young assistant called Frank Coombs, an architect who had worked as a draughtsman for Hampshire County Council. After four years he had decided to give up his job and move to the island of Sark in order to dedicate himself to becoming an artist. He met Ala Story there when she was on holiday, and she offered him a job, so he followed her back to London. After six months Frank was allowed to organise an exhibition of his own. His show, including pictures by significant contemporary British artists – or artists resident in Britain – such as Ivon Hitchens, Frances Hodgkins, Christopher Wood, Victor Pasmore and John Banting, moved the gallery in an entirely different direction.

Mrs Story eventually decided to leave. Despite his doubts over the attractions of a gallery where rats could be heard scuttling behind walls which were covered by nothing more than hessian stretchers, Eardley bought a stake for £300 with assistance from Lord Hambledon. Fortunately, his fears proved groundless, as people were curious about the Bohemian squalor. Eardley had memories of Lady Ottoline Morrell getting badly entangled with the lead of her small dog as she made her way down the very rickety staircase, and of a friendly cat which became a regular visitor and helped discourage the wildlife. Soon afterwards Eardley and Frank brought back an André Derain and a Christopher Wood from Paris and then sold them both in twenty-four hours. After this success, Eardley became confident that, as far as the gallery was concerned, anything might be possible. The following year Frank and he became yet more ambitious and staged a show of eighteen pictures by Amedeo Modigliani; *Le petit paysan*, for sale in the Storran Gallery for £800, was subsequently acquired by the Tate Gallery. (Their finest Picasso was priced at £2,000, and only one Modigliani reached £1,000; most living British painters were on sale for between fifteen and thirty guineas, from which the gallery took 33 per cent.) In October 1937 the gallery moved to more salubrious quarters at 5 Albany Court Yard in Piccadilly. Exhibitions were widely reviewed in the press, including by Raymond Mortimer under the pseudonym of 'Roger Marvell'. Two years later, however, after a show which included works by Pierre Bonnard, Georges Rouault, Pablo Picasso, Henri Matisse, Maurice Utrillo and Chaïm Soutine, the gallery was forced to close just as it was starting to be profitable. In September 1939 Eardley and Frank sent out a circular saying that all the Storran's best French and English paintings had been sent into the country about fifty miles from London and were now hung in a private house.

Frank Mundy Coombs – he was also known as 'Frankie' – and Eardley Knollys were more than just business partners, they were lovers. Frank was born in Radstock in Somerset and attended the King's School, Bruton. His parents lived in Poultney Street in Bath. There is a portrait of Coombs by Glyn Philpot – an artist who exhibited at the Storran Gallery – in the Victoria Art Gallery, Bath. It dates to around 1930 when he was twenty-four. (He was four years younger than Eardley.) The sitter has reddish-blond hair, fine features and a high forehead; he is wearing a blue shirt. The background behind Coombs is divided, with a white curtain to the left, but to the right, the direction towards which he looks, there is nothing but blackness.

Relatively few of his letters to Eardley survive. The earliest was written on the reverse of some old notices which he said he had found in his suitcase. The address he gives is 'The Mill Studio, Sark'. At the top of the page Frank wrote 'Friday 7.45 pm', otherwise the letter is undated:

My dear Eardley,

Here I am at the top of the middle of the Island frying steak and onions for myself. I have to keep the door open as the steak and onions are rather too much for this small room, & the whole of the Island benefits. I arrived safely yesterday, it wasn't a very good crossing but I managed not to be sick. It rained all day after I arrived so I primed five canvasses, but it doesn't look as if the weather will let me do much. This letter I feel is going to be a bit disjointed as I have to keep getting up to prod the steak. I was very tired last night and went to bed quite early after having lots of beer with the fishermen and much handshaking and slapping on the back. Today I have been working on a picture outside the Bel-Air, it was rather cold and I had to wear a coat, but it was very healthy although [*sic*]. The visitors seem a mouldy lot. It is a large picture with the avenue in the middle, on the extreme left is the Bank (Old Guernsey Branch) (open every other Monday in November), on the right Mr Firth's house, and a very odd looking carriage on the left, and on the right a nice old fisherman with a wooden leg (Philip Hannan) dashing into the Bel-Air for a drink. You look about three miles up the avenue, but you stay in the wilds of Little Sark because the centre of the wheel of the carriage brings you right back. Several chimneys, windows, stones, Philip's hat and the wheel are all in their appointed places like stars in the firmament and they sing accordingly.

I caught a fast train to Southampton on Wednesday night, flopped into a corner seat, fixed my eyes on a button in the upholstery opposite and thought about you. On my left dark trees and lights were whizzing past, and on my right a nice old gentleman was reading a newspaper of which I could just read the headline WIDOW STUNNED THEN STABBED, in the centre I sat facing Southampton and thought how nice it was to be coming back to see you again. Gradually my thoughts were merged in the music of the wheels, and became a part of that harmony in which it is impossible to be out of time, then all my thoughts about you and all the things I cannot say, still less write, flowed out and I became a poet until we reached Basingstoke, where I felt like the

77

young woman 'who often said that she would choke if she remained at Basingstoke', but the music began again and I became a singer as well before reaching Southampton. Eardley, if you want to know what I want to say to you, next time you're on a train, just fix your eyes on a button in the upholstery – and listen.

Saturday 8.30 am.

Congratulate yourself that the steak and onions just saved you from getting a love letter from me. I got up very early this morning and walked down to the Harbour, fetched the milk on the way back and am waiting for the eggs to be boiled.

I have eaten the eggs and drunk a pint of milk.

I am just off to start painting my picture, the sun is quite strong and it looks like being a fine day so go out and buy yourself a carnation with love from Frankie.[10]

At the outbreak of war Frank was thirty-three and Eardley thirty-seven. All males between eighteen and forty-one had to register for service, but farm work was one of a number of reserved occupations. Without a gallery to run, Frank Coombs and Eardley moved down to Dorset to work on a farm instead. They hoed sugar-beet and took part in haymaking on a farm adjoining Maiden Castle. '[I] am simply loving it,' Eardley told Eddy. 'When I feel I must do my bit to help the war I hoe faster and harder. So I am back sore and recumbent but as far as one can be – happy – I live with Frank in a lovely room at Weymouth.'[11] Each day he bicycled back and forth on 'a most dignified machine curried out in black and gold – not a fast mover'.

Eardley's happiness was short-lived. After a few months Frank joined the navy as an able seaman. Eardley was both appalled and deeply hurt. 'Frank has gone back today,' he wrote to Raymond:

It makes me shudder to think of what he has let himself in for . . . I feel I have been an awful bore to my friends about it all during the last month and am rather ashamed of my behaviour.

When I think of the things we said to one another in those happy days in France it still seems impossible Frank of all people can have done anything so unwise – at least I can't help from any point of view thinking it so, though I am getting to be able to adjust myself to it.[12]

Eardley continued to work on farms, and when his contract in Dorset came to an end he found another job in Stanford Dingley, Bob Gathorne-Hardy's home. He wrote to Frank:

I have been put to hoeing again – which I hate. I do it very slowly and badly exactly 1/3 as fast as I should. I can't think how the others get along so quick and on top of that it tires me out and makes me ache all over. And I think I shall be at it nearly all this month! In bad moments I curse everyone and everything – then I compare the torture with that of the boys at Calais and Dunkirk and feel better.[13]

But threshing was a great experience – although exhausting, he said there was something 'biblical' about watching the sacks of grain accumulate. Every few days Eardley wrote Frank long, detailed, densely written and informative letters which run for several pages. It was as if he felt the need to communicate as much about himself as he could and writing it down came as a relief. Frank's letters to Eardley are brief – probably he had much less time to himself. In December 1940 they had some time together, but Frank had to leave again before the end of the year, and Eardley spent New Year with his sister-in-law and her children. (Vernon, Eardley's brother, was in a prisoner-of-war camp in Poland.) 'This will just be a little happy New Year letter my sweet as I have no news,' he wrote. 'I think I have never been so happy as in our 10 days together. It is lovely to know we still like each other as much as before.'

A few weeks before Christmas, the National Trust advertised for a new member of staff to help look after their growing portfolio of properties. In a very short space of time Eardley applied for the role of Assistant Secretary, was interviewed and then offered the job. Within weeks he took up his new post at West Wycombe. He told Frank in a letter that he was happy in his work – its only drawback was Lady Dashwood, who was 'hellish mean and bad-tempered'. She had just cut off both the jam and marmalade at breakfast time:

> There is a fascinating social embarrassment at lunch . . . at the centre table today were Lady D, son and daughter, Eddy & Rebecca West while Matheson & I and the head woman secretary, the head filing clerk & the accountant Mr Finch were at the other round table in the corner. The food is all put on a side table & you help yourself so there is an ugly rush. After each course the ladies at our table knit madly & each group is much more interested in the conversation at the other table than in their own.[14]

Lady Dashwood allowed Eardley to go shooting in the park, but it was 'poorish fun'. She could not shoot anything except sitting coots, and these were horrible to eat, but she fed them to the National Trust staff whenever she could.

He also wrote to Monroe Wheeler. The National Trust, Eardley explained:

> owns country mansions, farms, estates, cottages, roman villas being excavated and all sorts of other trash and beauty for the public to enjoy, hike over, litter with paper, scratch their names on, and get sunburnt among. It is really land agency work. It suits me down to the ground and I do not think I will be conscripted. I live in a little pink cottage built in 1750 in strawberry hill style with Raymond, and his London housekeeper, bombed out, looks after us and she is one of the best cooks in Europe, how lucky I am . . . I live in a rarefied atmosphere of highbrow bookishness and get a

good deal of fun out of being a lowbrow and cultivating a vegetable garden. London is too horrible, and only madmen, and those who have to, sleep there. The curse so far of this war is being separated from all one's friends, as with them all in the middle east or shooting at aeroplanes in Scotland or in the country, and [with] the telephones not working very well it is difficult to meet, and of course hardly any petrol. When we are all killed we shall look back to these as luxury days.[15]

Frank was serving on HMS *Caroline*, the naval headquarters in Belfast Harbour, although both the administration and accommodation had outgrown the ship and occupied various establishments throughout the city. After leaving Eardley at the start of January 1941 he returned to Belfast. The journey took nearly twenty-four hours, and he stood most of the way from Euston Station. He told Eardley that he thought the 'Big Crisis' seemed very near. Eardley, meanwhile, had been thinking 'quite a bit about life after the war'. The prospects of reopening the gallery were remote, so he instead considered selling privately from home: 'I visualise our house in Dorset, simple life, super works of art for the few rich boys . . . and of course enormous sums for the oil paintings of F. M. C. [Frank Coombs]' He said he was:

very very taken with Sherborne and am inclined to think it must be our district . . . You will be glad to hear I am now responsible for the Cerne Giant and I strolled up and down his cock. He is in a bad way and needs some attention. I am expecting some fun from a correspondence about his respectability in the local papers, some by the National Trust saying he is a disgrace and should be destroyed.[16]

The Cerne Giant is a hill figure near the village of Cerne Abbas in Dorset; the figure depicts a nude male with a prominent erection and wielding a club. A few weeks later Eardley went back to Sherborne:

[I] think I shall have time to try and see a house or two. God knows where we can find the money if I do see somewhere we want. I am inclined to go for a small nice place with a couple of acres well placed and then for us to build or adapt it rather than strain the last penny to buy a place we can barely afford. We wouldn't want much commitment and I would like it to be somewhere we could live all right with no money and no servant.[17]

Frank replied that he had played rugby against Sherborne School and he liked the place. At the beginning of February Frank wrote: 'Thinking of all the things we have in common I was suddenly reminded of OYSTERS and decided that my aversion must be conquered and the reproach reversed. So I jumped in a tram and went to the Waldorf Oyster bar and had half a dozen with delicious brown bread and a glass of Chablis and enjoyed them enormously. As you probably guessed I had never tried them before although! [sic]'[18]

He also told Eardley that he was about to do a picture of a camouflaged American destroyer with a background full of hills. Perhaps it was this destroyer which gave Frank the idea of applying for release from the navy in the hope of being accepted as a camouflage artist by the Air Ministry – but with so much going on he feared that his application would be overlooked. At the beginning of April, however, and rather to his surprise, Frank was informed by his commanding officer that the Admiralty had written to the Air Ministry on his behalf. If they selected him, he would get his discharge: 'All of which is splendid and quick too.'[19] Frank was called back to England for an interview, and this gave him a brief chance to see Eardley again. On Good Friday, 12 April 1941, Eardley wrote to say he had been told the 'odds are you will be doing aerodromes and aeroplanes . . . There will be tons of air fields all over the place when the American planes arrive. Raymond says you *must* get some leave between jobs & come and stay here [The Bothy]. There seems no doubt you will be an RAF officer.'[20]

Frank replied the following day, 13 April – the envelope bears the censor's label, 'Examiner 2047':

175 Clifton Park Avenue

Darling Eardley

I arrived safely after a comfortable and fairly quick journey to find I had missed Belfast's first air-raid. I was indeed lucky to have moved digs and to be away at the time as the bombs fell very near my old place.

I did enjoy the very short time we had together and was frightfully pleased about my interview. We have been awfully busy since I got back and shall be working all this weekend . . .

Your lovely postcard from Polperro arrived to-day.

All my love, Frankie.

Belfast had survived the first two years of the war more or less unscathed. Although the city was only two and three quarter hours' flying time away from the Continent, there had been little preparation for an attack, and many continued to believe, almost perversely, that Belfast was out of range and raids would not happen. Yet Belfast had legitimate targets. Harland & Wolff was one of the largest shipyards in the world and had built liners such as the *Titanic* for the White Star Line, as well as aircraft carriers and cruisers for the Royal Navy; Short Brothers manufactured aircraft; Harlands Engineering built trucks; and there were a number of factories which manufactured aero-linen for covering aircraft, ordnance parts and ammunition.

Broadcasting from Hamburg, William Joyce, the German propagandist known as 'Lord Haw-Haw', announced that there would be 'Easter eggs for Belfast'. On the night of Tuesday, 15 April more than 150 Luftwaffe bombers left their bases in France and the Netherlands and headed for Belfast. Their targets were supposed to be military and manufacturing, but poor visibility meant that explosives often fell on densely populated areas. Incendiaries and bombs rained down from the sky and continued to fall until five in the morning. That night between 900 and 1,000 people were killed, and 1,500 more were injured. More than 200,000 refugees fled the city to neighbouring towns or walked into the fields. It was the greatest loss of life in any night raid during the Blitz outside of London.

On 22 April, a week after the Easter air raid, Eardley wrote again to Frank from The Bothy: 'My darling Frankie, I have become like your mother and am feeling very worried about you though I keep telling myself that I am sure that your lucky neckwear and your lucky star were in action last Wednesday.'

There had been a bomb in Sackville Street during a recent raid and the London gallery had been damaged but not too badly. The windows were all smashed and the shutters torn off, and several panes of the roof lights broken. Throughout the war Eardley had continued to encourage artists like the young Francis Bacon and Graham Sutherland ('the pressure of doing a number of war pictures in a given time has improved his drawing and [Sutherland's] work out of all recognition').[21] He also continued to deal in pictures, and most of this letter to Frank relates to some pictures by Frances Hodgkins,* a New Zealand-born artist in whom Eardley took a personal interest: 'four absolutely outstanding beauties' which he had just bought from the Leicester Galleries:

> I fully expect to hear tomorrow that we have got them. I only hope the whole thing will please you. Seeing the four upstairs together I seemed to think they were as good as four Cezannes of equal importance. They need a lot of light. I have felt so pleased all day about them, it is funny how buying or selling a picture gives me a kick that nothing else does . . .
>
> With tons of love, is it too Audreyish of me if I ask you to send

---

* Frances Hodgkins (1869–1947) spent most of her working life in England. During her lifetime, she had a very high reputation. 'By prodigious efforts' Eardley secured for her a civil-service pension.

me a p. c. after any other formidable raid on Belfast, my sweet, well anyhow you have written I am sure and you know I don't want to be tiresome, E.[22]

There were so many bodies and so much hurry after the Belfast raid that there was no time to lay the corpses out and treat the dead with any kind of dignity. Bodies were bundled into their coffins in old sheets or blankets, or in the torn and filthy clothes they were wearing when they were found. The gravediggers worked until late in the evening and started again in the early hours of the daylight. For the unidentified and the unclaimed there were mass graves. During the funeral procession the streets were lined by silent crowds of mourners: hearse after hearse, coffin after coffin, there were so many it was impossible to count. Most of the dead were buried in Belfast City Cemetery.

Frank had also been killed in the raid. When Eardley wrote to him full of his own news and asking Frank to let him know that he was safe after any future raid it was all too late. Frank had been dead for days. He too was buried in the City Cemetery.

On 14 May, a month after his death, *The Times* published a brief tribute written by Raymond: 'Frank Coombs . . . did much to introduce to the public young artists of promise. His friends will feel his loss the more profoundly because his enjoyment of the beautiful and the comic was so acute and infectious. He was a man with an uncommon talent for happiness.'

5

The Sackville Glove

B ecause so great a number of their friends belonged to the world of the arts, and because the Crichel Boys themselves were such good company, and the food and drink so generous, the house became a kind of wholly informal literary salon. A weekend visit to 'Crichel' (as it was usually called) was guaranteed to mean a couple of nights of enjoyment, at the same time both restorative and invigorating. In December 1949 Rosamond Lehmann stayed at Long Crichel with her lover Cecil Day-Lewis and a few days before Christmas she sent her hosts a – not wholly serious – letter of thanks:

> Oh, my dear, dear Boys, how remiss I am not to have written to thank you for my heavenly 2 nights . . . it demoralizes me dreadfully to stay with you, I look on it as one of my treats & pleasures. I return so discontented with my dwelling & its contents, with my couple [Lehmann's staff], with my lack of beautiful lamps and gramophone records and bath towels etc. etc. etc. etc.
>
> You are such perfect hosts, and your delicate consideration for your guests and one another is a shining example to this coarse, violent and predatory age. I love you all. I spent a happy time on the way back trying to decide which of you I'd like best of all to marry SUPPOSING I was asked . . .

Hugo & Sally [her children] are decorating the banisters & adorning a Xmas tree. I think of you all doing the same. Sally was telling me last night that the young Matron at her school, to whom she is devoted, lost her fiancé in the war. I said sympathetically I did hope she'd find another young man. S. (firmly) 'No, no. She's not the type who'd love twice.'

Happy Christmas and very much love to you all – Your grateful Rosamond.[1]

Long Crichel had strong links with Bloomsbury. Both Vanessa Bell and Duncan Grant painted there – and had their pictures on the walls. Grant also designed the curtains, and plates were painted by Bell. John Piper was responsible for some of the textiles. One weekend the Cambridge don Dadie Rylands, another Bloomsbury figure and a frequent visitor, came with Dame Peggy Ashcroft, and they gave readings from Shakespeare.

When, in 1950, Somerset Maugham visited Long Crichel he was probably the most famous writer in the world. Maugham was a friend of Raymond – in a letter to Monroe Wheeler, Eardley mentions that Raymond has just returned after spending three weeks with Willy [Maugham], 'enjoying himself madly with American sailors from Villefranche'. Frances Partridge found herself sitting next to Maugham at tea. She said she was charmed by him but saw him as belonging 'in a reptile house, a chameleon by choice, with his pale deeply furrowed brow, sunken glittering eyes and the mouth that opens deliberately and sometimes sticks there – as he has a distinct stammer'.[2]

'Conversation reaches a high level in this house,' Frances wrote, although 'both Raymond and Eddy admit that they often don't hear what other people say. At breakfast this morning Desmond suddenly burst out in comic desperation, "Raymond never hears a *single* sentence I say, even if it's only three words long!" Raymond beamed sweetly but didn't deny the charge.' The conversation could also be rather confused. When the historian Hugh Trevor-Roper came to dinner Rose Macaulay asked him if he remembered William Laud – Laud was appointed Archbishop of Canterbury by Charles I in 1633 and beheaded at Tower Hill in January 1645. According to another story in the Long Crichel anecdote book the conversation turned to lavatory graffiti. Raymond asked Rose Macaulay, 'Women don't do it at all. Is that true?' Unfortunately, her response was not recorded.

Another early visitor was Nancy Mitford, a close friend of both Eddy and Raymond. *The Pursuit of Love*, published to great acclaim in December 1945, was an idealised romance about a failed marriage and then falling in love again. The book caught the public mood. A semi-autobiographical story, the novel is peopled by figures based on Nancy's family and friends from her own life: her tyrannical father is caricatured as Uncle Matthew, while Uncle Davey, the hypochondriac – 'such a clever cove, literary you know, you wouldn't believe the things he does' – is based on Eddy, habitually surrounded by his pill-boxes and forever worrying about his diet: '"You shouldn't," said Davey, "read in trains, ever. It's madly wearing to the optic nerve centres, it imposes a most fearful strain. May I see the menu, please? I must explain that I'm on a new diet, one meal white, one meal red. It's doing me so much good."'[3] However, chocolate creams always seemed to count as white when he wanted them to.

Fabrice, Duke of Sauveterre, the hero of *The Pursuit of Love*, was based on Gaston Palewski, with whom Nancy had an affair. Although Palewski was never more than very fond of her, and pursued other love affairs, he was the great love of Nancy's life. The money she received from *The Pursuit of Love* gave her the means by which she could turn her back on England and start a new life in Paris, where, although Palewski strongly discouraged her from coming, she could be close to him. For the first time in her life Nancy was able to buy couture clothes from fashion houses like Dior and Lanvin and look truly elegant. Not that she could ever look anything other than English: her French friends used to call her '*la bougie anglaise*', 'the English candle'.

Nancy told Eddy that she was writing another book and suggested that, as Davey would once again be in the novel, it would be useful to have him around for a while. He fully appreciated and encouraged the joke, and was delighted to help. Like Eddy, Davey was a critic, and never one to spare even those closest to him. Davey's most savage reviews appeared under the pseudonym 'Little Nell'. In 1949 the new book, *Love in a Cold Climate*, was published. Apart from Uncle Davey, several other characters reappeared from *The Pursuit of Love*, but the new and central character, the appalling Lady Montdore, with her 'thick skin and ambition and boundless driving energy', was very obviously based on Helen Dashwood at West Wycombe.

Raymond was also in Paris after the end of the war. He was at home there, looking very much like the typical talkative, chain-smoking Left Bank intellectual, his clothes covered in cigarette ash. Nancy appreciated how well he understood the French. She said that while the English ignorance of French matters never ceased to astound her – and even pundits like Harold Nicolson and Cyril Connolly did not know as much as they pretended – Raymond was different and really understood what he was talking about. Raymond and Evelyn Waugh were Nancy's two literary mentors. Both were always willing to give advice and share their opinions on the frequent carelessness in her writing – not that she necessarily took any notice. In 1952 and 1953 Nancy spent much of her time in Versailles, researching a book about Madame de Pompadour. She sent a passage of her writing to Waugh, and thanked him for his reply, saying she would study his remarks about her execrable punctuation, then she added:

Raymond most kindly read the MS. He says the book is extremely unorthodox & reads as if 'an enchantingly clever woman were telling the story over the telephone', that many people will dislike it extremely but that as far as he is concerned I have got away with

murder. He says perhaps I should have left out wars & Jansenism*
which read as they might if written by Fragonard.

I was taken aback – I had seen the book as Miss Mitford's sober
and scholarly work – but then I saw him and he had obviously
enjoyed it though he says the whole exercise is questionable &
many will find it very shocking. He says don't rewrite, it won't be
any better if I do, but he has made a lot of suggestions (in the text)
& I'll take it back to Paris & work on them.[4]

She also told Waugh that someone had said to Raymond they
had heard he had taken a lot of slang out of Nancy's book. He
replied, 'Not really. I suggested she might not say Louis XIV was
perfect heaven 3 times on one page.'[5] However, such was Nancy's
reputation that in 1966, when the eminent art historian Kenneth
Clark's *Rembrandt and the Italian Renaissance* – which left Raymond
'dumbfounded with admiration' – was published at the same time as
The Sun King, Nancy Mitford's biography of Louis XIV, Raymond
was obliged by the *Sunday Times* to review the Mitford rather than
Rembrandt.

Nancy used to call Long Crichel's residents 'the Brontës'. This was
intended as a joke, but it was true that everyone in the house seemed
dedicated either to the production or the encouragement of the arts.
Raymond could often be found on his knees consulting one of the
many encyclopaedias or dictionaries, and when he sat at his typewriter
his sighs of despair rang throughout every room.

Unfortunately, the first joint attempt at publication by members
of the Crichel coterie ended in failure. In October 1945 Desmond
wrote to Kenneth Clark, a friend of both Eddy and Raymond, from
the offices of Lund Humphries & Co, where it was planned:

---

* A French theological movement which proposes that human sin and depravity can only
be absolved by divine grace.

I believe you know all about the new art quarterly which is being brought out, & that you very nearly consented to come on board. I very much hope that you will become a fairly frequent contributor to the publication – for which by the way we have decided on the title of 'Flair' . . . PS Is FLAIR terrible or rather good? Not my idea, so can't take offence whatever you say. It's not too late to change the title – if only we could think of a better one!

A fortnight later he wrote again: 'You will be pleased to hear FLAIR is dead, and that we have fixed on a title which should be stodgy enough to please even you; namely, THE ARTS QUARTERLY.' Articles, he wrote, were to be lavishly illustrated and payment was to be six guineas per 1,000 words. The following week he told Clark, 'One of our ideas is to forge links between the various arts which too often remain aloof from one another, and we have invited several poets to produce an original poem of about fifty lines in length to be illustrated by contemporary artists. Cecil Day-Lewis was one – please get in touch.'

The Arts – it was never a quarterly – first went on sale in 1946. It was a folio-sized, high-quality magazine. The price, ten shillings, was exceptionally high. The editorial board consisted of Desmond, who was the editor, Eddy and Herbert Read, a writer on art and culture and editor of the *Burlington Magazine* from 1933 to 1939 (Virginia Woolf thought he looked like a shop assistant). The full-colour cover design of the first edition was by the artist John Tunnard, and inside there were twelve articles. These included an essay with colour illustrations on the work of the artist Édouard Pignon by Read, who regarded Pignon as an 'existentialist', the most fashionable of post-war philosophies. There was also the first part of an essay on the 'Architectural Backgrounds in Italian Painting' by Kenneth Clark; a piece by Eddy on a Henry Moore sculpture; a review by Desmond of a performance of Benjamin Britten's opera *Peter Grimes* in Stockholm; and an essay by Raymond on 'The Desirable Life'

– reflections on half a dozen old master paintings, including ones by Claude Lorrain and Fragonard. '"Oh to have lived when frivolity could be thus poetical,"' sighs the modern rake – but it never was,' he wrote. There was no poetry, however.

The second edition of *The Arts* was not published until the following year. It had a cover by Edward Bawden and fewer articles. The pieces of writing there were included the second part of Kenneth Clark's essay; an essay by Eddy on the Catalan composer Roberto, together with a section of a score; Roger Hinks on Mannerism; a Clive Bell essay, 'Festina Lente'; and an article by André Gide on 'The Lesson of Poussin'. This second edition of *The Arts* turned out to be the last. Eddy resigned, telling Herbert Read that he had allowed himself to join against his better judgement, and he felt there was not enough for him to do: 'I am not cynical enough to take a director's salary for doing nothing, or next to nothing; nor do I believe that my name in itself, on the cover of the magazine, is worth £200 a year!' Although its intellectual quality was undoubted, it was difficult to see exactly who the magazine was aimed at – other than the owners of Long Crichel House and their friends. There was neither an editorial column, which might have set out a manifesto, nor any explanation of its intentions. The only advertising it had managed to attract came from the Lefevre Galleries in London and New York. No links between the arts were ever forged. It was as if the magazine had been dreamt up one evening over a dinner-party conversation and its contributors were writing predominantly for one another.

Desmond had more success with an illustrated book on Covent Garden, which he published in 1948. At the end of the year he was broadcasting in a series called 'Writers and Music' on the BBC Third Programme,* which the *Listener*'s radio critic called 'at the same time

---

* The BBC Third Programme was the BBC's third national network service, which was broadcast from 1946 until 1967 when it was replaced by Radio 3.

solid and light; serious criticism and extremely comical entertainment'. Meanwhile, Eddy and Desmond were also in the midst of compiling their *Record Guide*. This was a substantial undertaking and took several years of hard work. The explanation they gave for its publication was that reviewers were frequently asked to name the best versions of a dozen or so standard symphonies or concertos – they themselves had been reviewing for over sixteen years, and during that time requests for advice and information about recordings had poured in. *Record Guide* was to provide a considered and very readable review and ranking of their judgements. It was also to include technical notes. On a visit to Long Crichel Duncan Grant painted a sketch of Desmond sitting at his writing desk. He did not pretend to pose but got on with his work as he darted about the room looking for facts and references for the forthcoming book.

Their research was painstaking and thorough, but it was also rewarding. In 1948, while in search of new equipment and records, Desmond made a journey to Brussels in order to see and hear a state-of-the-art gramophone. He wrote home to Eddy and Eardley, 'My dear boys':

> [The chateau stands] in a small pleasant park with a wide view of trees and fields – in fact country. Most enjoyable and comfortable, with a lot of so-so modern pictures everywhere, a beautiful Afghan & a Maltese terrier, and Enoch's gramophone in the most whopping form imaginable; it really is the perfect gramophone, to which one can listen at huge volume without discomfort and also (which is nice) reduce the volume without losing the quality. Hiss not all bad by 'expert' standards, hum practically nil; new speaker, like a queer-shaped refrigerator made of white wood and taller than me, plus most elegant new pick-up with a long thin slightly curving arm (like the brown sticks of bread one used to get in Soho restaurants) seem, between them, to have done the trick. After hearing Britten's Young Person's Guide and Lipatti's B minor Sonata,

I think you would be wholly converted: absolute clarity and un-
forced tone right into the middle, and *more* bass and *less* boom
than I should have imagined possible.[6]

The *Record Guide* was published at last in 1951. The work involved
was exhausting. Desmond said later, 'It became absolutely awful. We
decided that unless the *Guide* was going to kill us we had better kill
it. It was very hard to keep Eddy on the rails, and I tended care of the
couplings and so on. It was the most awful sweat.'[7] Although the
book could never have been encyclopaedic, and the judgements
Desmond and Eddy made were inevitably partial, the results were
highly readable. Even after the information had long become obsolete,
the brief compilers' comments were still pithy, instructive and
frequently amusing. Percy Grainger's music was flavoured by 'good
natured malice'. Jacques-François-Fromental-Élie Halévy's opera *La
Juive* 'is typical French grand opera, enormously long with big
ensembles, processions and crowd scenes, and a tremendous final
catastrophe in which the heroine is thrown alive into a boiling
cauldron. But Halévy was a fine musician; his style is solid and
learned; and he could rise with genuine emotional fervour to the big
melodramatic scenes.' Of Felix Mendelssohn, the writer (in this case
probably Eddy) said, 'It is sad that these graceful & melodious pieces
which have enabled so many amateur pianists to give so much
pleasure to themselves (if not to their friends), should have fallen so
completely into disfavour.' And Ralph Vaughan Williams 'is now a
solitary figure, for his influence has served to produce a steady trickle
of pentatonic wish-wash. In this form British music is demonstrably
less vulgar than the bad music of other countries; but it is more
soporific, more negative . . . and like a hawk in repose – of some
seventeenth century bishop whose portrait testifies less to benevolence
than to a passion for truth.'

The dedication within the *Record Guide* to Eardley Knollys and
Raymond Mortimer was doubtless made out of gratitude for their

forbearance during the authors' labours. However, the effort had been worthwhile, and the book was widely praised. For the *Times Literary Supplement* it was 'at once practical in aim, useful to the amateur-musical-gramophone-record-collector (diskophile for short) and of the greatest literary distinction', and the reviewer commended 'this extraordinary book's merits, its readability, compounded of humour, the just epithet and control of biographical fact [which] places it in a class of its own'.[8] For the *Observer*'s critic it was 'the most enjoyable book on music in general I have read for years. I would recommend it as a general music-lover's and a connoisseur's companion . . . a rich source of instruction and delight.'[9] The authors stated in the introduction that they intended to keep the *Record Guide* up to date by issuing completely revised editions at regular intervals. In the event there were only two more editions, appearing in 1955 and 1956, but both were compiled with the help of assistants and both were much shorter than the original. Desmond and Eddy were probably sick to death of the whole project.

From 1950 to 1955 Eddy was a trustee of Covent Garden; his fellow trustees included Sir Kenneth Clark and the Earl of Harewood, the King's nephew, who was still in his twenties. It was Eddy who first recommended that Michael Tippett's opera *The Midsummer Marriage* should be staged, and its first performance at Covent Garden in January 1955 was evidence of the esteem in which his opinions were held. This was a golden era for British opera. Tippett, Benjamin Britten, Lennox Berkeley and Ralph Vaughan Williams were all creating major works, but Britten was always first and foremost, and his promotion was another Long Crichel cause. During his 1948 visit to Belgium Desmond attended the Belgian premiere of Britten's comic opera *Albert Herring*. 'I expected a tepid sprinkling of avant-garde types, but not at all, the large and ornate house was pretty well packed with all sorts of people,' he wrote. 'The delightful thing was that they all took it in their stride; I heard no muttering, saw no shocked shaking of elderly heads but on all sides smiles, rib-digging and plenty of open laughter. It's quite evidently a success.'[10]

Eddy probably first met Britten before the war and began to see more of him when he joined the Features and Drama Department at the BBC. They were close enough friends for Britten to invite Eddy to stay at the Old Mill, his house at Snape in Suffolk. Britten had lent the house to his sister Beth as somewhere to bring up her small children in safety from air raids. Eddy helped in the kitchen and taught Beth to make sauce. Meanwhile, he continued to compile his 'Gramophone Notes' for the *New Statesman*. During his years as a reviewer Eddy had shown little interest in British composers, preferring to write about twentieth-century Europeans like Béla Bartók and Paul Hindemith instead. Britten was the great exception. Eddy was not a lone voice in extolling the talents of the young homosexual composer. E.J. Moeran was also a Britten enthusiast. Moeran, who had known and supported Britten personally for some years, was a composer of English pastoral music which was generally well received – although not by Eddy. For Eddy and other denigrators his compositions were 'cowpat' music of a kind he and like-minded critics despised. In January 1943 Eddy included in his 'Gramophone Notes' a review of a newly released recording of Moeran's first – and only – symphony. It was written in the acidic manner ascribed by Nancy Mitford to Uncle Davey's pseudonym 'Little Nell':

One must congratulate both the Gramophone Company [HMV] and the British Council for their willingness to further the cause of English music but, at the risk of seeming ungrateful, one must question the wisdom of spending a lot of money and precious shellac on so dubious a work as EJ Moeran's enormous G minor Symphony. Apart from the fact that the boneless and romantic style which this composer affects is not representative of what is best in contemporary English music, much better examples of this style can be found among the six symphonies of Sir Arnold Bax, not one of which has ever been recorded . . . I can see nothing to be said for Moeran's characterless reflection of his greater contemporaries. Indeed, this symphony, for all its elaborate orchestration and display of 'profound' feeling, bores through its own lack of conviction . . . Instead of dealing a series of well-aimed blows, the symphony flops around like a jelly-fish.

Britten, seeing Eddy as a more useful connection than Moeran, not untypically, broke off his friendship as being of no further use. Unsurprisingly, Moeran felt insulted and was furious. When *Peter Grimes* was first performed he described it as the 'music of a shit'.[11]

Britten's songcycle 'Serenade for Tenor, Horn and Strings', which is widely regarded as a masterpiece, is another wartime work. Britten dedicated it to Eddy, who had both helped choose the words – poems by Alfred, Lord Tennyson, William Blake and John Keats – and written about the 'Serenade' in an article for Cyril Connolly's magazine *Horizon* in 1944: 'The subject is Night and its prestigia: the lengthening shadow, the distant bugle at sunset, the Baroque panoply of the starry sky, the heavy angels of sleep; but also the cloak of evil – the worm in the heart of the rose, the sense of sin in the heart of man. The whole sequence forms an Elegy or Nocturnal (as Donne would have called it), resuming the thoughts and images suitable to evening.'[12]

For all its beauty, this 'sense of sin' imbues the work. And the love which is given a voice in both the words and the music is secretive, disturbed, never quite a 'natural' love. It is 'queer' in every possible way. It was more than just a work of imagination; it also related to Britten personally, in the shame and fear he felt about his sexuality. Michael Tippett recalled how Britten and Peter Pears 'shared the same bed – it was quite open, though it was illegal. They ignored everybody, lived their private life as though the law hardly existed.' Homosexual acts were not just sinful – whatever one meant by that – they were also, whether in private or not, against the law at that time and regarded as criminal behaviour. Buggery carried a maximum sentence of life imprisonment. Yet Britten's relationship with Peter Pears was an open secret, however circumspect their behaviour may have been in public. The biographer of Pears, Christopher Headington, recalled seeing scrawled across a poster for one of the Britten–Pears London concerts in the 1940s the single word 'PANSY'.

When Eddy first met Benjamin Britten he had not recovered from his obsession with his previous lover, Sir Paul Latham. Latham, who was married, had inherited a baronetcy and millions from Courtaulds, the textile and clothing manufacturing firm. He was also the Conservative MP for Scarborough and Whitby. But he was a bully who, as Eddy told Raymond, had taken pleasure in making him utterly miserable: 'it is so disconcerting to be with someone who suddenly looks at you like a fixed bayonet . . . but there it is – *c'est plus fort que moi*: I feel an absolute compulsion to sacrifice myself to him'.[13] When war broke out Latham volunteered for the army and joined the 70th Searchlight Regiment in Sussex but was arrested for improper conduct with three gunners and a civilian. He tried to kill himself by driving into a tree, but he survived and was court-martialled. Found guilty of ten charges of indecent conduct, he again attempted suicide and was sentenced to two years in prison. His wife divorced him.

Peter Pears was often separated from Britten by concerts and opera tours which might last for weeks on end. Eddy, on the other hand, was frequently in contact with Britten. Needing another object for his thwarted emotions, Eddy now fell in love with Britten, although he was obviously unobtainable. Following his pattern of previous emotional disasters, Eddy soon succeeded in making himself unhappy again. In December 1942 Eddy wrote to Britten, addressing him as 'My dear White Child', a reference to Britten's *Hymn to Saint Cecilia*:

My dear White Child,

Your sweet letter was a great relief to me. I thought you were never going to speak to me again . . . The fact is, I am quite easy to deal with as long as I *know* when I am going to see you again, or if I can be sure that you are busy – or I am busy – you will at least give me a ring and say hullo. What I can't bear is silence & uncertain absence. So, if you love me, you must try for my sake never to let the rally stop. Once the ball is allowed to fall into the long grass, I begin to feel the snow falling around me, cutting me off. So, this week, until this morning when your letter came, I went through an extreme of misery such as I had hoped never to feel again. I can't help imagining things, & then I tear myself into long strips . . . I know it is all unreasonable & very hard on you; but after the betrayal, the cheat, the wicked cruelty I suffered six years ago, I have to re-learn confidence in the good will of others.

But it is simple really and you will succeed – of course it will. I am not such a fool as not to know my luck in possessing your affection. And what is all that nonsense about being a bore & inadequate?! Why, I consider you one of the most consistently intelligent people I have ever met. You never say a dull thing & your mind – your outlook is endlessly sympathetic to me. I never tire of talking to you – whatever the subject – or of walking with you, or making toast, or playing 2-handed Mahler (even if I do look cross when you play loud while I am playing soft), or just sitting reading when you are composing. It is just your presence – your intimate companionship – that I need to remake my life, so that I may be reasonably happy & get on with my work. And since friendship means giving as much as taking, I will say what I believe you know; that I have a good deal to give – particularly at this most important point in your career.

But don't forget: *you must not let the ball fall to the ground again.* Otherwise snow, & silence, & madness, & death come crowding round.

Good-night, my dear. A thousand blessings on your head . . .

My love as always,

Eddy [14]

In another letter from Eddy – again addressed to 'my dear White Child' – he informed Britten, with a peculiar insensitivity, that he had always loved people inferior to himself in every way – 'except one and he died'. It was therefore a new experience for him to love someone whom he regarded as a 'heavenly genius' and potentially the greatest genius of the new era: 'It is wonderful to have come up against you at this moment when, your long apprenticeship over, you are at last launching into a series of masterpieces.'[15]

The advice, assistance and occasional criticism which Eddy was able to give Britten during the wartime years were all undoubtedly creatively helpful for the composer, but as soon as the war ended Peter Pears came home and Eddy was more or less superfluous again. In June 1945 Britten's opera *Peter Grimes* had its first performance at Sadler's Wells Theatre. The opera was first conceived while Britten and Pears were living in California, and Britten chanced to read an article by E.M. Forster about the Suffolk poet George Crabbe in the *Listener* magazine. He subsequently read the narrative poem 'Peter Grimes' from Crabbe's book *The Borough*, and he said he knew instantly he must write the opera. Grimes, the protagonist, is conceived of as an outsider in society which, regarding him as a criminal, ultimately destroys him. Once again the subtext appears to be homosexual guilt. 'There are plenty of Grimeses around still, I think,' Peter Pears later wrote.[16] The opera was mostly composed at Snape where Britten composed in spite of the constant distraction from the noise of RAF fighter planes from nearby aerodromes – 'the aeroplanes are bloody, bloody, all the time'. The whole three hours of the first performance was spent by Britten standing in evening dress at the back of the stalls too nervous to sit down. At the end there were thirty seconds of silence followed by wild applause. One of the critics counted fourteen curtain calls. Britten's fame was assured. That season the box-office takings for *Peter Grimes* matched or exceeded those of *La Bohème* and *Madame Butterfly* with which it was performed concurrently.

However, after the first performance at Sadler's Wells in June 1945, Britten, who was almost as thin-skinned as Eddy, made it known that he had yet to receive any praise from him. Eddy replied with a long series of complaints of his own – about his hurt feelings on not being invited to the party which Britten's publisher had held for him:

And finally, when I passed you outside the Wells last Monday night, you pretended not to see me. Small things, you will say. No doubt; but they add up, and they also remind me that you have never troubled your head about me except when you wanted me to do something for you. Do not misunderstand me: devoted as I have long been to you and your music, I ask nothing better than to help you in every way I can; my pen was, as you know, at your service at a time when I incurred a good deal of ridicule and hostility for my championship of your music; I hope I shall always have the privilege of writing about it, and in other ways furthering it. It is a great satisfaction to me to have recognised your genius considerably in advance of other critics. But now that *Peter Grimes* has established your position beyond question, I think the moment ill-chosen to give so intimate and devoted a friend the impression he is no longer of the slightest consequence to you.

How tiresome and difficult Eddy is! you will say. No doubt I am; but if I were not hyper-sensitive in every way, I should probably not appreciate your music either![17]

At the end of 1945 Britten and Pears stayed at Long Crichel for four nights. It was not a great success – Eddy was in bed with flu for most of the time. When he had returned home Britten thanked Eddy for the rest – 'it is a most lovely happy home that you have, & I am delighted to be able to think of you there'.[18] He added that he intended to write a piece of music titled 'Serenade for Topaz'

– Topaz was a Jersey cow. But he and Pears never returned. In later years Eddy continued to attend his concerts and write about Britten's music, and, from time to time, there were further tiffs, but Eddy's protégé had long flown the nest. *Peter Grimes* came to be considered as part of the standard repertoire and the composer's reputation was assured. Eddy was never fully ejected in the way that Moeran had been from the magic circle with which Britten surrounded himself at Aldeburgh, but he was no longer close to the heart of it. Desmond Shawe-Taylor was another matter. He too was always an enthusiastic reviewer of Britten's new works, especially of his operas, but, in the opinion of the prickly composer, his enthusiasm was often found wanting, and between themselves Britten and Peter Pears referred to him as 'Desmond Shaw-failures'.

In the 1950s Eddy started to keep a journal. As well as being a record of the events of his life and his thoughts and reflections, the plain school exercise book which he used was also a scrapbook for newspaper cuttings. Among the pages, he stuck pictures of handsome rugger players and one of Marlon Brando, and an essay by E.M. Forster on the afterlife he imagined for the Honeychurch family from his novel *A Room with a View*. There are obituaries of Paul Latham (who died in 1955), and also of Noel Mewton-Wood, an Australian pianist and interpreter of Benjamin Britten – after the death of his lover from peritonitis, Mewton-Wood threw a glass of gin and cyanide at the wall of his flat in Notting Hill, killing himself by breathing in the fumes.

On one of the pages Eddy pasted a letter in verse by Patrick Leigh Fermor published in the *New Statesman* at the end of January 1953. The verses had been inspired by a letter from the poet Kathleen Raine which the magazine had published a few weeks earlier. She had expressed her strong objection to what she regarded as the over-free use of Christian names. She felt that the literary world had little to do with one's private life and that there must be others who would prefer Christian names to be used only by personal friends. This had set off a long correspondence. Among those who wrote letters were a 'T. Cobley from Widecombe, Somerset' and Leonard Woolf. Leigh Fermor contributed a long poem but kept his anonymity by signing himself as 'A Struggling Young Poet':

> Sir –
>   Dear Kathleen Raine, though we haven't yet met
> I worship your verse and we'll all be upset
> I'm giving a do at the Cri,* at ten-thirty and asking a few
> Sister souls to drop in while I read one or two
> Of my poems out loud – Do you think you could take it?
> There'll be lashings of bubbles so do try to make it.
> Tom and Aldous and Clive will be staying to eat
> – They all like my stuff and I'd like you to meet,
> There's Cyril and Raymond and Desmond and Alan
> All longing to know you, and Wystan and Dylan
> Are coming on later with Louis and Stephen and
>   Christopher too . . .

Sixty-three names were included, Raymond, Desmond and Eddy among them. Most were from the world of literature – 'Angus and Harold and Edith and Vita/Are all packing into Rose's four-seater', although this was a joke in itself, since Rose Macaulay was such a notoriously bad driver that many people would not get in the same car as her. There were also names from the worlds of art ('Lucian and Francis') and politics. The verses were witty and clever, and, despite their anonymity, everyone in the London literary world would soon have discovered the identity of the author – which is exactly what Leigh Fermor would have wanted. They also brought the *New Statesman* correspondence to an end.

---

* Criterion Restaurant, Piccadilly.

Although Paddy Leigh Fermor was by no means religious, he had written some of his first book *The Traveller's Tree* at the Abbey of St Wandrille de Fontanelle near Rouen in France and had then suggested to Eddy that he might also enjoy the experience. In the autumn of 1950 Eddy went on retreat to St Wandrille. On his return he wrote to Paddy, telling him that 'le commandant Fairemaure' had obviously made a lasting impression: 'The great sign of their affection for you was the gales of laughter that sprang up whenever your name was mentioned. Clearly you raised their spirits.'[19] Unfortunately, however, the meals at St Wandrille had not suited Eddy's digestion.

On one of the pages Eddy pasted an anonymous letter in verse which had been published in the *New Statesman* in January 1953, and underneath he made a note that it had been written by Paddy Leigh Fermor. The lines had in fact been inspired by *The Traveller's Tree*, an account of a journey through the Caribbean islands by Leigh Fermor, his partner Joan Rayner and the photographer Costa Achillopoulos. On its publication in 1950 the book was widely praised, especially by Raymond, who thereafter became a great supporter. Despite the generous financial help Paddy received from Joan, he had neither any fixed income nor profession he could turn to. He also lacked all sense of financial responsibility. Aware of his problems, Raymond recommended him to Secker & Warburg as someone who could translate two novellas by Colette, *Julie de Carneilhan* and *Chambre d'hotel* (translated as *Chance Acquaintances*). Although Paddy did not much care for either story, and found the work boring, it was easy. 'It's like some awful imposition at school,' he wrote. 'I'm beginning to think she's fearful rot.'[20] However, the two stories together were only about 40,000 words, and the book took him no more than a couple of weeks. At £2 per thousand words he earned about £80.

Raymond became so entranced by Leigh Fermor that his letters to him begin 'My dear, my dazzling, Paddy', 'My cherished Paddy', 'My glorious Paddy'. However, Leigh Femor was such a slow and painstaking writer that his next substantial book *Mani: Travels in the Southern Peloponnese* did not appear until November 1958. Raymond wrote to him:

> Your book is the best that has appeared this year . . . if I had been able to review it, I should in my usual senile pedantry have groaned over the unorthodoxy of your grammar but everything else enchants me. I adore the bravura passages, and admire equally the art with which you modulate from one tone to another. Parts of the book are Flaubertian, others like the best of Norman Douglas – but with a far richer texture and music. Really a glorious addition to Eng. Lit. upon which I cannot congratulate you too enthusiastically. Now I pin my hopes on being able to prostrate myself beyond the second volume when that appears.* You are the best writer we have under eighty, or (to be prudent) the one who gives me most delight.[21]

Paddy and Joan – who did not marry until 1968 – became regular visitors to Long Crichel. Since the visits Paddy Leigh Fermor had made with Balasha Cantacuzene to Crichel House in the late 1930s to visit Napier Alington, who was a friend, everything had changed. On the outbreak of war, Paddy had returned to England from Romania, hoping for a commission in the Guards but, like many a junior officer in the First World War, it had seemed likely that he too might be killed within weeks of being sent into action. Instead, before long it was Napier Alington who was dead. Balasha had been forced by the Communists to surrender her house and her estate at Baleni in Moldavia. The house was razed, leaving little trace of its former owners other than the Cantacuzene family monuments and the old curtain wall around the property. For the rest of her life she

---

* *Roumeli: Travels in Northern Greece*, the successor to *Mani*, was not published until 1966.

lived with her sister in an attic room in Bucharest, managing to survive by giving French and English lessons. When at last Leigh Fermor saw her again he found her 'a broken ruin' of her former self, but they continued to write to one another, and in the letters there are passing references to his Crichel past: 'Long Crichel (3 miles from Napier's house) has always been a sort of Mecca for me . . . all working hard, as in a lay-monastery, except for the delicious food and funny conversation.'[22]

In the dying months of the war Paddy had met Joan Rayner in Egypt. They were attracted to one another immediately. Joan was already married but, as with so many others, her marriage had failed under the strains of war. Frances Partridge observed the relationship between the two: 'I was touched by Paddy's obstreperous devotedness, leaving all decisions to Joan, only wanting her to decide and looking at her expectantly like a curly wet dog that has just fished a stick out of a lake and bounces about as if to say, "Only tell me, mistress, where to put it and I'll do it at once with joy."'[23]

Paddy, who never liked living in London, was always looking for somewhere quiet to work, and he found Long Crichel conducive for writing. In the evenings after a day's work and dinner there was conversation and games. One night, on the analogy of Wellington and Sandwich, somebody wondered what the surnames of the owners of Long Crichel might represent. A 'Mortimer', it was thought, might be a kind of hat, and a 'Knollys' a new kind of footwear; 'Shawe-Taylor' would be a kind of harness ('got a short tail, see?'). A 'Sackville-West' was more of a problem: what could someone so gentle and sensitive and willowy suggest? Then Desmond came up with the idea that it should be a new kind of boxing glove. Everyone applauded, and that night Paddy wrote a poem he called 'The Lay of the Sackville Glove'. The original was lost until an incomplete version was found at Lismore, the Duke of Devonshire's castle in Ireland. Paddy rewrote and finished the poem at his house in Greece long after it was first composed:

THE SACKVILLE GLOVE

'Twas a summer's day at Long Crichel
And Phoebus vas shining bright
And the 'ole of the Dorset Fancy
Vas gathered to see the fight.
II
Shawe-Taylor vas there on 'is bobtail mare
In the flashiest of nankeen suits
And Mortimer, too, in 'is beaver 'at,
And Knollys in 'is Blucher boots.
III
There vas many a bang-up Corinthian,
And many a milling cove,
But the gamest of all vas SACKWILLE-VEST,
As invented ve SACKWILLE GLOVE!
IV
They pitched the ring on the welwet lawn,
And the gemmen was crowding thick,
For BATTLING BEN from Blandford
Vas meeting the VIMBORNE CHICK.
V
'*Up with yer dukes!*' cries SACKWILLE-VEST,
And their maulies met with a bang –
And down goes the CHICK, as the BATTLER's right
Connected 'is neb vith a clang.
VI
Now this clang vas caused by a doorknob
Concealed in the BATTLER's right,
But nobody spies it, and everyone cries:
The BATTLER AS VUN THE FIGHT!
VII
But over the ropes jumps SACKWILLE-VEST
Vith 'is right 'eld be'ind 'is back,
And 'is left up'eld in preclusive spar
Vot prowokes th' impending vhack.

VIII

'Is long, left daddle was 'eld on 'igh,
Manoowering in the air
Clad in a newly-fangled mitt,
MADE OF LEVVER AND 'ORSES 'AIR!

IX

Forty-two rounds they milled and slogged
Like the pugs of 'oom poets sing
At the War of Troy, and their slammin' dukes
Fair made the Velkin ring.

X

Ben's proboscis vas 'ammered flat
Vith many a well-aimed stroke;
Both 'is peepers vas black and shut,
And 'alf of 'is ribs vas broke.

XI

'Is ears swole up like cauliflowers,
'Is gnashers vas down 'is froat
'Is claret vas tapped like a stove-in keg
At the wreck of a wintner's boat.

XII

They carried BEN off on a five-bar gate,
And round the 'ERO pressed
All the covies, bawlin' fit to bust
'THE WICTOR IS SACKWILLE-VEST!'

XIII

So fill up your glasses, gemmen all,
And all you milling coves,
And drink long life to *SACKWILLE-VEST*,
As invented the *SACKVILLE GLOVE!*

XIV

So fill up the blushin' bumpers
And empty ve blowin' bowl
To SACKWILLE, VE SEVENOAKS BRUISER!
To bashin' VEST, from KNOWLE![24]

When Joan's brother became ill with dementia Paddy found staying with him too depressing. While Joan stayed behind with her brother in his house in Gloucestershire, Paddy sneaked off guiltily to the delights of Long Crichel. In a letter to Deborah Devonshire he wrote about 'endless croquet in midsummer weather, glass-in-hand, with pigeons and rooks overhead, and pretty well non-stop cuckoo (thanks to its being May) seldom out of earshot'. A game on the croquet lawn was always a revelation of temperament – and Paddy in particular not a good loser. At Long Crichel croquet was played by its own particularly vindictive house rules.

Frances said she had a photograph of Eardley and Desmond in the midst of a croquet game which always made her laugh because it captured their contrasted characters so perfectly. They were arguing a point – and had been doing so for ages – but whereas it was plain that Eardley would hold to his position until kingdom come and nothing would budge him, Desmond was obviously on the verge of desperation. And Desmond wrote about Raymond that 'despite lacking dexterity he became (as he would have put it) "quite a dab-hand" at croquet; he revelled in long drawn-out contests which he was unashamedly eager to win. On the lawn his strategy was impeccable, and it was an understandable source of irritation when the physical toll of advancing years caused him to squander, in a single stroke, some advantage long and carefully prepared.'[25]

The contrasting dispositions set out in a croquet game could be described as a sort of metaphor for underlying tensions among the residents of Long Crichel House.

6

Perfect Life

Some years after his conversion to Catholicism, Eddy wrote a short essay, 'A Fragment of Autobiography', about the experience:

> Even today the course of my progress towards reception into the Roman Catholic Church remains at some points obscure like a path through a wood lit only partially by moonlight. Born in 1901, I was brought up an Anglican, in what was then known as the Broad Church, which was in fact a good deal higher than the so-called Church of Ireland but at the same time resolutely opposed to anything it regarded as Popish practice. My mother was religious in the sense of saying prayers every night, but my father had no religion of any kind, though as a young man he sometimes accompanied my mother and me to Matins on Sundays, as a matter of convention. Later in life he abandoned even this attempt at formal religion and ended his life as some kind of stoic.[1]

He went on to say that as a very little boy he had the odd ambition to become a monk despite never having seen a monk and knowing nothing about monastic life. Yet the ambition was there, and it formed an important part in the secretive imaginative life of a rather 'lonely, invalidish and apprehensive child'.[2]

In the summer of 1948 Eddy and Evelyn Waugh corresponded

about Graham Greene's recently published novel *The Heart of the Matter*, which Eddy had just reviewed. The novel revolves around the spiritual struggles of Major Scobie, a police deputy commissioner in a West African colony during the Second World War. Scobie, who is caught in a loveless marriage, has an affair with a younger woman. Various complications of the plot make his feelings of guilt only worse, and eventually he commits suicide by taking an overdose of sleeping pills. Despite the apparent dark pessimism of the novel, it ends with reflections on the mercy of God and the unknowability of the heart. In his final letter to Eddy about the book Waugh wrote: 'Of course you are at the heart of the matter when you ask what right Catholic authors have to try to interest non-Catholics in their work. The real answer, which must sound pretentious to anyone outside the Church, is that the Church is not, except by accident, a little club with its own specialised vocabulary, but the normal state of man from which men have disastrously exiled themselves.'[3] Both Waugh and Greene were converts to Catholicism, and although Eddy did not mention this in his letters to Waugh, over the years there had been various times when he had expressed an interest in the Roman Catholic Church, and he too was considering conversion.

The following year George Orwell's dystopian novel *1984* was published. Eddy found this even more disturbing. He became convinced that the agents of the Devil, who had so recently been associated with the Nazis, might have been conquered on one front but they were still very much present elsewhere. He decided that it was high time to declare himself and take the side of Christ against the gospel of materialism. The obvious next step for him was conversion to Catholicism. The only Catholic priest he knew, Father Martin D'Arcy, who was attached to the Jesuit church in Farm Street, advised him to get in touch with the nearest Jesuit parish church to Long Crichel, which was in Bournemouth. He underwent a rapid conversion. On 5 August 1949 Eddy wrote to Waugh:

In view of the letters we exchanged a year ago, it may be of some dim interest to you to know that I am 'receiving instruction' preparatory to being (I hope) received into the Catholic Church. It has taken me twelve years – a long time – to reach this point, & I am thankful to have got there at last. I have not forgotten your kind invitation to visit you & one of these days I hope I shall do so. Meanwhile all sorts of work keeps me chained to my writing-table – or so it seems to me.[4]

In his reply the next day Waugh thanked Eddy for his great good news, which was by no means of 'dim interest' but of intense delight:

It always seems to me to be the natural and inevitable thing for anyone to become a Catholic and the constant surprise is that everyone does not. Conversion is like stepping across the chimney piece of a Looking-glass-World where everything is an absurd caricature, into the real world God made; and then begins the delicious process of exploring it limitlessly.

Please let me know the day of your reception so that I can pray for you. Please pray for me.[5]

His house, he continued, was currently overrun with children and barely habitable, but Eddy would be most welcome to come for a visit. Waugh added a postscript, saying how puzzled Nancy Mitford would be. Nancy, however, was far from bewildered. She wrote to Eddy saying that it must be like having a lovely new love affair. He did not reply but, given the disastrous course of Eddy's love life, the analogy was probably not one he greatly appreciated.

On 17 August Eddy was received into the Roman Catholic Church by Father Hubert McEvoy. Evelyn Waugh sent him a copy of Ronald Knox's explanation of the Mass, *The Mass in Slow Motion*, as a welcoming gift. If Eddy was still attending Mass in Bournemouth, which was a long drive from Long Crichel, he must frequently have been exhausted by the time he arrived. Within a few months of his conversion he received from the Vicar General a dispensation from the Eucharistic fast, which obliged Catholics not to take food or drink – including water – after midnight when receiving Holy Communion the following morning. The faculty from the Holy See stated that, on account of Eddy's state of health, he was allowed to take liquid, non-alcoholic refreshment.

In May 1950 Eddy took up Evelyn Waugh's offer of a visit to Piers Court, Waugh's house in Somerset. Father Ronald Knox, a priest who was well known in society circles, was a fellow guest. Knox had been born into a family of evangelical Anglicans but had become attracted by High Church ritual while still at Eton. Ordained an Anglican priest in 1912 he was received into the Roman Catholic Church five years later. His writings included both theology and detective stories. He had also loved word games from childhood. Waugh sent Nancy an account of Eddy's stay:

> [Eddy's] visit was a heavy responsibility. I gave him fresh meat at every meal but he took a great number of pills. Were they in order to ameliorate the cooking or reinforce the vitamins? He only drinks whisky in tiny quantities and I generally count on large bumpers of goodish wine dulling my guests' consciousness of their discomforts . . . He looked very elegant, & except for pimples, pretty. He had a dear little dinner jacket with a velvet collar & tiny black suede shoes. I took him for a breathless hot walk and he seemed to enjoy the countryside but he moaned pitifully with the pain of my picture books. He got up at dawn and sat in the drawing room before the fire was lit. Oh dear I don't think he can have enjoyed himself at all. I do like him so.

Frances Partridge, who had lost all religious faith as a child and become an outspoken atheist, found Eddy's Catholicism oppressive. Sometimes when she was staying at Long Crichel she was given

Eddy's room, and she said that the powerful aroma of his personality stifled her in a way that the impersonal atmosphere of the spare room did not. Eddy's feminine side was expressed in having hundreds of tiny knick-knacks arranged all around the room, such as little white china pieces, Victorian shell decorations, enamel boxes and even jewels. An ivory Christ hung on the wall, and there was a prie-dieu with a rosary standing in front of it. She found the effect of the objects unpleasant: 'Why is it not mere neutral? Why not think of it as a mere *object*. But I can't; it's swathed and crowded with emotional debris.'[6]

Few of the Long Crichel visitors had strong religious convictions. Desmond and Eardley had none at all. Raymond had converted to Catholicism as an undergraduate at Oxford – he found the byways of religion and people's credulity endlessly fascinating, and the often self-deceptive ambitions of Victorian divines were a particular delight – but, probably under the influence of his new Bloomsbury friends, he soon lost his faith.

In April 1951 Eddy wrote about a weekend visit from Graham Greene in his diary:

> Very easy & as happy as he ever seems. Evident need for incessant conversation, veering round always to Catholicism. He thinks Heaven may be the union of body & soul in a single point of love. Odd how every place he talks of seems sinister or squalid. Told me an extraordinary story of equivocal episodes in Lyons, with a *louche* businessman & a mistress & a rich widow. Also – a fascinating detail – that the large rosary of leaden beads with which a renegade priest (c. 1890) used to murder people.[7]

Jim Lees-Milne was a guest the same weekend, so Raymond was outnumbered by Catholics. He later told Desmond, who was absent, that he had been bored, as nothing was talked about except religion.

***

The writer Rose Macaulay, a regular visitor to Long Crichel, was exceptional in that she also attended services at the parish church next door. Unlike the bombed and fire-scarred empty shells of churches within the City of London which haunted her imagination, here in secluded Dorset St Mary's had survived the war unscathed. A small wooden plaque commemorating two Long Crichel men, Stanley Lever and James Goddard, who had been killed in the Second World War, had brought about its only change. The plaque was hung underneath the much larger Great War memorial brass.

Rose's father was Assistant Master at Rugby School and the historian Thomas Babington Macaulay her grandfather's cousin. She spent seven years of her childhood at the seaside town of Varezze near Genoa. As a child she was a tomboy and had thought that she would grow up to be a boy. She later went to Oxford High School for Girls and Somerville College, Oxford, where she studied history and discovered a passion for the seventeenth century. Although slightly older than him, she was a close friend and companion of Rupert Brooke. Her father, who had become a Cambridge don, was Brooke's tutor. She would regularly cycle over from her family home in Great Shelford to Granchester, where Rupert lived. They both loved poetry, language and talking, as well as tramping through the countryside and outdoors swimming – preferably naked. For Rupert she was a companionable friend and a relief from his sexual confusion. After starting her literary life as a poet, Rose became a prolific and successful novelist – in two of her books she made clear the depth of her feeling for Brooke. Success allowed her to buy a flat in London, and from the 1920s she was very much a stalwart of the London literary scene. In 1935 she began writing a weekly column, 'Marginal Comments', for the *Spectator*. At the same time she wrote literary history and criticism, including a biography of Milton and, in 1938, a study of the writings of her friend, E.M. Forster. She also encouraged a younger generation of writers like Elizabeth Bowen and Rosamond Lehmann.

Among Raymond's papers there is a postcard from Rose dating from the 1930s inviting him to a sherry party. At the time she was having an affair with an Irish writer called Gerald O'Donovan. In 1916 Rose had joined the War Office, and when she met her lover he was head of the Italian section of the Ministry of Information. O'Donovan was a former Roman Catholic priest. After his ordination he had been appointed as administrator of Loughrea in County Galway, and such was his reputation, both as a priest and an enthusiast for Irish causes, that he became a national figure – even though to some extent he blamed the impoverished condition of Ireland on the clergy themselves. When in 1903 he left Loughrea rather than submit to a new bishop he disliked, hundreds of townspeople gathered along the road to the railway station, some on their knees to be blessed by him. O'Donovan went to London but was unable to find a job as a writer–priest, and the very fact that he had taken holy orders made it difficult for him to find other work. Eventually he became both unemployed and bankrupt, and after five years in London he chose to become laicised. He then married and had three children. In 1913 O'Donovan published *Father Ralph*, the first of several novels expressing his bitterness with the hierarchy of the Roman Catholic Church – although not with religion itself. As intended, the Catholic hierarchy was outraged.

H.G. Wells said that O'Donovan's blue eyes under a heavy dark brow looked like 'two gun barrels from behind a hedge'.[8] He was also balding and ten years older than Rose. They fell in love and had a long affair, but he would not leave his wife. Under the stress of the relationship Rose lost the certainty of her faith and stopped taking communion in the Anglican Church. In 1939 the couple were motoring in the Lake District when Rose had an accident. O'Donovan was injured, and this was followed by a stroke. In 1941 he was diagnosed with terminal cancer and given only months to live. Rose was only able to visit the great love of her life occasionally as a concerned friend, and when he died the following year it was in the presence of his wife and children.

In the 1930s Rose had been an active member of the Peace Pledge Union. In 1938, however, she wrote 'Damn the Nazis, they are making pacifism impossible', and then she resigned and recanted.[9] During the war she wrote little and instead she spent nearly three years as a voluntary part-time ambulance driver, waiting night after night at the wheel as victims were pulled from burning wreckage. She fell ill and became depressed. In the midst of everything else her flat in Hinde Street, just south of Oxford Street, was bombed. Although Rose herself was safe all her treasures and mementos and O'Donovan's love letters were lost in the destruction. She felt that the experience of war – and the loss of love – had been like the death of civilisation itself. At the end of the war she learned that she had been on a list of writers who, after a Nazi invasion, would have been exterminated.

Rose eventually returned to writing and wrote two travel books, *They Went to Portugal* and also *Fabled Shore*, which was an account of a journey through Spain at the end of its civil war. Then she wrote a novel, *The World My Wilderness*, set among the devastation of the City of London in the shadow of St Paul's Cathedral in which Macaulay's heroine Barbary and Raoul, her younger brother, wander among the wreckage: 'Fragments of hymn books, torn and charred, were scattered about the church and the belfry floor. Out of one of the cracked bronze bells lying on their sides Barbary picked a grimy clump of pages spread open at the Dies Irae. "Day of Wrath," she read aloud. "Oh day of mourning! See fulfilled the prophet's warning, Heaven and earth in ashes burning! Oh what fear man's bosom rendeth when from Heaven the Judge descendeth . . ."'[10]

The World My Wilderness clearly betrays the spiritual pain of the writer and her longing to be back within the now ruined Anglican fold:

St. Vedast's, St. Alban's, St. Anne's and St. Agnes', St. Giles Cripplegate, its tower high above the rest, the ghosts of churches burnt in an earlier fire, St. Olave's and St. John Zachary's, haunting the green-flowered churchyards that bore their names, the ghosts of taverns where merchants and clerks had drunk, of restaurants where they had eaten – all this scarred and haunted green and stone and brambled wilderness lying under the August sun, a-hum with insects and astir with secret, darting, burrowing life, received the returned traveller into its dwellings with a wrecked, indifferent calm. Here, its cliffs and chasms and caves seem to say, is your home; here you belong; you cannot get away, you do not wish to get away, for this is a maquis that lies about the margins of the wrecked world, and here your feet are set; here you find the irremediable barbarism that comes up from the depth of the earth, and that you have known elsewhere. 'Where are the roots that clutch, what branches grow out of this stony rubbish? Son of man, you cannot say or guess . . .' But you can say or guess, that it is you yourself, your own roots, that clutch the stony rubbish, the branches of your own being that grow from it and elsewhere.[11]

By 1950, the year in which the book was published, the craters and cellars were being filled in or built over – if not by taverns and restaurants then by concrete office blocks. But she thought the 'irremediable barbarism' must rise to the surface elsewhere again, for it is latent in man.

That same year Rose began a correspondence with Father Hamilton Johnson, a distant cousin who was living in a religious community in Boston, Massachusetts from whom she had been long estranged. Although they had not met for over thirty years and were never to meet again, Johnson helped her, as he put it, to enter '*inside* the church door, instead of standing in the porch'. All Rose's friends were, of course, made aware of Rose's re-entry into the Church of England, although Ivy Compton-Burnett said that she couldn't understand why Rose couldn't remain 'a perfectly sound agnostic like everybody else'.[12]

For the writer V.S. Pritchett, Rose was 'a jolly skeleton'.[13] Jim Lees-Milne said that she was like a 'wizened damson' but she was 'very spirited in spite of her desiccated appearance . . . She can and will talk of anything. She is wizened in feature and her lower jaw – false teeth, ill-fitting – juts out at you in speaking. But do not be alarmed. She has no airs of any kind and fills her intellectual inferiors with enthusiasms that flatter their mean understanding.'[14] She was also, he said, intensely loveable as well as very clever. Although not somewhere obviously sympathetic to her religious beliefs, Long Crichel became a kind of refuge for Rose, a place where she could sit and read, talk and think. In May 1951 she wrote to Father Johnson:

I took away with me for the week-end your letter of 11th May, but not my typewriter, so will write to you in my best hand instead. I am sitting in a beautiful library, looking out on a beautiful garden, and beyond it to a beautiful buttercup field, and beyond that to a small grey perpendicular church, to which no one in this house ever goes, and which I gather is almost Tractarian in the rarity of its services. One of my 3 hosts is R. C., the other two are nothing – they are 3 friends (male) living together, very delightful people their interests literature, architecture, art, and music. I am here to help them entertain the editor of the *Sunday Times** and his wife, whom none of us knew very well. We talk and read and write and play a little tourniquet, at which I am becoming rather a dab. But mainly we talk, and talk, and talk. Last night we talked about how nearly all specific *religious* writers to-day (novelists, poets, etc.) were R. C. ('Catholic,' they all call it but me) and how few were definitely Anglican in tone and view-point. Why is this, I wonder? I think because people 'vert to the R. C. Church – the Anglican is what we were (mostly) brought up in, and many take no notice of

---

* Harry Hodson, Editor 1950–1961.

it, or just lapse from it and don't come back. So it doesn't seep into their writing. If they begin to believe Christianity, then they do something dramatic, like going R. C. I can't help feeling that going Anglican is better; anyhow I could never have done the other myself . . .

Later. A discussion occurred at supper tonight about whether Corpus Christie was (a) a feast in the P[rayer] B[ook] calendar (b) a feast commonly observed in the Anglican Church. I thought it *was* in the P. B., and knew it *was* kept in the Anglican Church. One of my hosts swore it was neither. So we rang up the Dean of Winchester, E.G. Selwyn (a cousin of mine) and asked him, and he said it was not in the 1662 book, but was (of course) in the 1928 Revised one, which is always used in many churches, and in his Cathedral. And he said it had been celebrated at Corpus (his college) for many years. So I think *I* won the bet, and Raymond Mortimer thought *he* had. The argument began because I went to evensong in the little church and heard the feast of C[orpus] C[hristie]. announced – quite an ordinary, moderate village church, with a congregation of about 10 people.

Rose returned to Long Crichel to look after Raymond when he was unwell. Both her own life and her flat in Hinde Street had been rebuilt after the bombing. Back in London she told Hamilton Johnson that she had recovered from her conflagration; she was sitting surrounded by 'its fruits' – new curtains, new carpets and a new cabinet with drawers for the new wireless to stand on; 'and on the new wireless stands my new and beautiful Parthenon of cork, under a glass dome like a bubble, which Raymond Mortimer gave me in Dorset'.[15]

Rose Macaulay's final book, *The Towers of Trebizond*, which was published in 1956, was partly inspired by a visit to Turkey two years earlier. She told Raymond:

My novel is rather odd and a lot of people will find it unaccountable & crankish, I think. I was surprised that the Book Society thought their members might like it, for I don't expect they will. However it contains a camel & an ape, & perhaps Our Members will like that; they certainly won't like the Anglican obsession of my central character, & I don't suppose they'll want Turkey. However it has a few jokes.[16]

The Towers of Trebizond is considered Macaulay's greatest book and was a literary sensation in Great Britain and the United States. It also won the 1956 James Tait Black Memorial Prize. The novel's first line, '"Take my camel, dear," said my aunt Dot, as she climbed down from this animal on her return from High Mass,' became famous. The book's narrator Laurie describes her aunt Dot's eccentric efforts to convert the Muslim women of Turkey to high Anglicanism. At times the story is strongly autobiographical. Laurie has become unhappily cast adrift from her faith on account of an adulterous affair: 'Adultery is a meanness and a stealing, a taking way from someone what should be theirs, a great selfishness, and surrounded and guarded by lies lest it be found out. And out of selfishness and lying flow love and joy and peace beyond anything that can be imagined.'[17]

In her seventies Rose was still diving from the highest diving board into the Serpentine on cold winter days. She was also still writing prolifically for the *Times Literary Supplement*, the *Spectator*, the *New Statesman*, the *Observer* and the *Listener*. In 1951 she was made an honorary DLitt by Cambridge University. In 1958 she was made a DBE, and in the last of her letters to her cousin, written on 19 June that year, she told him about having been invited to Buckingham Palace – to her great amusement – to dine with the Queen. However, she fell ill again and went down to Long Crichel to recuperate. On 30 October Rose Macaulay's name appeared in *The Times* as a signatory to a letter condemning the Soviet Writers Union for victimising Boris Pasternak after the award of the Nobel Prize for

Literature. Other names included T.S. Eliot, E.M. Forster, Sir Kenneth Clark and Bertrand Russell. She died suddenly the same day of a heart attack. She had started a new novel to be called *Venice Besieged* but only the first chapter had been written. In her will Rose directed that her personal papers should be burnt after her death. The instruction was carried out by her executors, and much of the rich evidence of her life was destroyed in yet another bonfire.

Eardley was shattered by Frank's death: there was nothing to be said or done but plenty to be suffered. Out of a population of about fifty million – and 25,000 killed in raids so far – it had to be Frank. As far as Eardley was concerned the war was lost. 'Without wanting to be silly I really do feel a sad indifference in watching the greater horrors approaching.'[18] He applied to join the Royal Air Force but, as Raymond said, conveniently for him, and luckily for him, it was not possible. Eight years had passed.

After a holiday in the south of France, Jim had just returned to England. He was exhausted from having driven most of the way home. The entry he made in his diary on Saturday, 23 July 1949 ended, 'It is difficult for me to know what to do. I am in great confusion.' Two days later, on Monday, 25 July, he wrote:

> I am back in the London office. Eardley dined and I told him all. He is so patient with me and listens to all my problems. We drove to Fulham at midnight, walked the river and drank coca cola from a night shelter, which he considered very paintable. It was on wheels besides some bollards on the embankment. E., who is incurably romantic, said that he would chuck up Long Crichel and his perfect life there for love and give all he possessed to the loved one. And he would too. The heat in London is as oppressive as lead.[19]

Apparently, Eardley's advice to Jim was that he too should give up everything for love. Jim was in love with a woman called Alvilde

Chaplin, but Alvilde was married and lived in France. Jim did not know which way to turn, hence the great confusion and problems.

Lees-Milne was attracted to both sexes. At the beginning of the war he had been in love with a man called Richard 'Rick' Stewart-Jones, a committee member of the Society for the Protection of Ancient Monuments. They met in March 1938 when each went separately to inspect a house in Queen Anne's Gate. Jim was expecting some 'venerable, archaeological greybeard'.[20] After entering the house Jim locked the front door, so Rick had forced open a window and climbed through. The man Jim encountered was someone who only looked eighteen, but Rick was 'twenty-four, slender, with a slight stoop, and nimble as quicksilver. A cigarette was dangling from his lower lip in a way the proletarians used to affect.'[21] Discounting the cigarette, the impression which Rick made on Jim that evening in Queen Anne's Gate, through the dust and smoke, was of the face and form of a young Shelley. It was a *coup de foudre*. They spent the evening, and probably the night, together. For a while they lived together, but they soon found that they were incompatible. Rick was a Chelsea borough councillor and, Jim said, he would just as happily go and rescue 'old Mr Simpleton, who had locked himself into a lavatory at The World's End and couldn't get out' than attend the sort of fashionable event Jim enjoyed.[22] They were both young men in a hurry. The relationship did not survive. And then there was war.

Alvilde was a year younger than Jim. She was given the Norwegian name after her mother discovered that her husband, a military-intelligence attaché stationed in Oslo, was having an affair with a ballet dancer called Alvilde. The daughter was to be a permanent rebuke to her father's adultery. Her father was subsequently appointed Governor of South Australia, where the family lived from 1923 to 1927. Alvilde was forced to succumb to her father's sexual advances, a trauma which had a lasting effect, and afterwards the men whose company she preferred were either sexually ambiguous or homosexual, a preference which included Jim.

In 1933 Alvilde married a man called Anthony Chaplin. It was through a family connection, the marriage arranged by their mothers: Chaplin had little money of his own whereas his new wife would inherit a great deal from both her parents. In 1937 Alvilde and Anthony moved to Paris in order for him to study composition with the renowned French teacher Nadia Boulanger. Although the couple were sexually unsuited, they succeeded in having a daughter they called Clarissa. Anthony soon became unfaithful. Alvilde reacted by going to live with Princess Winnie de Polignac. Winnie was born Winnaretta Singer, the twentieth child of Isaac Singer, the sewing-machine magnate. She had lived most of her life in Paris, where she became one of the greatest hostesses and patronesses in the city, especially for musicians. Many of the scenes which Marcel Proust evokes of Parisian salon life were born from the concerts he attended in her drawing room. She married twice. On the wedding night to her first husband, Louis de Scey-Montbéliard, she climbed onto the armoire and threatened to kill him if he approached further. Her marriage to her second husband, the Prince de Polignac, was much happier. She loved him, but he was homosexual, and both marriages were unconsummated. Jim met Alvilde because he had become friends with Winnie, and he wanted to hear her memories of Proust. Winnie, whom Jim described as 'rather like a large Buddha', had many lesbian relationships, and Alvilde was the last of her lovers. The age difference between the two was enormous. When the affair began Alvilde was twenty-seven and the princess seventy-two. However, Anthony encouraged the relationship, since, as an aspiring composer, he was in need of all the patronage he could get. When war broke out Winnie and Alvilde were in England, and they decided to stay for the duration, living in a block of flats next to the Dorchester Hotel. Alvilde trained as a hospital nurse, and Anthony joined the RAF as a rear-gunner. Winnie died of a heart attack at one of her soirées in November 1943. She bequeathed Alvilde her jewellery, her summer house at Jouy-en-Josas outside Paris, together with its contents, and a substantial portion of the residue of her estate. Alvilde had already inherited the estates of both her parents who had died a few years beforehand, although the contents of their house were lost in an air raid.

Alvilde was tall and slim, and she was handsome rather than beautiful. She was also shy and vulnerable, but she could be prickly and had a reputation for being difficult. She took offence easily, offending people in return, and once friends felt slighted by her they did not always try again. At the end of the war she returned to France, becoming a tax exile in order to avoid the punitive British taxes on her very substantial income. She also found life pleasanter in France. Nancy Mitford, having moved to France herself, befriended her and even considered moving to Jouy, which was in the countryside but only twenty minutes from Paris. Alvilde – or 'Alvee', as Nancy called her – and she moved in the same circles, and Alvilde and her contrariness are mentioned frequently in Nancy's letters. She told Gerald Berners that Alvilde had much improved since Princess Winnie's day and she thought he would like her now. She had said to Nancy that she suffered dreadful remorse over having been horrid to the princess but never thought it was quite her fault – it was just that they thoroughly got on each other's nerves. Then a few weeks later Nancy wrote to her sister Deborah about her Christmas: 'I went to A for the actual day. I'm getting up a tremendous hate against her, really I mustn't as she's my only English buddy here – and she's very like Helen Dashwood, greedy & possessive, fond of one & yet never stops denigrating, hinting that the Col[onel] is treating me badly & so on. You know, perpetual pricks. Such a bore.'[23]

After Princess Winnie's death, Alvilde mostly had lesbian affairs, although she had occasional encounters with other men. Then there was Jim Lees-Milne. In his diaries Jim mentions long dinners, visits to the theatre, evenings *à deux*. They went to Rome together; Anthony was also present, but he and Jim got on well – they were like 'blood brothers', Jim said – and Anthony was happy for his wife's sake. He also talked about his sex life in front of his fifteen-year-old daughter.

Jim was appalled, but Clarissa did not seem embarrassed. Anthony introduced Rosemary Littleton, his new mistress (and later wife), for a weekend at Jouy, and once again everyone got on well together.

There were times, however, when not everything went so swimmingly. In September 1949, a few weeks after Jim had confided his anxieties to Eardley, he and Alvilde took a three-week holiday in Italy. It was not entirely successful:

> At times we had rows, mostly slight, but some of them deep. Since I do not know which of my tiresome habits rile her I cannot enumerate them. No doubt there are plenty, for she gets cross and snaps at me like a spoilt child. This conduct has a most unfortunate effect on me, makes me want to escape, turns me in on myself, makes my love grow tepid. A. instantly recovers from these bouts which leave me unhappy and disturbed. Dwelling on them I say that I do not think after all I can live with her permanently . . . There was a night on Lake Garda when I left her in the garden in anger, and walked by myself under the moon along the shore, and sat on the shingle praying for help from the lapping waves. When I returned A. was in tears. Then I was all penitence. There were other moments when she taxed me angrily with not loving her. I could give no honest answer for during those moments I had temporarily ceased loving her.[24]

Jim consoled himself 'with the certitude that no true and enduring love affair ever runs entirely smoothly'; he also accepted that 'marriage is a very unnatural state'.[25] As a Catholic, he needed a Papal annulment before he could marry Alvilde; otherwise, in the eyes of the Church, his marriage would have been not only an 'unnatural state', it would also have been bigamy. In 1950, as Anthony and Rosemary now wished to live together, Alvilde began divorce proceedings against her husband, and Jim applied for an annulment of the Chaplin marriage.

The divorce came through, but there was no sign of the annulment. Anthony had promised not to remarry until after the annulment, but he went ahead anyway. Alvilde was furious, because it meant that she still had Anthony's name although there was a new wife, and she felt this was insulting. She therefore urged Jim to marry her as soon as possible, even though, under these conditions, he would be excommunicated from the Catholic Church. Months passed, still no annulment came through and Alvilde continued to nag. Eventually, Jim agreed to go ahead with the marriage, and their wedding took place at Chelsea Record Office on 19 November 1951. Among the small party of guests there were three husbands and two bachelors. All five men were homosexual and three of them were Jim's ex-lovers. One of those present at the party was Rick Stewart-Jones, who had also recently married, and both Rick and Jim returned the letters they had previously exchanged. With an uncharacteristic lack of enthusiasm, Desmond wrote to Jim a couple of days later: 'Congratulations on having taken, however quietly, the decisive step. Heathen that I am, I have no view about it being good or bad theology; but I am sure it is good sense and will make you both happier.'[26] Neither Eardley nor Raymond liked Alvilde. This lack of enthusiasm for the marriage was widespread. Vita feared that during their first marital row Jim would say to Alvilde, 'And to think that for you I was prepared to sacrifice my immortal soul.'[27]

Alvilde continued to spend all but ninety days abroad in order to avoid paying British taxes. She sold her house at Jouy and bought a little house in the village of Roquebrune, just outside, and formerly within, the Principality of Monaco. Jim now decided to resign from his job as Secretary to the National Trust so that he could divide his time between France and England. For his sake in December 1950 the Trust's Historic Buildings Committee agreed to the creation of a new part-time post of Historic Buildings Adviser and agreed that its first appointee should be Jim. The job took effect from 1 January 1951. When he was not working for the Trust Jim could devote his time to writing, which was something he had long wished to do. Inevitably, however, the fact that Jim was working fewer hours for the National Trust meant that he was obliged to take a drastic reduction in his salary to only £700 a year. This made him even more reliant on his wife's wealth and good will. Jim grew to hate the house at Roquebrune. Whenever he returned to England he first of all spent a few days at Long Crichel. The house was his safety valve, where he could let off steam and recover from the stresses of married life. He would arrive anxious and preoccupied, but after a few days in the welcoming company of Eardley, Eddy, Raymond and Desmond, together with their other friends and house guests, he was another person altogether.

7

The Ecliptophiles

In the summer of 1954 the four Crichel Boys joined a party of friends to go on an expedition to Sweden. They spent a couple of days visiting museums and art galleries before going on to Jönköping in the south of Sweden to see an eclipse of the sun, where they were joined by others including the eye surgeon Pat Trevor-Roper and Ben Nicolson, who, as well as being the elder son of Vita and Harold Nicolson, was editor of the *Burlington Magazine*. Despite his reservations, which he listed in a long letter to Frances – '(a) a vile voyage out, (b) of course we didn't see the sun, (c) Sweden is simply one pretty view' – Eardley had enjoyed himself hugely:

> The stimulus of being abroad made even us old Crichels rather jolly & the variety of the company made me long for expeditions when we all push off to France or Italy & join & separate & meet again in new places . . . Purpler prose than mine will have been read by you – I heard it shouted down the telephone to the Sunday Times through the wall of my bedroom! But I expect my impressions were very different and far more sentimental. Raymond, Jimmy, Ben & I spent Tuesday afternoon scouting round for a good view point and as the roads were full we decided not to venture too far. It was a glorious afternoon with white cumulus clouds very rarely obscuring the sun. At dinner after the

others had arrived it became quite clear & so on Wednesday [30 June 1954] it was especially shattering to wake to very low dark grey unmoving clouds with frequent showers. As it was broad daylight at 3 a.m.

I got up about 5.30 and had some hopeful moments but it soon resettled glum. We packed 7 into Jimmy's car & they reached the aussicht punkt [viewing site] at 11.30. It was a little grandstand overlooking the lake on the eastern side & was already a scene of great activity. Not only Swedes with all sorts of cameras on aluminium tripods but a German group setting up a telescope they had brought in a huge packing case. The owner with a great beak nose swathed in tweed & covered with a cap with buttons & a scarf had cut his chin shaving & was a wonderful mummified mass of enthusiasm, his wife fussing at his side. Eddy, buttoned high in a burberry & with an infinitely unbecoming brown beret fitted well into the picture. It was throughout a Victorian or even an ageless scene of enormous charm. I adore picnics & expeditions and this occasion was the absolutely perfect instance with a miscellaneous set of all ages & nations assembled for a God-made inevitability – so unlike a race meeting or tournament – something from which no-one could make money directly, no seats to be sold etc. Soon the indefatigable old Mortimer saw that a rock protruded on the hill far above us and we scrambled up the course of a stream through the wood . . .

About 1 one began to think it was getting darker and colder (like a summer day at Crichel said Raymond). At 1.15 we deserted our picnic nook & went to stand on the rock . . . We kept looking across the lake & then up at the scudding clouds & here suddenly there was a 3 second glimpse of the sun with the moon right across it except for a sickle of light on the left.

All this time it was like the lights lowering in the theatre, slowly & then very fast indeed as we saw IT coming across the lake. As they went right out the lake turned the most amazing blue and heliotrope & then it swept across us. As soon as this most dramatic moment passed one glanced round and saw near at hand everyone silent & open-mouthed, the tow headed kids too. Behind on the horizon one saw a band of light on the land it had not reached – and absurdly lights twinkling in farm houses & all streetlights of Jönköping on! Next across the lake in the distance one saw a band of yellow like the dawn & then very quickly the light came back to its depressing grey & soon to something which seemed quite light. The whole incident was in a sense nothing – its import seemed very personal & almost as big as death or life – things you face alone and mean just what your personality makes them mean. It was enough to make me an écliptomane or is it écliptophile (this was debated & settled) & if I could I would join Raymond whose thoughts are set on Bangkok this time next year when it happens again.[1]

Eardley had taken up painting a few years earlier. His absolute absorption – according to Eddy – made him much happier than he had ever been, or at least since Frank had died. He built a simple wooden studio in front of the house where he could indulge his hobby, and such was his excitement at its planning and construction that during the course of the work he took more than fifty photographs. Although Eardley was never more than a talented amateur and his work never really progressed, he had a strong feeling for colour and at his best some of his pictures have an energy: they convey the pleasure he achieved from what he was creating. For the most part he painted still life and landscape. Apart from his work for the National Trust and his painting, he continued to deal in art works, and he also looked after the interests of other artists. At the end of Frances Hodgkins' life, Eardley corresponded with John Piper about her care. She had once been one of his favourite artists but later she suffered from what he called 'a clear case of persecution mania'.[2] She was unable to recognise anyone and believed that she was being poisoned. Eardley also kept in touch with artists such as John Banting, Matthew Smith, Graham Sutherland, Henry Moore and Ivon Hitchens, whom he had known since the 1930s. They were all his friends, but he had no sentimental compunction about selling on pictures which had been given to him as presents – which sometimes strained his friendships.

One morning in May 1953 Aldous Huxley sat down in his study and swallowed four-tenths of a gram of mescalin dissolved in half a glass of water and then sat down to wait for the results. The following year Huxley made a report on this first psychedelic experience in his book *The Doors of Perception*. He described how, an hour and a half later, he was staring intently at a small glass vase which contained only three flowers – a pink rose, a magenta-and-cream-coloured iris, and a purple iris. At breakfast that morning he had been struck by the 'conflicting colours. But that was no longer the point. I was not looking now at an unusual flower arrangement. I was seeing what Adam had seen on the morning of his creation – the miracle, moment by moment of naked existence.' Someone asked him if it was agreeable. '"Neither agreeable nor disagreeable," I answered. "It just is."'[3]

Huxley had been introduced to psychedelic drugs by the British psychiatrist Dr Humphry Osmond, who was a pioneer in the treatment of alcoholics (Cary Grant, among others, was prescribed LSD for his drink addiction).*

The Doors of Perception became immensely popular and had considerable influence on a great number of fashionable people, especially in California where Huxley lived. It also made a significant impression when it was first published in Britain. Pat Trevor-Roper's medical and scientific interests went beyond the care of the eye. He asked Raymond if for the first time in his life he might be willing to

---

* In 1957 Dr Osmond coined the word 'psychodolic' (mind-opening); it was later amended to 'pyschedelic' in order to remove the psychotic connotations of LSD.

Napier Sturt, Lord Alington. *(© The Cecil Beaton Studio Archive)*

Crichel House, 1925. *(Alfred E Henson/Country Life Picture Library)*

Eddy Sackville-West, July 1929.
(Private collection)

Raymond Mortimer, 1932. *(Private collection)*

Leigh Ashton, Paul Hyslop, Eardley Knollys, Raymond Mortimer and Donal Rolfe.
(Norman Coates)

The Bothy. *(Norman Coates)*

Frank Coombs, *Chapel des Relgieuses de Notre Dame (Chartres)*. *(Radev Collection)*

Eardley Knollys and
Frank Coombs.
(Norman Coates)

Glenway Wescott. *(Norman Coates)*

James Lees-Milne, 1930s. *(© Michael Bloch)*

Mrs Audrey Knollys. *(Norman Coates)*

Storran Gallery, 5 Albany Court Yard, Piccadilly. *(Norman Coates)*

THE AUTHOR

James Lees-Milne at the
National Trust, 1940s.
Frontispiece to *Caves of Ice:
Diaries 1946 & '47.*
(© Michael Bloch)

Edward Le Bas, *Interior at Long Crichel*, 1952. *(Private collection)*

Rosamond Lehmann. *(Hulton Deutsch/Getty Images)*

Elizabeth Bowen. *(Hulton Deutsch/Getty Images)*

Desmond, Raymond and Eddy at Long Crichel. *(Norman Coates)*

E.M. Forster and Mattei Radev at Long Crichel. *(Norman Coates)*

Eddy in the drawing room at Long Crichel. *(Norman Coates)*

experiment with drugs and act as a guineapig for some research he was doing into mescalin. Raymond readily agreed. He was fifty-nine, but he remained endlessly inquisitive. Huxley and he had been contemporaries at Balliol and were old friends. Even as a freshman Raymond found Aldous 'formidably sophisticated – he was dazzling, *dazzling* . . . The erudition: he had read everything.'[4]

Under the heading 'Report on Mescalin: An Experiment with a Nightmare Ending' Raymond described the results of the experiment in an article for the *Sunday Times*. 'The proposal was made by a doctor who knew me to be alert in my visual impressions and well used to describing them,' he wrote, adding that he had been eager to accept the proposal:

> The increase in visual perceptiveness did prove staggering. I did not respond more vigorously to paintings or to the patterns on materials; but colour took on a prodigious intensity, and form appeared more three-dimensional. The room looked like a rich Impressionist picture, so sensitive was I to the gradations in tonal value and reflected colour. Otherwise the vision was the reverse of Impressionist: the outlines were very sharply defined. The leaves in a vase seemed made of metal, so did the persons in the room; and their heads and the folds in their clothes were sculptural, as is seen in a stereoscope. I was reminded of certain Mannerist pictures of the sixteenth century. My vision I must emphasise was not distorted: I saw only what was there, but I saw it with unprecedented acuteness . . . I felt that I had been lent the eyes of a great painter, seeing colour like Renoir or Monet, and form like Michelangelo or Bronzino. This was an unforgettable experience, and I believe moreover that it has left me able to use my eyes better than before.
>
> Another effect was at least equally extraordinary. Thought and memory remained; emotion entirely vanished. I remembered without pleasure or pain; I looked forward without desire or fear. I was shown photographs of Italian architecture; I listened to

Chopin on a gramophone; I repeated lines from a favourite poem: though I recognised the excellences of these works, was entirely unmoved by any of them. I thought without the faintest affection of the persons to whom I am most attached; I could muster no resentment against persons who had treated me badly.

Whereas Mr. Huxley felt that he had blessedly escaped from self, I remained highly conscious of self, losing merely my emotional responses (except to colour and form). I was acutely interested in the experience I was undergoing and in nothing else. My personal opinions and beliefs remained unchanged. Complete emotional detachment might be expected to make one think more clearly and thus to modify one's opinions. It did nothing of the sort. Though my thoughts about Hitler were not coloured by any of my usual disgust, my intellect calmly condemned him. I *knew* but I did not *feel*, the difference between right and wrong, or between love and hate . . . In my experience it did not diminish self-control, remove inhibitions, or increase suggestibility. My mind had become neither less individual nor weaker, but emotionally I had ceased to be a person.

Mescalin, it is said, produces some of the same symptoms as schizophrenia. According to Mr. Huxley it brings to most people the heavenly part of that disease – and 'hell and purgatory only to those who have had a recent case of jaundice, or who suffer from periodicals or chronic depressions or chronic anxiety'. To the best of my knowledge I am free from all of these yet the drug eventually produced the most horrifying experience I had ever known. The dose had certainly been too strong for me: I suffered from recurrent nausea and often felt on the point of passing out. This hampered my delight in the revelation of visual beauty, and was presumably responsible for the misery that followed.

Some five hours after taking the mescalin the inability to feel suddenly became alarming in the extreme. Had the drug merely paralysed my emotions, I wondered, or had it perhaps destroyed them for ever? Life without them would be unendurable. Then I decided that this terror was itself an emotion, and that its appearance meant that I was emerging from the influence of the drug. This realisation brought momentary relief, but I now began to suffer a generalised apprehension amounting to panic. I was not frightened of pain or death; I was frightened only of continuing to exist in my present unmotivated anguish. Though my brain was lucid, I was suffering the torments caused by some forms of madness. A sleeping-pill at last brought a merciful unconsciousness.[5]

On the day Raymond's article appeared a young man had arrived on his doorstep at eight o'clock in the morning wanting to talk to him. Raymond was away, so Paul Hyslop answered the door. The man said he had been so agitated by the description of what he had experienced when he had lost his sanity, that he could still reproduce the state of mind at will. 'Presumably a schizophrenic, still on the edge of madness,' Raymond suggested. Pat told Raymond that he had sent a copy of his article to Huxley and asked him for any facts he could obtain about the effect of an overdose.

Rosamond Lehmann persuaded Pat to have a similar session with her in her flat. There were just two of them taking the drug, but a young psychiatrist friend of Rosamond sat in to observe and take notes. Pat recalled that it was all fairly dramatic: 'Rosamond looked increasingly beautiful and statuesque, and her hair seemed to move in solid blocks. She kept saying, "The stone in my womb is getting heavier and heavier. Oh my womb is weighing so much." . . . It went on like this for two or three hours.'[6] Rosamond herself was both intrigued and repelled by her experience. She remembered:

a hard-edged semi-mineral disparate world of artefacts and coldness . . . phenomena that astonished me and yet had no meaning, and from which I was *horribly separated* so that I could feel no love or pleasure in them. And the visual hallucinations I had for a time were of reptilian or crustacean forms of life i.e. P.T.-R.'s hands became crawling lobsters. His face and also the psychiatrist's looked *knowing*, crafty-eyed, although archaic images of stone.[7]

Pat described the experience as 'down to Hell and up to Heaven'.

In 1958 after the death of her daughter Sally in Java, Rosamond was prostrated with grief. In order to gain a glimmer of hope she became obsessed with psychical research. With the help of a medium she convinced herself that not only did Sally survive on 'the other side', she sometimes even managed to establish contact – with her daughter condescending, as Nancy Mitford said cruelly, to slide down to Rosamond on a sunbeam. She persuaded Pat to experiment yet again with hallucinogenic drugs in order to bring about a much hoped-for spiritual encounter. Inevitably the experiment was a failure. Pat continued to see Rosamond, however, and she found his kindness and interest so comforting that she started to rely on him entirely. Eventually she suggested they should marry. 'I think she fell slightly in love with me,' said Pat.[8]

After the 1930s Eddy never wrote another novel. In 1950 the writer Julian Maclaren-Ross wrote to the BBC Talks Department telling them that he had written an article about Edward Sackville-West for the *Times Literary Supplement*, and he thought they might like him to give a talk about his subject as well. Failing this, he proposed Anthony Powell, 'another very interesting writer', whose new novel was to appear later in the year; he also suggested that Eric Ambler might be an interesting subject. However, the *Times Literary Supplement* piece on the novels of Edward Sackville-West never appeared, while the literary careers of Powell and Ambler continued to thrive. Despite his achievement with the *Record Guide* and all his other activities in the worlds of art and music, Eddy feared that he had 'dried'. In February 1953 Eddy wrote in his journal: 'Unrequited love is the only relationship [in] which I have ever been able completely to realise my complexities as a human being.' And: 'I feel fully alive only when obsessively unhappy.'[9] He made a second visit to Wandrille, but it was a disappointment, and the depression which descended on Eddy persisted throughout the early years of the decade. 'I have been practically alone with Eardley,' he wrote, '& have felt closer to him than I think – ever, in the years we have lived here. I believe he guessed that I was suffering from a severe attack of *Weltschmerz* [world pain], and wanted to help.'

It was around this time that Graham Sutherland painted Eddy. It is a portrait which combines both a certain melancholy vulnerability and a sense of aristocratic entitlement (Eddy once told Frances that he had never met anyone who would not rather have an inherited title than one bestowed by the Queen; Frances was shocked). The writer Sybille Bedford said that Eddy 'sometimes had the look of a fragile and ageless princely child'.[10]

In August 1953 Elizabeth Bowen wrote to Raymond from Bowen's Court, her rather austere house near Kildorrey in County Cork, telling him that she would love to see him again. Her husband, Alan Cameron, had died the previous year, and she had been devastated:

> I haven't really lost myself, to real friends, in Ireland. This last year has been of the kind simply to live through, and it seemed best to stay here and work hard. I'm trying to finish my present novel by Christmas. But after that I shall be emerging again, and hope to be for some time in England. I needn't say, I know, dear Raymond, how *very* welcome you would be here if you ever felt like undertaking the journey. Flying, it's not too bad; this house gets a degree more comfortable each year; I *would* take care of you, and it really is a nice quiet place to work in [the] meanwhile.[11]

The novel when it was published the following year was called *A World of Love*.

Ireland also began to attract Eddy. With the typical enthusiasm of a convert, he seemed keen to be surrounded by a Catholic environment, and he also had Irish ancestry on both sides of his family. Bowen was a close friend and a frequent visitor to Long Crichel, and he had stayed with her. In the spring of 1955 Eddy decided to buy a house of his own in Ireland, and it seemed obvious to start looking in the vicinity of Bowen's Court. He first considered Shanbally Castle. One of the great houses of Ireland, it had been built for the 1st Viscount Lismore in the first decade of the nineteenth century by John Nash, the architect to the Prince Regent and the builder of Regent Street. It was also complete and in good condition, having been lived in until recently. In August Eddy's father wrote asking him if it was true that he had bought, or was contemplating buying, an ancient castle in Ireland? 'If so do tell me about it. I need hardly tell you that ancient buildings cost much to repair & maintain.'[12] Eddy's plans for Shanbally came to nothing, since he was unable to purchase enough land with the castle to make the property self-supporting. Instead, by the end of the year, he had bought Cooleville, a much more modest house in Clogheen, a nearby village. Cooleville was in County Tipperary, eighteen miles from Bowen's Court, and like Shanbally it was built at the beginning of the nineteenth century. As well as the house, there was a gate lodge, a courtyard and 'a vast ruined mill . . . full of wood pigeons cooing noisily'.

This new and startling development in Eddy's life brought about considerable consternation among the other members of the Long Crichel household. In February 1956 Elizabeth Bowen was in London and staying in Eardley's flat in West Halkin Street, which she was using to meet her lover Charles Ritchie, a Canadian diplomat. Before she left London she lunched with Raymond and Paul Hyslop at the house they shared in Canonbury. She told Ritchie that

Raymond had been extremely fussed and agitated, burning to have a chat about Eddy's affairs.

[Raymond said], what we fear is, that when Eddy goes to live in Ireland he may *Take to the Bottle*. 'Good heavens, Raymond,' I said, 'why?' 'Because, Elizabeth, everybody in Ireland drinks so much.' 'Really, Raymond, do you mean that *I* am a drunk?' 'Good God, no . . . but the fact is that in the last two years, since Eddy has started being so much in Ireland, he has started *Drinking Far More Heavily*.'

Yes, he said, they (the Long Crichel boys) had observed that the whisky at Long Crichel was *steadily going down*. At first they thought it was Deverell (the butler) but finally it had become plain to them that it must be Eddy.

The idea that these dear old cissies at Long Crichel all rushing to measure the decanter with their thumbnails, every time poor Eddy has one then goes out of the room, really did seem funny. But also grim. It really is time poor Eddy *did* have a house of his own! And really they need not be so fussy; this is not the first bolt he has made – did he not [pop] off and quietly join the Church of Rome?

I laughed inwardly during the conversation and out loud when I was alone afterwards, at finding myself cast in the role of an elderly rake. I think this must be the result of Eddy's artless unwitting prattle. I said somewhat briskly that I thought Eddy was well able to take care of himself. 'Yes, in a way he has a will of iron,' said Raymond, 'but he is also *rather easily influenced*.' I said: 'Of course, Raymond, *you* are the great influence in his life.' Which at once mollified the old boy and spiked his guns.[13]

In the middle of March, however, Elizabeth told Ritchie she had begun to understand that, although she thought Cooleville was a very nice place and Eddy had every chance of being very happy there, Raymond might have had a point after all:

The only thing is, I'm afraid Raymond has got something in this thing about Eddy and the bottle. I don't mean he really drinks such a lot – I mean, by what I regard as normal standards – but it does *affect* him tremendously: the last two or three evenings he's been what I suppose anyone would call tight: not stupid but madly exhilarated. I think he's already punch-drunk with excitement over this house . . .

If he really is 'drinking', I've no idea how to stop him. I refuse to nag anyone in my house – in fact I refuse to nag anyone. I suppose the fact is, he always has had someone in a nurse-or-governess relationship to him, in one form or another, and is now fairly far on in life to be a free agent. Really he's no fool, and one would be a fool to treat him as one – he'll find his own equilibrium, don't you think? Only in a sense one cannot feel responsible, partly because he is so young for his age, partly because he's in his own way so fond of me and does, I know, react to what I say or do . . .[14]

Eddy was fifty-five, only two years younger than Elizabeth Bowen. The previous night, on their way home from a visit to friends, he had been so drunk he lost his way. He also drove 'like a bat out of hell'.[15]

Elizabeth was helping Eddy to furnish the new house, and her letters to Ritchie are full of references to him. She also continued to make disparaging remarks about Raymond, although they had known one another socially for many years and had many mutual friends. He had also always supported and praised her writing. In his diary Ritchie recorded that Raymond had once said to him how Elizabeth had such charm and was so kind and made most of one's friends seem irremediably vulgar. At the end of the month Elizabeth went to Long Crichel, despite the distaste she expressed both for her hosts (Eddy's 'keepers', she called them) and her fellow guest, Hester Chapman, a writer of history books whom she found '*most* unpalatable'. She approved, however, of Desmond and thought he agreed with her dislike of Raymond:

140

He's an Anglo-Irishman: very conventional outwardly, looks like somebody in the Kildare Street Club, Dublin. I remember being told what indeed becomes very clear during the weekend, that Desmond can't stand Raymond, resents his having moved into Long Crichel . . . I am now clear that Eddy's fundamental reason for wanting a life in Ireland – so fundamental that he either hasn't realized it or doesn't want to – is to get away from Raymond and all that whip-cracking organization.

Elizabeth Bowen had married Alan Cameron, a local government official, in 1923 at the age of twenty-four, but the marriage was never consummated. She only wanted to write, and Cameron, after his experiences in the First World War, thought it irresponsible to bring children into the world. She later took a number of lovers, of whom Charles Ritchie, who was cultivated and suave, was the most satisfying both emotionally and sexually. Ritchie had been appointed to London in January 1939 as private secretary to the High Commissioner, and he remained in England only for the duration of the war before returning to Ottawa. In 1948 he married happily and had children, but he and Elizabeth continued to correspond and saw one another when they could.

Elizabeth also saw a great deal of Eddy and wrote about him often. She reassured Ritchie, however, that Eddy was not in love with her 'in any usual sense'. He had told her that he loved her very much, but she thought it was 'that happiest kind of love which contents itself with the happiness they have with a person'. In fact, love had always made him frenzied and miserable. Norah Preece, a cousin of Eddy and close friend of both Eddy and Elizabeth, claimed that each had proposed marriage to the other and how embarrassing it had been. For Elizabeth Bowen, who had no 'proper money' (by which Eddy meant capital and unearned income), marriage would have given her financial and even a certain emotional protection.

Elizabeth Bowen's own marriage, despite its apparently unsatisfactory nature, was not unhappy: she continued to rely on her
husband, and, until his death, there had been genuine understanding
and affection between the two. Eddy for his part, despite his homosexuality, liked the idea of being married and had considered it
before. He also very much liked the idea of being looked after, but
the constant nursing he would have demanded was not a role which
Elizabeth, so recently widowed, would have wanted. Furthermore,
she was a Protestant. Bowen's Court had always been a bastion of
Protestantism in the midst of not entirely accepting Catholic neighbours. She would not have converted. The scope for mutual
awkwardness was all too great.

Meanwhile, Ritchie remained in love with Elizabeth. He confided
to his diary:

> I have been disturbed – frightened – by E's letter about Eddy. I do
> hope I may be spared that confrontation . . . If he wanted to marry
> her – no, what I dread is that she might want to marry him – security,
> that's it, and a title. How could I deny that it would be the 'ideal
> solution' for her, remove the strain – the financial one – and there he
> is installed in the neighbourhood. Have I been a fool all this time?
> She imported him, she installed him; she sees him every day and
> every night . . . If she married him, I should know what she knew
> when I married, and should not 'behave' half so well. It would be
> justice all right if that means anything. Mind you, I don't think he
> intends to. Though what he intends matters much less than what she
> intends . . . At the very thought of her marrying the ground cracks
> under me. I think I should fight it selfishly – unless that way I
> thought I should lose her for good, in which case I might do what she
> did, and we should lose one another by inches – aren't we already?[16]

From the evidence of the entries he made in his diary not long
after he moved into his new house, Eddy was happier in Ireland than

he had been for years. On 13 June 1956 he wrote: 'I have been here now since May 25 & have sunk ever deeper into the *strangeness* of this country, which bears no resemblance whatever to England.' Ireland became something new to live for, a new cause for him. He took pleasure in 'its backwater quality' and 'the equally warm, intensely religious peasantry (for they are that still whatever they may call themselves)':

> The inhabitants of Clogheen, whether employed by me or not, have been uniformly kind & welcoming. Intensely curious too of course: if I sneeze in the library at 11. 15 a.m. & go into the shop at 3 p.m. I am commiserated with for having caught cold! . . . Imagine the villagers of Long Crichel saying "Welcome to LC!" – our relations with LC are pretty negative: the people are not interested in us, nor we in them. But it would be impossible for me to have anything but a positive relationship with the Clogheen people, for they would insist on it.

In fact, the neighbourhood was agog at Eddy's arrival. He decorated Cooleville in a suitably Victorian manner. The house, said David Cecil, was a mixture of Eddy's room at Eton and Mr Rochester's house in *Jane Eyre*. Mr Rochester had a very lush crimson-and-gold drawing room, and the Cooleville drawing room was the same: there were huge 'man-sized roses' on the flock wallpaper and a rose-coloured carpet. The library was Prussian blue; there were orange floor-to-ceiling bookcases and a Graham Sutherland landscape hung over the fireplace. A young man called Julian Jebb came over from England to sort out the books. Eddy dressed his four maids in a red uniform. He himself wore a red dinner jacket in the evening. 'My word! What good servants they are,' he wrote in his diary, 'the sort Mrs Knollys had until the war. The house is marvellously well kept & Miss Slattery cooks in the best country house style of 1925 (so she ought at £6 a week!).'[17]

Eddy even developed an interest in gardening, making notes among his diary entries:

> Fuschia on the west wall of hall; clematis on mill remove: shrubs in front of mill (phlox); variegated laurel; elder & laurel in front of beech; sample conifers; saxifrage extend bed at least 6ft; Love-in-the-mist; anemones; lobelia; 3 dark red roses (grand gala) cineraria and red rose – conservatory; pelargoniums

On his return from a short holiday in England in July 1956 he said that although his time had been very enjoyable, it had only made him miss his own green garden, and that he had returned 'in a passion of excitement'.[18]

A couple of months later Frances and Ralph Partridge came to visit. Frances thought that Cooleville was 'a beautifully constructed, smoothly-working toy', but Eddy sat in the midst of it all like a little rich boy with 'great sad eyes, ringed around with ill-health, as thin as a sparrow and with spots on his poor face'.[19] It made their hearts bleed to see him look so ill and exhausted, all the while forcing himself to be charming, intelligent and the most amusing of hosts. He still railed against the state of things from a purely aristocratic point of view, and often declared his disbelief in, or dislike of, equality, but in Ireland he could live in a way that existed nowhere else, nor had done for about a hundred years. 'No two sets of values could be more different than ours and Eddy's,' she added, 'especially now he's become Catholic, yet very warm affection – I believe mutual – exists between us.'[20] On the night the Partridges arrived Elizabeth Bowen came to dinner and they decided that that they both liked her very much. She was 'horse-faced, with big hands and a clumsy body in a short black evening dress and flashing diamond corsage; she has an attractive stammer which makes her words beginning with "r" with a whirring sound like a clock about to strike'.[21] A couple of evenings later they were invited to dine with her at Bowen's Court, 'at a candle-lit table in a vast room full of shadows, servants waiting, and Elizabeth in a white evening dress and emeralds'.[22] Afterwards they played Scrabble in front of a roaring fire in an equally vast drawing room.[23] In September Elizabeth told Ritchie that Eddy had endured seven weeks of non-stop visitors all summer and was 'cracking up'. The worst thing for him was Raymond and Eardley arriving like a couple of witches on broomsticks: 'Raymond was all over me, full of compliments. But I'll never trust that little creature again.'[24]

Although Eddy went back regularly to Long Crichel, the others were still concerned about him, and he feared they regarded his desire to be a landowner in Ireland as an 'absurd caprice'. 'I can't think why they should mind,' he wrote in his diary. 'Of course I daresay my surprise is partly due to my inability – & unwillingness too! I fear to believe in others' affection for me. I do everything in my power to make people love me – and then am surprised if I they do!'[25] In June 1958 he wrote to Desmond:

Your wistful and forbearing letter made me sadder than ever. Probably one should never try to explain one's motives beyond a certain point; but since both you and Eardley, by use of the word 'happy', seem to have misunderstood me, I suppose I'd better say more.

I never was and never could be happier than I have been at Long Crichel. But happiness is only a by-product and I have never sought it directly. What I do seek is a justification for my existence, and this is exactly what I have missed – with increasing distress and bitterness – since I ceased to be a writer. The only thing left to me, from that point of view, is this place – the farm, the garden, the house; they are an occupation which prevents me from feeling utterly futile. It is not much, you will say, – and you will be right. But it is the best I can do, now that a lifetime of ill-health has at last destroyed my powers of concentration and what creative gift I ever had.

I still cherish a dim hope that Long Crichel may be saved from disintegration. I have always favoured the idea that Dadie [Rylands], as you know: apart from anything else, he might go far to console Raymond for my absence. If you took my bedroom, Dadie could have yours to sleep *and* work in; the fortissimo noises elsewhere in the house would not reach him there. But you may have a better idea by now . . .

I quite agree with you that for the present we should mention this matter to nobody. One knows only too well the avalanche of miscellaneous gossip which any step of this kind always causes.

George 'Dadie' Rylands was a literary scholar and a theatre director. He was called 'Dadie' because as a small child he was unable to pronounce the word 'baby'. The name stuck and was used by everyone. From Eton, Rylands had won a scholarship to King's College, Cambridge, and he continued to live at the college as a fellow for the rest of his life. Attracted by Rylands' intellect and great good looks, Lytton Strachey introduced him into the world of Bloomsbury, and Leonard and Virginia Woolf published his verse and his dissertation at the Hogarth Press. As a teacher at Cambridge, Rylands was popular, and as a theatre director he was immensely influential.[*] However, although a friend of everyone at Long Crichel and a very frequent guest, he was never to live there.

Elizabeth Bowen's 1954 novel *A World of Love* is about the subject she knew all too well – the failure and decay of an Irish country house. The house in the book is called Montefort:

the small mansion had an air of having gone down: for one thing, trees had been felled around it, leaving space impoverished and the long low roofline framed by too much sky. The door no longer knew

---

[*] Ian McKellen, Clive Swift, Eleanor Bron and Derek Jacobi were all directed by him.

hospitality; moss obliterated the drive for the turning carriage; the avenue lived on as a rutted track, and a poor fence, close up to the house, served to keep back wandering grazing cattle. Had the façade not carried a ghost of style, Montefort would have looked as it almost did, like nothing more than the annexe of its farm buildings – whose slipshod gables and leaning sheds, flaking whitewash and sagging rusty doors made a patchwork for some way out behind.[26]

Such decaying, redundant houses were all too real and all too near at hand – in Ireland just as much as in England. The success of Elizabeth's wartime novel, *The Heat of the Day*, had allowed her to install a bathroom at Bowen's Court for the first time, but the curtains in the drawing room were made from corset satin. Despite all her frantic efforts – journalism, lecture tours in the United States and periods as a writer-in-residence at American universities – the money was never enough to enable the upkeep of the house she had inherited from her father in 1930. In 1959 she sold Bowen's Court to a farmer in the vain hope it would still continue as a family home. Elizabeth had, quite simply, run out of money. She had lived well, entertaining her friends with fine wines and excellent meals, but no one knew about her unpaid bills and her true predicament, and she was too proud to share her anxieties. The only likely relation of the next generation, Charles Bowen, farmed in South Africa and had no desire to accept another responsibility. In April 1960 there was a two-day auction in Cork of the contents of Bowen's Court, accumulated by generations of Bowen ancestors. She asked her friend Derek Hill to paint a picture of Bowen's Court to hang in her new home in England, but by the time he arrived he discovered that the roof had been taken off by its new owner, Cornelius O'Keefe. O'Keefe had only wanted the property for the land and the timber, which was quickly felled. By the end of the summer the whole great house had been demolished. In 1942 Elizabeth had written a history of Bowen's Court, then twelve years later in 1964 she published a revised version in which she said that the destruction of the house had been 'a clean end'. But it was not 'clean', of course, it was a catastrophe for her, a complete failure of all her hopes and efforts.

Eddy was deeply hurt at not having been forewarned, but neither was anyone else. Elizabeth had scarcely admitted the matter to herself. After leaving Ireland she went to live in Hythe in Kent, a town she had known and where she had been happy as a child.

Some years later Eddy's librarian Julian Jebb, who was by now working in television, went to stay with Elizabeth when he was making a programme about Virginia Woolf. He wrote to Frances:

Elizabeth's house is a tiny villa – two up, *one* down – in a row on a very steep hill – built in 1962. It is a doll's house, modern, complete with tiny lawn and borders from which spring up through spotlessly weeded black soil a mass of many coloured tulips. Inside there are many books, a gold wall-papered sitting room and an air of scrupulous orderliness and cleanliness. Elizabeth does everything – cook, wash up and will, slightly worryingly, let me do nothing at all to help. So that when I went to bed last night at about 11.15 she was downstairs at least an hour tidying with a transistor radio pumping out pop music while she crashed about.[27]

In his diary Eddy mentions making several visits to Shanbally, the castle he had considered buying. He had not been the only prospective buyer: a religious order had also been interested in purchasing the property for its own uses. However, the Irish Land Commission decided that Shanbally should be demolished. Civil servants sold the castle to a Limerick firm, and instructions were given to dismantle the house and its fittings; the battlements were hacked down; the trees on the lawn were carted away. Explosives had to be used to demolish what was left, and 1,400 holes were bored into the walls about 18 inches above the ground. In fact, the castle could easily have been restored for a fraction of the cost of its destruction.

On 15 March 1960, at Cooleville, Eddy recorded in his diary: 'At 5.30 p.m. a loud bang, like a bomb going off in the distance. I was in the drawing room. All the [sound] away from the direction of Parson's Green. Went in to the village to post daffodils to Jim and Cicily. Mr Sweeney told me they had blown up Shanbally . . .'

This was the last entry in Eddy's journal.

8

The Crichel Down Affair

At the end of June 1948 Jim and Eardley drove over to see Crichel House, where they were shown around by Miss Galston, the headmistress of the girls' school. Few of the Alington contents had been put away. It seemed that everything was still used by the girls – nothing had been spoiled, not even the carpets and curtains. The girls, who were 'pretty and sweet', sat out of doors reading, walking or playing musical instruments.[1]

The house was stuccoed with some grey texture, and there were dull, nineteenth-century additions. Only the south colonnade, imposed in 1774 upon a George II wing, was noteworthy, but Jim thought that the interior was very good indeed, with some rooms of high quality:

The dining room ceiling beautiful . . . blues and greens and plasterwork clear and not over-fussy, all white, the walls biscuit. The school tables are certainly not ornamental. I certainly see no reason why they should not be so, yet simple. The drawing room ceiling reminds me of Adam's at no. 20 St James's Square; green silk walls (modern), crimson upholstered gilt chairs. The mirrors throughout the house are fine. We walked round the grounds, lovely lake and woods.[2]

Bryanston School, an equivalent school for boys, was in a village some twenty miles away from Crichel House but within cycling distance, but the Bryanston boys and the Crichel girls were not allowed to meet. Thorold Coade, the headmaster of Bryanston, was terrified of the sexual consequences of any possible encounter. Girls were even banned from joining the boys' weekly dancing classes. The boys had to lust and fantasise from a distance, and they learned to dance using long-handled brooms, shuffling around the floor with bristles pressed against their cheeks.

After they left Crichel House, Jim and Eardley drove on to the village of Wimborne St Giles. In the parish church every tablet on the walls was dedicated to a member of the family of the Earls of Shaftesbury, the Ashley Coopers. They had tea at St Giles House with Lady Shaftesbury, Napier Alington's mother-in-law and the grandmother of Mary Anna Sturt. Her husband, whom she referred to as 'Shaftesbury', was away. Jim wrote in his diary:

> She is old, rather fat, bandy legs for she is lame, and *maquillée* [wearing cosmetics] in the Queen Alexandra fashion. Eyes very made up. Must once have been pretty, and has enchanting manners. Is a sister of the Duke of Westminster. Clips every 'g'. 'G-clippin'' has become a favourite joke at Long Crichel. After tea she showed us round the state rooms. They are *superb*; late seventeenth-century and early eighteenth-century . . . A magnificent house. Pray God the contents are never dispersed. Lady Shaftesbury told us that, their son having died last year, they are faced with £250,000 death duties. Presumably they had rashly made over the estate to him. Her exquisite personality impressed me strongly.[3]

The Shaftesburys were offering to make over to the National Trust a massive and remarkably ugly eye-catcher called Horton Tower, or 'Sturt's Folly', which was on their land. The first member of the Sturt family to arrive in Dorset, Sir Anthony Sturt, had built a manor house in the village of Horton in 1718. His son, Sir Humphrey, the man who had repaired and enlarged Long Crichel rectory, had also built the red-brick, hexagonal tower to use as an observatory. When Humphrey married and moved to Crichel on the death of his father-in-law, both house and tower were abandoned, and he embarked on a large building programme there instead. In May 1762 the historian Edward Gibbon visited the folly. Such was the nature of the man, he said, that Humphrey Sturt had already made 'a granary of his turret'. Jim and Eardley found that the interior of the tower had completely disappeared, and only a burnt beam or two was left. Shrubs were growing out of the broken parapet. Eardley thought it best not to accept the building.

Although Mary Anna Sturt was brought up with the family of her guardian, Lord Hardinge, who had three daughters of his own, the early death of both of her parents meant that she had a lonely childhood. She joined the Brownies pack at Buckingham Palace with Princess Margaret and attended Miss Faunce's Parents' National School at Lancaster Gate. On the outbreak of war the school had moved to St Giles House, which served as both a hospital and as a school. Afterwards she attended Cheltenham Ladies' College. Throughout her youth she longed to reach her majority and have the Alington estate and properties returned into her possession. She was tall and dark and had taken after her father – and presumed grandfather – in looks and she had a strong, determined character and knew precisely what she thought about everything.

After leaving Cheltenham she went to Oxford to read history, where she joined each of the main political parties at the same time. However, on her very first day at Somerville College, she was introduced to Lieutenant Commander Toby Marten – a man as tall as herself – at a lunch party. Instead of finishing her degree, she left Oxford at the end of the university year in order to marry him. The wedding, which took place in November 1949 at Holy Trinity,

Brompton, was attended by a large contingent of members of the Royal Family, including both the King and Queen, who was her godmother. Mary Anna also had exceptional political connections: in the first Conservative government after the war when Churchill was again Prime Minister, the Minister of War, Antony Head, was her uncle by marriage, and James Stuart, the Secretary of State for Scotland, was an executor of her father's will.

Soon after their marriage the Martens moved into Falconer's Cottage, the house rebuilt by Paul Hyslop for her father – and in time Mary Anna, who had a considerable interest in the arts herself, also became a good friend and regular visitor to the Crichel coterie. Marten had spent nearly his whole life in the navy. He had entered Dartmouth Naval College as a boy and remained a serving officer until 1953. He spent the whole of the war in destroyers. In August 1941 during the siege of Malta he had helped a crippled tanker find rescue in the Grand Harbour, Valetta, for which he had won the Distinguished Service Cross. According to the citation he had shown 'bravery and dauntless resolution'. He now took up the running of the estate – 500 acres were farmed in hand while the rest was let out to tenants. In 1941 the coalition government had passed a law giving it the power to take over agricultural land. The bill contained a specific provision that within five years of the war ending the Minister of Agriculture should give the owner, or successor, the opportunity to repurchase the land, unless the Minister certified that, in his opinion, return to the original owner would lead to inefficient management or cultivation. But the intention was clear. Land, however acquired, would be put in the hands of the newly created Agricultural Land Commission.

In early 1950 one of the tenant farmers pointed Crichel Down out to Marten on the scrub-covered hillside to the west of Long Crichel. The tenant explained that 328 acres of the down had once belonged to the Alington estate and made up more than half of Middle Farm in Long Crichel. Formerly, part of the land had been cultivated, while the rest was used for grazing by sheep and cattle. Once the Air Ministry took over in 1937 the down became a practice bombing range, and the local cottagers became used to the sound of exploding bombs and the roar of planes overhead. As all cultivation ceased so the land deteriorated, gorse began to spread freely and rabbits multiplied. When bombing trials ended in September 1948 the RAF began a surface search for explosives until, by the end of 1949, they had cleared more than 200 tons of live or inert bombs from the area. Having seen the land and heard its history, Marten decided it would be a good idea to try and buy it back, and restore it to its original place as part of the Crichel estate. However, by chance, only a few weeks before Marten's arrival, the Air Ministry had decided to divest itself of the land and pass it over to the Ministry of Agriculture. The formal transfer had taken place on 9 January 1950. All this had been agreed in Whitehall, without the estate having been informed. On his way home from seeing Crichel Down Marten called in at the estate office and told his agent to send a letter to the Ministry of Agriculture, asking for an opportunity to negotiate for Crichel Down if it was offered for sale.

Towards the end of 1949 Colonel Norton-Fagge, the Land Commissioner who was responsible for state-owned land in Dorset and Somerset, suggested to his superiors that, whatever the long-term plan was to be, the Dorset Agricultural Committee should be instructed to plough as much of the down as possible and sow to spring corn for the 1950 harvest. Norton-Fagge's reply to Marten's letter was noncommittal, and Marten never heard from him again. It had already been decided that the whole of Crichel Down should be farmed as one entity, and when this fact became known in the county a number of interested parties wrote applying to farm the land. One of the applicants was a bespectacled, round-faced young farmer called Christian Tozer. He was thirty, married, and he farmed with his father and brother at Woodyates a few miles away. He had also made several trips to Europe to study agricultural methods and been particularly impressed by the efficiency of farms in Scandinavia. As it happened Harold Thomson, the Bridport agent of the Permanent Commissioner of Crown Lands, already knew of Christian Tozer. In 1950 when the Crown Lands took over the Bryanston Estate, Tozer applied to farm there, but he was too late. However, Thomson kept his name in mind for the future.

Marten returned briefly to the navy, but when he returned in 1952 he once more requested to buy Crichel Down. A Conservative government was back in power, which, he assumed, would provide an atmosphere more propitious to the repurchase of nationalised land, but he failed to appreciate the lingering, almost obsessive fear of food shortages left over from the war. The Land Commission were now of the opinion that they had an opportunity to build a modern farm unit on this bare land – albeit at considerable expense – which would turn Crichel Down into a model for modern farming methods, and in Christian Tozer they had already decided they had the ideal man to farm it. Donald Brown, a junior official, was sent to Crichel and told to make a report. Since the matter was regarded as extremely confidential he was instructed to speak to none of the locals, let alone the previous owners, and to base the report solely on information supplied by the ministry's officials. Unfortunately, if unsurprisingly, since he had been so poorly briefed, Brown's report was full of errors – not the least of which was a statement that the land had previously been badly farmed.

Marten kept writing. There were far more applicants for the land than just Christian Tozer, but all of them, aside from Tozer, were kept in the dark. The matter returned to Whitehall, and the Minister of Agriculture, Sir Thomas Dugdale, began to have second thoughts. At the end of October he sent Lord Carrington, the second Parliamentary Secretary, to Dorset to make an inspection. Carrington sat in the House of Lords rather than in the Commons, which meant that he was less tied to Parliamentary duties and freer to travel. It also meant that he found himself with the odd jobs which no one else wanted or could cope with. At the time he was much concerned about myxomatosis in rabbits – 'a hideous and incurable disease sweeping the country clean of these delightful, furry little creatures'.[4] Carrington based his judgement relating to Long Crichel on Brown's critical report and sided with the bureaucracy: big farms, he believed, were better than small farms and the way of the future. The fact that the national emergency had passed and that the previous owners might now have a legitimate interest in having the property restored to them apparently occurred neither to Carrington, who was a landowner himself, nor to anyone else. But because of the rumours and the expense and Marten's persistence, Crichel Down was becoming a priority, and the now bulky file was passing through the hands of every civil servant of consequence at the Ministry of Agriculture. Marten made as much fuss as he could. He even telephoned Christopher Eastwood, the Permanent Commissioner of Crown Lands when he was on his holiday (his address having been extracted from a hapless member of his office staff). Harold Thomson wrote to Eastwood from his office at Bridport:

> From the correspondence alone, I should say that Commander Marten was the last person we should want as a tenant. I can only report that we are committed to Tozer. The row which Commander Marten is determined to make is clearly going to be very unpleasant for Tozer and, to a lesser extent, for ourselves, and there is no doubt that everything possible will be done to embarrass both of us . . .
> If Tozer decided to withdraw, you certainly could not have Commander Marten after the way he has behaved. We should have to find someone else as a tenant who combined Tozer's farming ability with a very thick skin.[5]

In another letter Mr Wilcox, an under-secretary at the Ministry, wrote to Eastwood saying that there was some concern about letting a further 726 acres to a family which already farmed a great deal of land in the county. He added:

Commander Marten, it is thought, will continue to make as much of a nuisance as he can, both to you and to us, so long as he thinks there is any chance of getting either of us to change our minds. He is described as being a 'pukka gentleman' and once he realises the game is up and that he has no chance of getting Crichel Down back, then he is unlikely to do anything that would be prejudicial to Mr Tozer's position.

The matter dragged on with an uninhibited exchange of confidences between civil servants determined to dispose of the Commander's campaign once and for all by obfuscation, secrecy and deceit.

In September 1953 Mary Anna Marten, the landowner, wrote to *The Times*:

There have been a number of references in the Press recently to what may be called the veiled nationalisation of agricultural land. An outstanding example of this procedure is taking place in this locality, which will, I believe, become a matter for much wider interest . . . As the area [acquired by compulsory purchase] was no longer required for defence purposes I, as one of the previous owners, applied to the Ministry of Agriculture in 1950 to buy back the 330 acres which formed an important portion of one of my tenant's farms. After a delay of nearly 18 months my application was refused, though neither then nor at a subsequent meeting with the Parliamentary Secretary were we told what was to be done with the area. At this meeting I offered to buy or rent the entire 700 acres and laid out my plans for doing so. I was told they would be given sympathetic consideration . . .

Once again I applied and after a serious delay was informed by the Commissioner that as a condition of the transfer he was committed to the Ministry to erect a farmhouse, cottages, and buildings which were of course superfluous to my needs as I already had them. He also said that though he had not bought the land he was committed to another prospective tenant.

To my own distress was then added a large number of local farmers who had applied or hoped to rent the land. One of them has a written assurance from the Land Commissioners personally that before the land was let it would be advertised in the public press and that his application would be carefully considered. No such advertisement ever appeared. A committee of protest has been formed and a public meeting is to be held this week to ask for an inquiry into the matter, as it appears that the rights of farmers and landowners and extravagance with public money may be involved.[6]

Marten was chairman of the protest committee and sent a telegram to Sir Thomas Dugdale requesting an inquiry. As he expected, the telegram brought a reply to the effect that the Minister could not withdraw from the existing arrangement without a breach of faith and, in those circumstances, he did not think an inquiry would serve any useful purpose. Posters began to appear on the walls of the villages around Crichel announcing a meeting in the village hall. At the end of September Marten addressed an audience of about fifty, made up of owners of estates, farmers and a few agricultural workers. 'No one could regret more than I do the necessity for this meeting,' he began. 'If any of you had told me a year ago that what has happened was going to happen, I should have said, "Nonsense, in England that is quite impossible," but it has happened.'[7] He caused amusement by his portrayal of Dugdale's position:

There he is as Minister, owning 700 acres of land, for which he has a number of applications to buy or rent. He ignores these applications and, as Minister, he turns to himself as Commissioner of Crown Lands, and says to himself: 'Provided you put up a lot of buildings and find your own tenant I, as Minister, will sell this land to you.' Then, as Commissioner, he turns to himself as Minister and says: 'All right, I'll buy it.' Thus is formed a commitment between himself as Minister and himself as Commissioner, and vice-versa. Six weeks later, when things are nicely settled, he turns to me as Minister and says: 'You can't have the land.'[8]

Almost immediately afterwards Marten fell ill and within forty-eight hours of his speech he was in hospital. The persistence of pressmen and the patient eventually overcame regulations, and a party of journalists, all protected with hospital masks, was admitted to his bedside. He not only answered their questions but sat up to make a recording for a BBC news feature. The Minister wrote offering sympathy on the Commander's illness. He also admitted that 'this case raises a general issue of principle about the disposal of land for a specific purpose', although, as far as he was concerned, events had proceeded too far in the case of Crichel Down. Dugdale was now under pressure from the National Farmers Union, the Country Landowners' Association and the Food and Agriculture Committee of Conservative backbench MPs. Two days after Parliament returned from its long summer recess he had a meeting with Commander Marten in his office. The following day he announced that he had changed his mind and a public inquiry would be held. *The Times* had an editorial comment under the headline 'A sorry tale'.

The man Dugdale selected to lead the inquiry was Sir Andrew Clark QC, a fifty-five-year-old lawyer and former Conservative candidate with a reputation for handling complicated cases. He conducted the Crichel Down inquiry without fee. He was an old Etonian who had served in both world wars and been an honorary brigadier in the Royal Army of Officers. After the First World War he went on the Stock Exchange for a time but abandoned it for a routine which enabled him to spend six months of each year in Monte Carlo. Then he married, was called to the Bar and settled down to his career. After the Second World War he stood unsuccessfully as a

Conservative candidate in the 1945 general election. Six feet tall and with a bushy moustache, legal colleagues regarded Clark as a 'card'. He was known for his magnificent collection of fancy silk waistcoats, including one – it was reported – in silver-blue satin, embroidered with pink rosebuds which he had designed himself. He also wrote and published poetry. He was invited one evening to dine at the home of Sir Thomas Salt, the High Sheriff of Dorset. After the ladies had retired to the drawing room and the port was being passed around the table, Sir Andrew eyed a collection of three eighteenth-century flintlock pistols. He told his fellow guests that he was an expert. The ladies were recalled and the servants told to stay in the kitchen while Clark gave a demonstration of blowing out a candle at fifteen paces with one of Salt's pistols. He followed this by shooting a half-inch hole into the mahogany dining-room door with a bullet fashioned from candle wax. The marksman and the witnesses engraved their signatures into the mahogany.

The hearings took place in the old Corn Exchange in the market square of Blandford Forum. Sir Andrew Clark sat alone on the platform, while county dignitaries, including the High Sheriff and the Chief Constable, sat on a row of wooden chairs up against the platform facing the body of the hall. Immediately in front of them sat the clerk, and facing him were counsel, in dark suits but without wigs, bands and gowns. To their right was a table for shorthand writers, with a chair at one end for witnesses, who remained seated, rather than standing, when they gave their evidence. On the opposite side there was a table for the press. The remainder of the hall was set out with chairs for the public. Altogether twenty-eight witnesses voluntarily came forward to give evidence. Voluminous correspondence and documents were produced, quoted from and examined by Sir Andrew and counsel's tables. The inquiry lasted seven days.

The witnesses were not under oath, but for many of them it was an ordeal:

A few minutes later Mr Wilcox [from the Ministry] was called to speak for himself and there began what was to prove the most painful episode of the whole week. He was a nervous witness, hesitant in his replies. A middle-aged man, lean-featured and wearing horn-rimmed spectacles, he had the air of a professor. His performance was such that the Ministry's counsel, when he came to sum up, made special reference to it. 'Professionally, you might say that whatever case he was giving evidence about, he would be a hopeless witness,' he admitted. 'He was harassed in cross-examination.' . . .

[Wilcox] declared his view that Crown Lands had no moral obligation to honour the promises made by the Ministry to would-be tenants of Crichel Down. Immediately he found himself under vigorous cross-examination by Mr Stevenson [counsel for Marten]. A new word cropped up, a heavy word with the implication of hypocrisy and bad faith, the word *dissemble*.

Mr Wilcox admitted that, in order to avoid ill-feeling among the applicants, they might have had to consider some dissembling. But, in fact, he added quickly, no dissembling was possible or feasible under the circumstances.

'As a matter of interest,' said Stevenson, 'I should like to know, is this technique of dissembling in your view in accordance with the highest traditions of the Civil Service?'

'No, it is not,' Wilcox replied. 'Dissembling covers a wide range of things . . .' The rest of the answer was lost in the laughter rising from around him.

Sir Andrew Clark broke in: 'Like charity it covers a multitude of sins.'

'I really had not addressed my mind, I must confess, to the question of what might have been involved here,' said Mr Wilcox quietly.

Mr Stevenson resumed his rapid fire of questions. 'Something had to be done in order to make a dozen or so applicants think that a promise made to them had been performed, although you knew that it had not,' he suggested. 'Was that the position?'

'The position was,' replied Mr Wilcox, 'that we had to consider in what way the people should be told in due course that the property had been let and they would not have the opportunity of tendering. We should have to consider what could best be done in such a way as to avoid, as far as possible, ill-feeling. As I say, if I had thought, I could have seen that, in fact, the only course was to tell them.'

There was irony in Mr Stevenson's voice as he abandoned this line of questioning with the remark: 'So the reason why this little campaign of dissembling was to be embarked on . . . was just spreading light and amiability in Dorsetshire.' . . .

Still the witness had to face more stern questions. Sir Andrew put it to him that he should have acted differently when he first heard of the early applicants who had been given a promise that they would be able to tender for Crichel Down. 'Surely the moment you knew of the promises made, it was your duty to say to Crown Lands: "In view of this coming to light, you will have to implement these promises and put it up for tender"?' Sir Andrew suggested. 'That must have been the proper course, must it not?'

Mr Wilcox agreed that there should have been more consideration given to the matter, but he added: 'As against that, one has to set the fact that Crown Lands had this moral obligation to Mr Tozer. It is balancing one against the other.'

'That,' said Sir Andrew Clark, 'was nothing to do with you.' And he added a moment later: 'The question for the Ministry was: "Who is going to be thrown overboard – the twelve people we promised a year ago and who have been applying ever since, or Mr Tozer, who came on the scene a week ago?"'

Throughout the afternoon the questions flowed. Not until tea-time did the ordeal of Mr Wilcox end.[9]

Eastwood's questioning, though briefer, was even more damning. Clark observed that if Mr Eastwood's moral standards were so high that he could not back out of a tentative offer made to Mr Tozer, which was tentatively accepted, it seemed to him incredible he could for one second think of inventing a story to deceive fourteen other people. Eastwood said, quietly, that he agreed. 'Really you were the serpent in the garden,' Sir Andrew continued. 'It was you who put forward this tantalising suggestion to Wilcox that something should be done to make it appear that promises were going to be implemented, and poor Mr Wilcox, being a very willing Eve, just acceded to the suggestion.'

'I quite agree I was the first author of this obnoxious sentence,' Mr Eastwood said.

Eastwood was followed in the witness chair by his 'lieutenant', Mr Harold Thomson, a partner in Sanctuary & Son of Bridport, Crown Receiver and professional land agent managing about 20,000 acres of agricultural land in Dorset and Somerset. Questioned as to the method by which Mr Tozer had been selected as tenant for Crichel Down, Thomson suggested it would not have been practicable to offer a farm for tender when farmers were unable to see what they were tendering for. This brought an explosive interruption from Sir Andrew Clark: 'The most complete nonsense I've ever heard.' Thomson was questioned on a Monday. Clark told him to have a night's reflection before the proceedings of the following day. On the Tuesday morning Thomson was given permission to speak. He explained that he made his remarks – 'I should say Commander Marten was the last person we would want as a tenant' and 'You certainly could not have him, after the way he has behaved' – because of Commander Marten's threats to call for a public inquiry if he did not get his way. 'I think now my language was intemperate and I should like to take this opportunity of apologising publicly for it,' he added. Sir Andrew Clark commented: 'That is a very proper attitude to take' and Commander Marten rose from his seat and bowed to the witness.

Sir Andrew Clark spent a fortnight drafting his 16,000-word report. When it came, it could not have been more damning: the Ministry had been unyielding in its view that it alone was right and that it should not be examined on the matter. It was also financially unsound. One of Clark's conclusions was that the Lands Service and the Land Commission had become 'so infatuated with the idea of creating a new model farm that they were determined not to abandon the scheme for financial reasons'. Lord Carrington had been in a position to bring to the Agricultural Ministry his experience as a reasonable farmer together with all the advantages of his committee work on the Agricultural Advisory Board. But he had failed and his failure lay in his inability to challenge his officials. Clark also published the names of the officials he criticised. Donald Brown was completely exonerated. He was comparatively inexperienced, but it had been impossible for him to do anything other than make a misleading report. According to Clark, this 'arose solely from the 'passionate love of secrecy inherent in so many minor officials'.[10] On the other hand he regarded the actions of Wilcox, Eastwood and Thomson as demonstrating 'a most regrettable attitude of hostility', an attitude 'engendered solely by a feeling of irritation that any member of the public should have the temerity to oppose or even question the acts or decisions of officials of a government or state department'.[11] The decision of the Agricultural Ministers, led by Dugdale, endorsed the concept that land that had been forcibly purchased from its original owners for one use (in this case a bombing range) could be kept by the state for an entirely different use.

On Tuesday, 20 July 1954, Sir Thomas Dugdale, who had been a near contemporary of Napier Alington at Eton, resigned as Minister of Agriculture and Fisheries, on the floor of the House of Commons. It was his fifty-sixth birthday. Richard Nugent and Lord Carrington, his junior ministers, also offered their resignations to the Prime Minister, but Churchill refused – to lose the whole of the ministerial team would have been unacceptable. Despite his ministerial disgrace, in 1958 Dugdale was made a hereditary peer – as Baron Crathorne – and went on to have a second political career in Europe. Toby Marten, on the other hand, was never forgiven and did not receive the Conservative seat he had been hoping for. The Martens did, however, get their land back. Mary Anna Marten celebrated her victory with a shopping spree.

Rarely can a few hundred acres of remote and mediocre land have received such an enormous amount of publicity. But despite its apparent triviality, in modern parliamentary history the Crichel Down Affair is regarded as being of momentous significance, insofar as it revealed a whole catalogue of maladministration and incompetence. During the wars the powers of state had expanded enormously but Crichel Down showed that government could nevertheless only exercise those rights which had been granted by legislation, there could never be an assumption that it could do as it liked.

The Crichel found themselves living in the midst of this scandal unfolding on their doorstep. There was, however, another more squalid affair which was in many ways even closer to home.

9

The Montagu Trial

J ust as the Crichel Down affair filled the newspapers with discussions on the nature of authority in post-war Britain, the papers were also filled with the salacious details of the Montagu case, which represented a challenge to authority in a very different way altogether.

In the autumn of 1953 Desmond was in the United States. After his arrival in New York he took a train to Washington from where he wrote home to Long Crichel:

> imagine my amazement to see Edward Montagu on the train; and my relief at having been fairly discreet when questioned (as I inevitably was in New York) about the affaire Beaulieu. He looked a bit harassed and plunged into a very different version of the story we have all heard; but it is a good thing (from his point of view) that he has got to America, where he has a sister married to a Texan. He proposes to lie low for a bit here, and perhaps try to get a job which might keep him here for a few years, by when the trouble might be presumed to be blown over. Don't talk too widely of his being here, as he doesn't want it immensely known.[1]

Unfortunately, however, the Beaulieu affair did not blow over. Worse was to follow, and the Montagu trial became the most notorious of its kind since the trial of Oscar Wilde in the 1890s.

Edward Douglas-Scott-Montagu, the 3rd Lord Montagu of Beaulieu, inherited his title at the age of two in 1928 and was to hold it for eighty-six years. When he was twenty-one he joined the Grenadier Guards. In 1946 he was posted to Palestine, a place which affected him deeply, so much so that his maiden speech to the House of Lords about the worsening situation between the Arabs and Jews proved to be far-sighted. After his army service Montagu went to New College, Oxford but in his second year there was a fracas between the members of the Bullingdon Club and the members of the Dramatic Society. Montagu was a member of both and his rooms were wrecked. The Dean suggested he should 'consider his position' and so he left. His time at Oxford, however, helped him come to terms with the fact that he was sexually attracted to both men and women. He took a job in advertising, where he discovered that he had a taste for publicity, and this led to a job promoting British car exports. He also fell in love with the United States. At the annual conference of the Public Relations Institute in Washington he was hailed as 'the most promising PR man in England'. On his twenty-fifth birthday Montagu took over the running of the 10,000-acre Beaulieu estate on the edge of the New Forest, and in 1952 he opened the first-ever motor museum, which unexpectedly soon turned out to be immensely successful.

Although in the 1930s homosexual activity was illegal and the penalties were fierce, in the Bohemian society in which Eddy, Raymond, Desmond and Eardley moved – the anachronistically but appropriately named Gay Young Things – homosexual behaviour was not only acceptable but fashionable. Since Wilde, and even on account of him, it was a sign of rebellion against Victorian and Edwardian conventions. It was easy to pick up soldiers, especially in Hyde Park on Sunday afternoons when they were out in their scarlet tunics – although they themselves were probably looking for nursemaids. They charged from two shillings upwards. If there were a couple of soldier friends together and they didn't want to be separated, they might go back to the client's room and one of them could fall asleep in a chair until his friend was finished.

Harold Nicolson was mystified by the partiality of the younger generation for what he called the lower orders. He told Raymond that the idea of a gentleman of birth and education sleeping with a guardsman was repugnant to him. Many of the clients were, however, well-to-do people. If a soldier or sailor was stationed abroad, he could make more money by the sale of his address book to a friend. Among society at large, many people would claim never to have met 'a homosexual' and would have little idea as to what homosexuals actually did that was 'wrong'. Men might have sex with one another without it occurring to them that it was anything other than normal. For the soldiers – and others – it was a bit of cash on the side, and for many homosexual men it might be the only opportunity for sex they ever had.

Post-war Britain was less accepting. Patriotism was about building a new future which celebrated family and the pleasures of domestic life. In 1951 the scandal of the much-publicised flight to Moscow of Guy Burgess, who was homosexual, and Donald Maclean, who was bisexual but married, shook the Establishment and the nation at large. Attitudes changed quite rapidly: society discovered 'the homosexual', a subject not normally thought a matter for discussion. Homosexuals if not actually traitors, were, at the very least, corrupters of public morals. Egged on by the popular press, the new Conservative Home Secretary Sir David Maxwell Fyfe decided that he must reassert 'normality' and made the prosecution of 'inverts' a matter of the highest priority. 'Positive vetting' was introduced in the Civil Service in order to uproot 'serious character weaknesses'. In December 1953 he addressed the House of Commons: 'Homosexuals, in general, are exhibitionists and proselytizers and a danger to others, especially the young. So long as I hold the office of Home Secretary I shall give no countenance to the view that they should not be prevented from being such a danger.'[2] The Commissioner of the Metropolitan Police,

Sir John Nott-Bower, was convinced that the British way of life was threatened by a homosexual conspiracy and swore when he took over at Scotland Yard to rip the cover off London's 'filth spots'. Police activity was intensified to a remarkable degree. Comparative figures for England and Wales between 1938 and 1952 increased significantly: cases of sodomy and bestiality rose from 134 to 670; attempts to commit 'unnatural offences', including indecent assaults, from 822 to 3,087; and offences of gross indecency between males from 320 to 1,686. When Alfred Kinsey visited Wormwood Scrubs he found that 30 per cent of the prisoners had been detained for homosexual offences.[3] These figures were considerably greater than in the USA.

In 1953 there were three high-profile prosecutions. Bill Field, the Labour MP for Paddington North, resigned his seat after having been found guilty of importuning for immoral purposes in West End lavatories. In the same year, just months after John Gielgud had been knighted in the Coronation honours, he was arrested like Field for cruising in a public lavatory in Chelsea and fined £10. Rupert Croft-Cooke, a prolific author of both fiction and non-fiction, had picked up a couple of sailors in the Fitzroy Tavern off the Tottenham Court Road. He and his partner invited them down to his house in Sussex. On their return to London, one of the sailors assaulted a policeman. In order to gain immunity from prosecution for assault charges the sailor agreed to testify against Croft-Cooke, who was subsequently found guilty of gross indecency. He was sentenced to nine months in gaol, which he spent in Wormwood Scrubs and Brixton Prison.

In Edward Montagu the Hampshire Constabulary saw the prospect of an even more enticing scalp in this moral crusade. First of all they tried to have him convicted of underage sex with a couple of Boy Scouts who had done some work for him on the Beaulieu estate. Montagu had gone to the police himself to report the disappearance of an expensive camera from his beach hut on the Solent. Instead he found himself being charged – a charge he always denied. When he claimed that on the given dates he had not been in

England the police pointed to his passport to prove him a liar, but the judge found that the passport had obviously been tampered with. Nevertheless, even before charges were proffered, rumours were rife. It was said that Chelsea was covered by a cloud of smoke created by the burning of compromising photographs and letters. While Montagu waited for the Director of Public Prosecutions to decide whether or not to bring a case he went abroad to France and the USA, which was when Desmond met him.

Rather than stay abroad, which would have seemed the safer course, Montagu returned home in order to attend his sister's wedding. He was rearrested, and together with Peter Wildeblood and Michael Pitt-Rivers, he was committed for trial at Winchester Assizes. This time all three were charged with inciting acts of gross indecency with two RAF servicemen during a weekend party at a beach hut on Montagu's estate at Beaulieu in Hampshire. Wildeblood was the *Daily Mail*'s diplomatic correspondent; Pitt-Rivers was Edward Montagu's cousin and the owner of a large estate around Sturminster Newton in North Dorset. The key prosecution witnesses were two airmen, John Reynolds and Edward McNally, who, because they turned Queen's evidence, were granted immunity. Despite having been involved in twenty-four other homosexual affairs they were also granted immunity by the Air Council. There was no suggestion that either Reynolds or McNally was ever seduced or were anything other than willing participants. The other twenty-four men were in London and Cambridge, none of whom was ever subsequently charged. It would have seemed unusual that the only charges ever made should have been in Hampshire, had it not been for the fact that what had attracted the police was the single word 'Beaulieu', which they had found in one of Wildeblood's letters. The intention may have been to underline the fact that social privilege offered no protection: 'toffs' were fair game just like anybody else, and Montagu in particular was to be targeted for prosecution in a way that was hardly disguised.

Ralph Partridge attended the trial, which began at the Assizes in March 1954. In her diary Frances recorded his impressions:

> It was not a very moving tale they had to tell. The two little tarts from the R.A.F. made a pitiful showing in the witness-box, saving their skins at the expense of their three victims, Montagu, Pitt-Rivers and Wildeblood, who sat with folded arms in the pillory. Wildeblood is the most to be pitied. Ralph thinks he will get a stiffer sentence than the other two; he has admitted to being 'in love' with one of the cadets. It may ruin his promising journalist's career, hard cheese indeed when no one can conceivably be said to have suffered in the very least.[4]

Frances and her son Burgo went two days later:

> The proceedings seemed to have a natural sluggishness of their own, and I was afraid that it might become intolerably boring waiting while the barristers swayed on the balls of their feet pondering the next question. But I am fascinated by the formality of the scene – though it tends to act like a bandage hiding the human element. Then this suddenly gushes out like blood, and with a start one realises what a crucifixion it must be for the three educated, personable young men in the dock to have their most intimate feelings dragged around the court by hostile, mocking, aggressive Counsel before a mass of indifferent faces. Poor Wildeblood is sensitive, nervous, emotional and intelligent. He clasped the edge of the dock with long thin fingers and listened intently to every question before quietly and thoughtfully replying. A clever grammar-school boy who got a scholarship to Oxford, he was obviously the pride of his parents and had a very good newspaper job. I was appalled at the cruelty of these proceedings, which seem morally wrong as well as painful, in a way that seeing stones thrown at a negro because he is black would be painful. But since it happened I am glad I went.[5]

The prosecuting counsel was G.D. 'Khaki' Roberts, who had a bottle of pink cough mixture always at hand. Not only were the proceedings about sex, they were also, in a way somehow typical of a British sex scandal, about class as well. Peter Wildeblood was asked:

It is a feature, is it not, that inverts or perverts should seek their love associates in a different walk of life than their own?

I cannot accept that as a deduction. I have never heard any suggestion that this is the ordinary rule.

I mean, for instance, McNally was infinitely – he is none the worse for it but infinitely your social inferior?

That is absolute nonsense.

Well, perhaps that is not a very polite way of answering my question.

I am sorry, I apologise.

Please do not apologise. I know very well that you are under a great strain.

Nobody ever flung it at me during the War that I was associating with people who were infinitely my social inferiors.[6]

Wildeblood had served in the RAF. The war years had given him a welcome taste of social inclusion. His fellow servicemen, seeing that he was useless at drill, covered his deficiencies. He believed he had the right to choose his own in life. Wildeblood was also fortunate to have Arthur Prothero as his solicitor. Prothero lent him a pair of long johns so that he would not shiver in the cold courtroom and seem frightened. Prothero's father was a chief inspector, and he may have chosen the case in defiance of his own father's values. Chief Inspector Prothero had been the only witness called in the prosecution of Radclyffe Hall's lesbian novel *The Well of Loneliness* in 1928. He testified that the very themes of the novel were offensive, and the magistrate ordered all copies to be destroyed. Arthur Prothero could scarcely have demonstrated a generational shift of attitude about same-sex relations more clearly and more publicly than to have his name associated with a case which made front-page news.

The jury considered the case for eight days before returning unanimous verdicts of guilty on various charges. After the jury had returned the counsels for defence made submissions. Mr Peter Rawlinson, for Wildeblood, called Dr Hobson, a consultant physician in psychological medicine at Middlesex Hospital. 'Wildeblood was not a typical type of homosexual,' he said. There was a better chance than most cases of homosexuality of curing him by treatment. That was because of his high intelligence and his willingness to be treated. If Wildeblood were imprisoned it would make it more difficult for the doctor there to treat him, whereas there was a good chance that the witness, Dr Hobson, could cure him. He said that he had Wildeblood admitted to hospital before his trial because there was a possible suicide risk and so his case could be better investigated. Counsel for Edward Montagu stated that he was a useful member of the House of Lords and a kindly landowner; he was now faced with 'a bitter future'. Counsel for Pitt-Rivers submitted that 'because of his high character his was a case for the exercise of a large measure of mercy. Whatever the punishment, this case must mean the complete and final ruin of his career.'

The judge, Mr Justice Ormerod, sentenced Montagu – who had, in law, only committed a misdemeanour – to twelve months. Pitt-Rivers and Wildeblood were convicted for conspiracy to incite acts of gross indecency (the first use of the charge since the trials of Oscar Wilde), and having committed felonies they were sentenced to eighteen months each. After the conviction there was a three-hour wait in the cells before they were driven in the Sheriff's Rolls-Royce to Winchester gaol. In a distant echo of Oscar Wilde's ordeal on the platform of Clapham Junction railway station Wildeblood had been spat at by a stranger a few days previously ('a middle-aged, tweedy person wearing a sensible felt hat').[7] This time the public sentiment ran the other way. It was McNally and Reynolds, the two RAF men, who as they left the court encountered a chorus of booing and hissing from about 200 people waiting outside, and their car was attacked, in a rather British way, with rolled umbrellas and newspapers. When finally Montagu, Pitt-Rivers and Wildeblood emerged the mostly female crowd was smaller, but to their surprise instead of being met with hostility there was clapping, back-slapping and cries of 'good luck' and 'keep smiling'. As they were driven away in the dark to prison the crowd went on waving and one or two gave thumbs-up signs. Once in gaol each was given a single cell, as was customary with sex offenders.

In his autobiography Lord Montagu recorded the practices with which he was to become familiar:

> The first morning gave us our first experiences of 'slopping out', which literally meant queuing up at a drain point, each holding a chamber pot containing liquid and solid excretions from the night before. This disgusting and humiliating procedure continued for many decades . . . We were then subjected to the usual new body regimes, visiting the doctor for body examination, having our hair cut and visiting the padre. By mid-morning we were sent to sew mailbags, which I confess I did very badly and this provoked many jokes about ability to sew 'male-bags'. During the lunch break a friendly prison officer, colloquially a 'screw', showed me some of the newspapers, which reported my imprisonment with glee.[8]

Sometimes it became more bearable. It was Easter soon after Montagu's arrival, and he arranged for a mass of daffodils to be brought from Beaulieu to decorate the chapel. A warder brought him a cake made by his mother. After a few weeks, Montagu, Pitt-Rivers and Wildeblood all left Winchester and were deliberately separated because, according to a warder, they were 'a dangerous conspiratorial gang of homosexuals'. The night before he left gaol, the governor sent for Montagu and gave him a long lecture on how he had disgraced his class and would be despised and rejected for ever – and he likened his disgrace to the way that the working-class men of London had rejected Edward VIII and spat on pub floors when they'd heard the abdication speech.

This was not the case. The trial became a cause célèbre. Many years later Lord Montagu claimed that the changes in sexual law and mores which the Montagu affair helped bring about were the greatest achievement of his life.

In the summer of 1953 Home Office senior officials decided that the 'growing shamelessness of prostitutes' in London should be subject to control.[9] The number who came before the courts in the capital increased from 2,966 in 1938 to 9,756 in 1952. Although prostitution itself was not illegal, prostitutes could be prosecuted if the act of soliciting annoyed other citizens. The Home Office were now seeking a new law which could increase penalties for women who were soliciting and include terms of imprisonment for repeat offenders. While accepting that public female prostitution was a necessary evil, they wanted a law to regulate public decency. To this end they proposed a Royal Commission both to investigate and propose solutions.

Homosexuality was another problem. The *Sunday Pictorial* published a three-part series on 'evil men' which argued that 'this unnatural sex vice' produced 'the horrors of Hitlerite corruption' in Germany, had ruined classical Greece and would in turn destroy Britain. Soon after the Montagu trial the Admiralty issued new Fleet Orders highlighting 'the horrible character of unnatural vice' and insisting that officers should 'stamp out the evil'. They recommended inspecting jars of Vaseline or hair gel for tell-tale pubic hairs. Officers were encouraged to secure 'the help of the steadier and more reliable men on the lower deck' in order to counter the regrettable tendency 'to treat these matters with levity'.

At the end of 1954 the twenty-seven-year-old Ian Gilmour became the new proprietor and editor of the *Spectator*. Gilmour styled himself as both a libertarian and a 'progressive Conservative' and was willing to take up unpopular causes like the abolition of capital punishment and decriminalising homosexuality from the very start. In January 1955 the magazine ran a frank autobiographical article giving 'a biological homosexual's view' in which the writer set out how homosexuals were 'debarred from a permanent and publicly esteemed cohabitation with a loving partner'. Gilmour also attacked the Montagu verdict and sentencing, and published a 2,500-word broadside in his own name asserting that the trial was prejudiced by police malpractice. Gilmour's attitudes provoked widespread hostility. John Gordon, the editor-in-chief of the *Sunday Express*, dubbed the *Spectator* 'the Bugger's Bugle' for vigorously trumpeting reform.

The *Spectator* also campaigned for a Royal Commission on the subject. The Home Office eventually gave way and decided that the new commission on prostitution should also study the laws relating to homosexuality – as well as schemes for cures and treatments. Sir David Maxwell Fyfe did not believe that the law needed altering, but he suggested to Cabinet that 'a dispassionate survey by a competent and unprejudiced body might be of value in educating the public, which at present is ill-informed and apt to be misled by sensational articles in the press'.[10] Needless to say, the British public enjoyed nothing more than sensational articles in the press – misleading or not – about such matters as the Montagu–Wildeblood–Pitt-Rivers trial and other high-profile 'outings'. It was feared that the government might lose votes if it associated with the subject, so it was suggested instead that a backbencher might promote a private member's bill to test opinion in Parliament and in the country to see if there might be support for an act to restrict the reporting of such trials. Ideally the Cabinet, including the Prime Minister Winston Churchill, would have preferred newspapers to ignore the subject altogether, but this was unlikely to happen. Maxwell Fyfe insisted that a departmental committee, if not a Royal Commission, would go ahead, and the decision was announced in Parliament.

The man the Home Secretary chose to head the committee was Jack Wolfenden, the forty-seven-year-old Vice-Chancellor of Reading University. The conversation in which Maxwell Fyfe asked Wolfenden to accept the post took place at midnight on a sleeper train from Liverpool while they sat side by side on the sleeping berth of the Home Secretary's carriage. Maxwell Fyfe was half-undressed, with an overcoat covering his underwear.[11] Wolfenden was reluctant to agree to the proposal and protested that he knew very little about the subject. And as a father of four children, he feared what they might have to put up with from their contemporaries if their father got involved 'in this sort of thing'.[12] Wolfenden was a man with a morbid fear of showing his emotions, but he was also highly ambitious. Although anxious lest the role should harm the progress of his career, he was finally persuaded by Lord Templewood, the Chancellor of Reading University, who had served as Home Secretary in the late 1930s and was now passionately interested in prison reform.

The Committee for the Examination of Homosexual Offences and Prostitution finally met for the first time in Room 101 at the Home Office. ('"Vice, sir? Room 101," said the doorkeeper at the Home Office entrance,' Wolfenden recalled.[13]) It was decided to refer to the committee as 'Huntley and Palmers' or 'CHOP' in order not to embarrass any ladies present – especially the secretaries who transcribed in strictest confidence. The fifteen members of the committee of eleven men and four women included the former Procurator Fiscal of Glasgow, the Vice-President of the City of Glasgow Girl Guides, the Psychiatric Consultant to the Royal Navy and the Regius Professor of Moral and Pastoral Theology at Oxford. Over the course of nearly three years the Wolfenden Committee met sixty times in both morning and afternoon sessions twice a month. Many thousands of words of committee proceedings were taken down.

Prostitution proved a much less distasteful subject for the

committee than homosexuality. A highly respectable society of lawyers arranged for a party of girls from the streets to come and give their point of view. Much to the lawyers' disappointment, however, the girls refused when they learnt they had to attend the Home Office. They declared that it would be bad for business, whereas Wolfenden had imagined it would help them acquire a certain cachet other girls lacked.

Wolfenden also thought that the vast majority of the population were probably unaware that there was such a thing as a homosexual offence. Doctors, psychologists, clergymen, policeman, politicians and all manner of moralists were offered the opportunity to give evidence. Wolfenden personally found the notion of homosexuality deeply repellent. This was not uncommon. When Peter Wildeblood – at his own request – gave evidence only eight members of the committee were in attendance. Since he was a criminal not everyone approved of his giving evidence at all, and it is probable that he was boycotted. It turned out that Wildeblood was also exceptionally priggish himself. He attacked effeminate 'queens' inside and outside prison:

> They just happen to have a male body. They think like women, and go to incredible lengths to get cosmetics and things smuggled in. I do not know why it is they are allowed to get away with these things . . . people of that sort are very often born like that . . . What they are responsible for is their nuisance value. I think they are only a very small proportion altogether, but they do attract a tremendous amount of attention – I do not mean just in prison but outside as well – and I think they cause a lot of public feeling against homosexuals.[14]

In his diaries Jim Lees-Milne, who had enjoyed many gay encounters with a considerable number of men, recorded an encounter with an effeminate male prostitute with similar disgust:

This afternoon in the bus going back to Thurloe Square, having completed my shopping and final jobs, I found myself sitting next to a male tart, rather handsome he was in a Modigliani-like way with a long, oval, pale face and almond eyes. He gave me one of those sidelong looks I know so well, expressionless and full of deep meaning; a second look was of the most languishing and seductive nature, yet one which if seen by a third person would not be noticed. That is so clever of this tribe; brought about by aeons of persecution, like the Israelites. They knew how to elude detection. They have to, and the consequence of their subterfuge is a terrible dishonesty. We were not alone on the bus, yet I noticed how he touched my arm without appearing to, or without actually doing so. I asked him where he lived and he said South Kensington. Then in mincing tones which made me feel a trifle sick, with a preliminary clicking of the tongue he asked, 'Have you done a little shopping?' I was strung with paper bags. After another languishing look as though satisfied that we had thereby clinched an engagement, nothing further was said. When at my stop I suddenly got off the bus without giving him a glance or fond goodbye I hoped he was not surprised or affronted.[15]

When it was known that Wildeblood had volunteered to give evidence – and it was realised that such evidence might be more damaging than beneficial – other homosexual men, who were rather more respectable than Wildeblood, were sought to speak for the cause. Wolfenden considered advertising in newspapers and magazines, but they were helped by one of the committee members, Goronwy Rees, a writer and the Principal of the University College of Wales, Aberystwyth. Rees had been a close friend of Guy Burgess, the Cambridge spy, and he was probably a former spy himself. He had also been a former lover of Rosamond Lehmann. The 'respectable' homosexuals Rees suggested were the art historian Carl Winter and

Patrick Trevor-Roper. (The novelist Angus Wilson had also intended to appear before the committee but was unable to.) Both Winter and Trevor-Roper were undoubtedly men of the same social standing as the committee members and were, without question, part of the Establishment. Given their public profiles, their evidence could not be ignored – Goronwy Rees commended their courage when he introduced them to the committee. Their identities, however, were disguised: Carl Winter was 'Mr White' and Patrick Trevor-Roper became the 'Doctor'.

The Australian-born Winter had come to England as a young man. He had worked as a keeper at the Victoria and Albert Museum, where he had become an authority on miniature paintings, until shortly after the end of the war when he was appointed Curator of the Fitzwilliam Museum in Cambridge and a fellow of Trinity College. Winter had been married and had three children, and when he gave his testimony to the Wolfenden Committee he had only been divorced for a couple of years:

> My point of view is that homosexual persons are a considerable portion of the population and so many I do not know what a normal person is. I do not now wish to meet a strictly normal person . . . I live and have lived for a number of years in a society of which many members are aware that I am a homosexual. I have many friends who are known to be so . . . I am content to know the sort of people I do know, which covers a very wide field, and we are all completely at ease in one another's company and the world in which we live, which is a much more extensive world than many people would suppose.[16]

When Winter died in 1966 his *Times* obituary said nothing about the evidence he gave to Wolfenden, only that 'To personal relationships he brought the freshness of a singularly unreserved nature, enlivened by a sharp mind which took very little for granted.'[17]

Patrick Trevor-Roper was born in 1916 in Alnwick in Northumberland. His father was a general practitioner, and the Duke of Northumberland was among his patients. Hugh Trevor-Roper, his elder brother, later became Regius Professor of Modern History at Oxford. He always supported his younger brother in full, calling the legal persecution of people for their private morals 'monstrous' and 'a highly farcical witch hunt'.[18] At the time Trevor-Roper spoke to the committee, he was a consultant ophthalmic surgeon at Westminster Hospital and a fellow of the Royal College of Surgeons. He had set up a private practice of his own and also lectured in ophthalmology at the University of London. He was very frank about his own sexual development. He told the committee that, as a medical student in London in the 1930s, he had been 'unaware except for an occasional comment in the *News of the World* of the existence of homosexuality', but now knew about 150 other homosexuals. The committee was interested in how homosexuals met – were they 'recruited'? Trevor-Roper replied that there was no mystery:

> One is introduced to them . . . my private life tends to be virtually restricted to almost the purely homosexual world and has become increasingly so . . . one meets by ordinary introduction . . . Two of my current students both approached me. Why do they approach me? They were frightened and felt out of society. They felt one would be sympathetic. They knew I was unmarried and because I had dealings with them in the ordinary way they were in a position to lead up to it. I do not ask students but over the last ten years one or two others have done the same.[19]

Both Winter and Trevor-Roper argued forcefully for a change in the law. Trevor-Roper suggested sixteen as the age of consent. He said he had collected evidence relating to the extent of homosexual blackmail and suggested that the current intolerance led to a lot of men taking their own lives. He also pointed out that statistics were indications of the extent of police activity, not evidence of the number of men who were actively gay. Most gay men, he argued convincingly and wittily, led normal lives and posed no threat to heterosexual youths.

The Wolfenden Report was published in September 1957. It was an immediate bestseller, and Wolfenden was repeatedly congratulated on his bravery and courage in chairing such a distasteful inquiry. Its first recommendation to the Home Office was that 'homosexual activity between consenting adults over the age of twenty-one in private be no longer a criminal offence'.[20] What happened in the private sphere should be free of regulation so long as it did not harm the participants. While the law on street offences should be tightened because they created a nuisance, male homosexual acts in private should be decriminalised. The press reception was predictable. The *Daily Mail* attacked the proposals 'to legalise degradation in our midst',[21] and the *Evening Standard* found the recommendations on homosexuality 'bad, retrograde and utterly to be condemned'.[22] The *Daily Express* thought the report 'cumbersome nonsense. Anyone would think prostitution and perversion were widespread problems. In fact the majority of British homes never come in contact with either. It is up to the Home Secretary to see that family life remains protected from these evils. If the law needs stiffening he should get on with stiffening it.'[23] John Gordon, a *Sunday Express* columnist who always went out of his way to be as provocative as possible, called the report 'the Pansies' Charter'.[24] Scottish MP, Mrs Jean Mann, warned television viewers that, as a result of the report, 'we may even have husbands enticed away from their wives.[25] The *Telegraph*, however, regarded the 'Committee's findings, though controversial, clear, conscientious and courageous'.[26] The *New Statesman*, *Spectator* and *Economist* were also supportive. Journalists were made aware before they even wrote their copy that the government would act only on the proposals regarding prostitution, and in 1959 the Home Secretary Rab Butler's 'Street Offences Act' duly became law. Wolfenden's recommendations regarding homosexuality were kicked into the long grass.

* * *

There was also an ironic, personal side to Jack Wolfenden's report. Wolfenden's claim that he knew very little about homosexuality and homosexuals was a lie . . . Jeremy, his eldest son, had been actively gay since Eton and had told his father so when he was eighteen. At Oxford, in his adopted uniform of dark glasses, black shirt and old Etonian tie, he was already famous. He was also open about his sexuality, as he was afterwards in London – even flagrantly so. Jeremy was prodigiously intelligent: his Finals examiners gave him eight alphas but one of them commented, 'Frankly I didn't enjoy doing it. He wrote as though it were all beneath him; he wrote as though it were such a waste of his time.'[27] On his appointment to the Committee on Homosexuality and Prostitution, Wolfenden wrote his son a letter making two requests: '1] That we stay out of each other's way for the time being; 2] That you wear rather less make-up.'[28]

Jeremy Wolfenden became a journalist, serving as a foreign correspondent in Paris, Moscow and Washington. In Moscow he befriended Guy Burgess. The two men put on their old Etonian ties, gossiped and got drunk together. They may even have been lovers but Burgess was by then such a physical wreck that was probably impossible. When Burgess died in the autumn of 1963 Jeremy was a pallbearer at the funeral, and was left the pick of Burgess's library. Having always been a heavy drinker, in Moscow he – like Burgess – became an alcoholic who drank brandy and vodka at breakfast time. He also became caught up in the world of espionage: it was as if everyone – the SIS (the Special Intelligence Service or MI6), the KGB and the FBI – wanted to use him. He said that his life had been ruined by British intelligence. Finally, in Washington at Christmas in 1965 he locked himself in the bathroom and drank himself to death. The funeral was in Washington Cathedral. Jack Wolfenden and his wife attended. Wolfenden made his stay in the US seem like a social affair by fitting in the funeral between museum visits and New Year parties. He made a terrible impression on Jeremy's colleagues and friends but Jack Wolfenden's attitude was that his son had been given a chance, a great chance, and that there was now no more to be said.[29]

The Sexual Offences Act of 1967 finally put into law a modified version of the Wolfenden Report's proposals on homosexuality. In his brief autobiography *Turning Points*, written a decade later, Wolfenden ends his chapter on the report with the comment, 'It is entertaining to have lived long enough to have made oneself obsolete.'[30] That these years had also encompassed the tragic death of his homosexual son was never mentioned.

10

The Buggery House at Crichel

Situated in the middle of nowhere, Long Crichel seemed to exist in its own little tolerant world. In 1952, after a weekend spent at the house with Raymond Mortimer and Desmond Shawe-Taylor, his colleagues at the *Sunday Times*, Cyril Connolly told his partner Lys Lubbock that he 'longed to stay there forever and become a King of the Queers'.[1] Nancy Mitford wrote to Evelyn Waugh from Paris, telling him that she was coming to England for Christmas with her sister Deborah. She was having a few days in London then going on to see 'the "lads" (Raymond, Eddy & Co)'. Waugh replied that if she wanted to visit him in Somerset, it was a fifty-mile drive from 'the buggery house at Crichel', and a long drive in winter. Within the artistic and Bohemian circles in which the Crichel Boys moved, and in the world at large, the terms 'bugger', 'queer' and 'invert' were all in common usage and more or less acceptable as terms for homosexual. And both Waugh and Connolly had enjoyed homosexual experiences as young men.

Unlike Eddy, Desmond was also always comfortable with own sexuality. He was also close to, and fully accepted by, his own family.* A friend described Desmond, who had started to go bald when he

---

* His brother, Brian Shawe-Taylor, had a distinguished career as a racing-driver, competing in three World Championships and numerous Formula One races.

was young, as having the 'face of an impatient cherub'.[2] Highly intelligent and quick-minded, he was also highly sexed: he used to say that he would invariably get an erection merely from the movement of travelling on the top deck of a bus.

In 1943, while still a serving officer, Desmond placed an advertisement in *Exchange & Mart* offering a pair of trooper's breeches for sale. He received a number of replies from all over the country. Desmond's invariable response was that the breeches had already been sold, but the breeches were not the only point of interest. 'Breeches', as the subsequent correspondence revealed, was a code word for quite a lot more:

> Dear Sir,
>
> I am interested in your Trooper's Breeches offered for sale, and would like to know the *fork measurement* as well as the waist, and *also where the breeches could be seen*, before making an offer for them. Have they been worn by a trooper or just yourself? I am keen on trooper's breeches, & would like to acquire a good pair, if I can get a pair; am 5ft 8 & slim.
>
> Awaiting your reply, yours faithfully, HR Coates. 84 Kensington Gardens Square[3]

> Dear Captain Taylor,
>
> Many thanks for your letter, although I was sorry to learn that you had already parted with the trooper breeches, which to me sounded a first class pair, with good shape and fit, the first thing one goes for in troopers. I have worn them on my motor bike and playing around for a few years now, also when horse riding. I enjoy the close tight fit and grip around the lower thighs etc and the smart strappings. Like you I wear spurs whenever possible. It is always good to see the boys pulling themselves into tight troopers and then admire the 'smashing finish'. Your snaps also sound exciting, I agree I should like to see them sometime, I am often in

Watford and around as I lived there for 15 years when a boy at School etc. so could easily come down one evening and see you, or are you in town at all?

Naturally have always been real keen on smart kit and enjoy wearing it. Shall hope to hear from you again soon.

Sincerely, F Selwyn-Keith, Flat 1, 21 Ladbrook Gardens, Notting Hill[4]

Dear Mr Shawe-Taylor

Thank you for writing. I feel we have very much in common and must arrange a meeting. I am all packed up to move . . . I will send you a snap when I get unpacked but can I meet you next Saturday Evening (I get most evenings off and Sat. & Sun.) You could come to my room at New Cross Gate & we could show each other what we've got, etc. I am 30 slim & fair. I like riding, smart kit, shorts & kilts. I have breeches and boots but not smart cut like yours. If I see you on Sat. I shall not wear kit, but fawn corduroy trousers, brown shoes, fawn American lumber jacket & have rain coat. I can meet you outside anywhere you suggest. Write soon. Have you got a whip?

Sincerely yours, John E Jarvis, Normanton, 314 Queens Road, New Cross Gate.[5]

The men usually asked for pictures of Desmond in his trooper's breeches and offered photographs of themselves in return. Coates and Jarvis both mentioned that they lived in lodgings – and were on the point of moving to other rooms elsewhere. It is impossible to know how many of the men who wrote to Desmond he actually met, but he also advertised in *Films and Filming* and was selling riding boots as well ('not seen in Bradford', someone replied). H.R. Coates was still writing – at length – to Desmond in 1954, more than ten years after his first letter. His personal enthusiasm was for the caning which he remembered, with apparent relish, from his school days:

We usually were reqd to bend well over the back of the chair & grasp the front legs as far down as possible. The Prefects had the power to use the cane on any boys who were not Prefects, any age. They usually carried canes out of school hours, when on duty to keep order. Boys told to go to their studies for correction had to knock & then go & bend over the chair in approved position & wait until the Prefect condescended to notice them. He usually pretended to be busy & kept them waiting on purpose. Prefect used to run his hands over the bottom cheeks & feel & squeeze them to see if boy had anything stuck down his pants, then took up a nice springy cane & delivered a no. of well directed & stinging cuts up & down the bottom stretched before him, & back of thighs, & usually end up with a hefty & well placed kick, like kicking a football, underneath between the cheeks, & toe of boot well pressed up, & very often a good 'kick off' through the door as well! It was called 'Rooting the Arse' & was quite a school custom among the boys & prefects! . . . it was good practice for football! Nobody said anything.

Coates continued his letter with more accounts of caning teenage boys by the grooms in Irish stables, and messenger boys and pages in pre-war German hotels, which he said took place on Sunday evenings in front of an audience of about 200 senior messengers and pages: 'Then they had to go and change into thin tight shorts & come back & mix with the guests. The Head Senior shook hands with them & gave them drinks (usually sherry), which were also served to the guests on these occasions.'[6]

Desmond's archive* includes a drawing of a man in riding breeches, high-heeled boots and spurs, holding a riding crop, and,

---

* DST's archive is in the Lilly Library, the University of Indiana, Bloomington, Indiana, USA. In the catalogue to the archive the letters from Coates, Selwyn-Keith, Jarvis and many others are classifed together as 'Personal ads correspondence. From members of the homosexual community instigated by personal ads in 1943, 1946, 1954 and 1965.'

according to the catalogue, 'snapshots of thirty-five unidentified men in military uniform'.

On 21 September 1953 Desmond arrived in New York on the SS *America* after having received a grant from the Smith-Mundt Leader Program* to go to the USA and travel widely for three months without any expectation of doing any work in return. For several weeks he travelled by rail back and forth across the States, visiting various friends and places. On 5 October he wrote to Long Crichel: 'Dear Old Folks At Home . . . The voyage was calm . . . and utterly uneventful . . . We arrived on a misty morning, and the Battery loomed out of the mist like Walhalla in Das Rheingold. Wonderfully beautiful and strange; and as we approached, it began to look as such a Venice as one might find on the canals of Mars.' In New York he stayed in the Algonquin Hotel in a $6 room rather than a larger one at $8.50. It was a mistake – the room was 'too dark and poky and claustrophobic and depressing',[7] and after four days he said that he had had more than enough. Among the friends he visited were Glenway Wescott and Monroe Wheeler:

> That night Monroe had a delightful dinner party for me, with Glenway (as nice as could be), Sam Barber[†] (delightful too), Alice Bouverie[‡] & a pleasant girl with a name like Elmergingen. About ten a rather handsome (but of course not my style) Japanese came in with a huge wooden musical instrument like an Eskimo kayak which he laid on the floor and proceeded to play with Landowska-like-virtuosity; the music, though supposedly genuine Japanese of

---

* The programme was set up with the aim of promoting mutual understanding between the people of the United States and other countries. In 2004 it was renamed the International Visitor Leadership Program.

† Samuel Barber, composer (1910–1981).

‡ Alice Pleydell-Bouverie, née Astor, socialite and patron of the arts, especially ballet (1902–1956).

fairly recent date (i.e. post 1800) sounded pretty Western to me. This was enjoyable but I hoped it wouldn't go on too long and fortunately it didn't. The party began to clear off & Glenway took me to a couple of non-Greenwich-Village bars called The Blue Parrot and Shaw's. I was rather taken with Shaw's especially with a short, fair, lively boy in levis (as jeans are always called now, it seems) and a black leather jacket; he turned out to be a Monroe regular, which was perhaps a pity, but we had a long and amusing gossip. [8]

After he left New York Desmond wrote to Glenway to thank him for the party. He also asked for Christopher Isherwood's address, and a list of names and addresses of contacts in San Francisco:

Your friend Robert Shaw (nice name) sounds delightful: at least, to be candid, about two-thirds of your list of adjectives do. The ones I *don't* immediately respond to are 'small' and 'fox-faced' – although the former, as you have doubtless noticed, is not insuperable by any means. What I really like is Audie Murphy[*] – if you know who that is – or a warm sweet-natured, slightly vain, and *not* too intellectual, college boy . . . Follie! follie! delirio Vano è questo![†] So perhaps a wild party for kids, especially the leather-and-levi kind, might be more my thing than anything else.[9]

Glenway Wescott, who was still writing, and Monroe Wheeler, who was now at the Museum of Modern Art, had returned to New York from Paris in the spring of 1934. 'I felt I had stayed abroad for too long,' Wescott said. 'I had spoken French for too long. I came back not only thinking but *dreaming* in French. And I'd had all that success with my Wisconsin material and with Paris and the luxury of Paris. That's when I decided it was the fault of my language. And I

---

[*] American soldier and actor who mostly appeared in Western films (1925–1971).

[†] Madness! Madness! This delirium is vanity!

wasn't able to write.'[10] Neither Monroe nor Glenway was completely faithful to their relationship, and Glenway had also just fallen out of love with one of his casual partners. After a visit to the Café Boeuf sur le Toit he wrote to Eddy, 'there were women with pearls enough; and journalists, and the sort of lovers people have nowadays. I am sorry to say Paris is as petty as that for me, for the moment . . . Everyone's absence has annoyed me and I myself have been absent-minded. I should have worked; and now when the family gets back, I shall automatically go into harness, and drudge for six weeks.'[11] There was a total lack of imagination for any new novel.

In Paris in 1925 Glenway and Monroe had met a would-be poet called George Platt Lynes, and Monroe had fallen in love with him. Rather than cause a rupture with Glenway, Lynes was accommodated into the relationship, and they continued as a *ménage à trois*, even if it tended to be Glenway who slept most often by himself. Monroe went to work for the Museum of Modern Art in New York, where he researched and designed books which helped introduce the public to modern art. Despite being back in America, Glenway's emotional unhappiness stifled his creativity for the rest of the decade. In 1938 he wrote a 14,000-word autobiographical short story 'A Visit to Priapus', which was never published in his lifetime. Its central character 'Tower' – with whom Glenway clearly identifies – considers his current relationships while he waits for his first illicit homosexual encounter:

Naturally, bitter regret for my great days as a lover assailed me. Also a fresh and terrible kind of sense of devotion to the two I love, who love me, who cannot keep me happy, whom I torment and disappoint year in and year out, ached in my grotesque heart. With which my pride also started up, at its worst. To think I should have come to this: sex-starved in a cheap provincial hotel humbly waiting for a total stranger: and it should be so soon, at thirty-eight![12]

The story continues with a long and awkward night of love-making. In 1940 Wescott published a short novel, *The Pilgrim Hawk: A Love Story*. According to the author, the hawk was 'a symbol of the aging process and sexual frustration'.[13] The book was described by Susan Sontag as 'among the treasures of 20th century American literature'.[14] *Apartment in Athens*, Wescott's final and most commercially successful novel, appeared in 1945.

George Platt Lynes failed as a poet but became a photographer instead. He photographed ballet dancers and other performers, but much of his work is defiantly homoerotic and unashamedly celebrates male desire for other male bodies – not least those of Monroe and Glenway, whom he photographed nude. The emotionally tangled existence of their three lives became a subject of study by Alfred Kinsey, whose *Sexual Behaviour in the Human Male* was published in 1948. Lynes eventually fell in love with his studio assistant and walked out of the Wescott–Wheeler *ménage*. The studio assistant was killed in the war, and in 1955 Lynes died from lung cancer. Many of his photographs were destroyed before he died, but his remaining studies were acquired by the Kinsey Institute.

On 2 December Desmond was back at the Algonquin Hotel, writing to the 'Beloved English kids' at Long Crichel. He apologised for not having written more often, but, he said, the two months of almost continuous sunshine all over the country made it seem sinful to sit indoors at the typewriter. In Los Angeles he had seen a lively Christopher Isherwood with a devoted and very young new lover in tow (Don Bachardy, who was exactly thirty years younger than Isherwood). On his return to New York he discovered that Monroe had gone to South America on an art goodwill tour for six weeks, but Glenway had invited him to Stoneblossom, his house on his brother's farm in New Jersey. Desmond said that it was 'delicious – very much like a larger Bothy in atmosphere, and the wooded hills across the valley decidedly Henley-ish'.[15] They ate their Thanksgiving Day dinner in a female penitentiary, 'cooked by a murderess: very good, turkey of course, the only qualm when my coffee tasted super-revolting, and it proved that I had been handed salt instead of sugar; "now" said our charming and eminent penologist-hostess, "there will be another murder in the kitchen when the cook discovers how her coffee has been spoilt."'[16] The following week, Desmond continued, he was going

> to Harvard for a few days to stay with Isaiah Berlin, who is THE great darling of every hostess, and no wonder since no-one has ever sung so splendidly for his supper. Really more in my line has been the shadier life, of which there is also no lack. A small clever boy of Monroe's called Ralph Pomeroy* (not a bad poet), has proved extremely sympathetic, and is giving me what sounds a rather divine dress-rough-in-jeans-and-such-like party on Monday. This is a big craze now, but is usually associated with a perhaps too serious brand of sadism – of course the American touch again.[17]

In the letter Desmond also mentioned Gore Vidal, Osbert Sitwell, Aaron Copeland and Elsa Maxwell, 'who says she will invite us to her party at which Victoria de los Angeles sings to her guitar . . .':

> Everyone here, when they hear of my impending return to the Land of Terror and Persecution, looks at me as if I were an incredible resistance man about to be dropped behind the Iron Curtain in a parachute. I must say I thought Kingsley [Martin] feeble on the subject, and even Morgan [Forster] nothing very much. People all seem to write in England as though Kinsey didn't exist; I don't mean that his researches *justify* any particular kind of behaviour; but surely once the idiots grasp how widespread and

---

* Ralph Pomeroy, poet (1926–1999); published an illustrated book of poems with Andy Warhol titled *A la Recherche du Shoe Perdu*.

universal the thing is, they would stop talking about it as if it were some strange fantastic fate visited upon a few unfortunates from the blue sky. Fearful rubbish nearly all the public comment seems to me to be.

But, despite all, I am looking forward hugely to the loved ones at Cosy Crichel. Now, I must start on my Quarterly Review for the Gramophone – a hateful task which however does begin to make me feel as though I were tapping in the study instead of on West Forty-Fourth Street.

Love and kisses to all . . .[18]

Following his arrest and fine for importuning, John Gielgud made a somewhat sheepish return to the Theatre Royal, Haymarket, where he was rehearsing N.C. Hunter's *A Day by the Sea*. The atmosphere of embarrassment was broken by Dame Sybil Thorndike. 'Who's been a naughty boy, then?' she said, wagging her finger at Gielgud, who was both acting and directing. The following Monday at the play's first out-of-town opening in Liverpool, when he was still terrified, Dame Sybil took Gielgud's arm and all but dragged him onto the stage. They were met by a standing ovation, and the play ran for nearly a year. No longer an MP, Bill Field moved down to Fontmell Magna in Dorset and followed his interest in Egyptology. And after he was freed from Brixton Prison, Rupert Croft-Cooke went to live in Morocco and resumed his career as a writer.

Lord Montagu was released from gaol in time for Christmas 1954. Although his sentence had been for twelve months, he received the customary remission of four months for good behaviour. Knowing that the press would be waiting for him at dawn, the governor, 'a decent man', released him at one minute after midnight instead. Having lost a lot of weight and grown a moustache, he hoped he would not be recognised. He said his worst experience was going home and coming face to face with his neighbours and employees: when he deliberately set about meeting them there were some who found eye contact very difficult. The first time Montagu went to London he was invited to lunch with a few friends at Mirabelle, a smart and expensive restaurant in Mayfair. As the meal progressed it was clear that one or two of the neighbouring tables disapproved. The atmosphere became unpleasant and remarks were being made which were obviously meant to be overheard. Hugh Gaitskell, who was Leader of both the Labour Party and the Opposition, could see what was happening from where he was sitting a few tables away. Although they did not know one another, he recognised Montagu and crossed the room. 'How nice to see you back,' he said, holding out his hand. The action silenced the surrounding hostility.

A few months later Peter Wildeblood and Michael Pitt-Rivers were also released. Sacked by the *Daily Mail*, Wildeblood made a new career of writing and scriptwriting. Subsequently he joined Granada as a television producer. Through his writing he became one of the first authors in the English-speaking world to identify himself as homosexual, rather than just admitting to homosexual acts – and making a stand for respect and for the acknowledgement of his human rights. Wildeblood's first book after his release, *Against the Law*, gave an account of his harassment and public humiliation, as well as the pointless nature of prison life. The book was widely praised, although many booksellers refused to display or stock it. On one occasion he received an elaborately packed parcel tied with string and sealed with tape containing tins of steak pudding, glucose, tea, cigarettes, vitamin tablets, a miniature bottle of yellow Chartreuse, a pair of socks, a typewriter ribbon and a message from an unknown reader of *Against the Law* saying that it was the duty of society to cherish its creative artists. There were also invitations to cocktail parties at the House of Lords:

The cocktail party had been given by Lord Pakenham for the members of an organisation which he had launched, called the New

Bridge, the subject of which was to assist ex-prisoners in their return to freedom. It seemed strange to be standing in a gilded and be-muralled room with a Martini in my hand, discussing the sanitary conditions at Wormwood Scrubs with the Chairman of the Prison Commission, but I had become accustomed by now to the violent fluctuations undergone by my social status. By going to prison, I had become what the statisticians call 'socially mobile', to an extent of which no statistician had ever dreamed.[19]

When Michael Pitt-Rivers was released from gaol, Mary Anna Marten held a party to welcome him home. He returned to running the extensive estates in Dorset and Wiltshire which his family had owned for centuries. Michael's great-grandfather, General Augustus Pitt-Rivers, had been distinguished both as an anthropologist and an archaeologist. His extensive anthropological collections were donated by him to Oxford University, where they form the museum which bears his name. Following the passing of the Ancient Monuments Act in 1882, the general also became the first-ever Inspector of Ancient Monuments. His grandson, Michael's father, Captain George Pitt-Rivers, was also an anthropologist, but this led him to both eugenics and a vicious anti-Semitism. In the 1930s he became convinced that an international Zionist race-war conspiracy was at the heart of contemporary political events. He held meetings in Weimar with Professor Karl Astel, a racial scientist and part of the German Eugenics programme which made decisions about who was to be sterilised. Among those Astel had in mind for experimentation were 'classified homosexuals'.[20] Along with Oswald and Diana Mosley, George Pitt-Rivers was incarcerated for two years during the war and forbidden to return to Dorset until it had ended.

Eight years after the death of George Orwell, Michael Pitt-Rivers married Sonia Orwell, his widow, in Kensington Registry Office on 12 August 1958. Stephen Spender said of Sonia – who preferred her name to be pronounced 'So-nia' – that she had the look of someone who was always struggling to go beyond herself: she wanted an escape from her own modest social background and the convent where she was educated into some 'pagan paradise' of artists and 'geniuses' who would save her. When Sonia met Michael Pitt-Rivers through his younger brother Julian, a social anthropologist, she found him charming, good-looking and amusing – and someone who clearly belonged to Spender's pagan paradise. Sonia had many homosexual friends, and she was shocked by his trial and imprisonment.

Like George Orwell before him, Michael now became another cause. Although he was not dying physically, she felt he could still be rescued from the shame of the social death of narrow-minded attitudes. Having fallen recklessly in love with Michael, Sonia set about restoring him to his rightful place in Dorset society, thereby demonstrating to the world at large that they were above all the prejudices and blinkered bigotry of the world at large. They held a wedding party on the Larmer Grounds at Tollard Royal, a village on Cranborne Chase on the Dorset–Wiltshire border, a few miles north of Long Crichel. The grounds had been opened by General August Pitt-Rivers in 1880 for 'public enlightenment and entertainment', and Thomas Hardy had danced there with the general's daughter Agnes. After the party with the airmen at the Beaulieu beach hut which had led to his eventual arrest and subsequent imprisonment, Michael had invited them to the Larmer Grounds to help clear some of the nettles and weeds. It was not a good omen for a marriage. All literary London – Sonia was a reader and editor for Weidenfeld & Nicolson – turned out in force for the party. However, not all literary London necessarily approved of the match. Just as her marriage to George Orwell, a man only weeks from death, had seemed shocking nine years earlier, so her new marriage to someone so openly homosexual, however wronged he might be, seemed peculiarly wilful.

After the wedding Michael and Sonia spent several months exploring South East Asia – a trip which included an expedition to Angkor Wat in Cambodia with Vita Sackville-West. In the spring of

1959 they at last returned to King John's House, an old hunting lodge at Tollard Royal, which was Michael's home. They set about a round of parties and lavish and generous entertaining. In December that year the couple came to a dinner party at Long Crichel with Eddy, Eardley, Raymond, and Frances and Ralph Partridge. Frances recorded her doubts about the marriage:

> In bed at Crichel, whither we came on Friday afternoon under a luminous peacock blue sky with a crescent moon . . . Between several walks, meals and much lovely gramophone music we got happily to the evening, when Michael and Sonia Pitt-Rivers came to dinner. Rather to our surprise the *Crichelois* treat this marriage between a lifelong homosexual and a neurotic forty-year old woman as if it were perfectly normal, and they would be happy ever after and why not? They certainly bounced in laughing and talking. At dinner I sat between Raymond and Michael, who is a great talker. There's hardly a subject he doesn't fall upon with the avidity of a starving man pouncing on a juicy steak, though in fact we mostly talked about trees or his travels in the far East. Lots of funny stories and excellent imitations followed one another without pause, and his memories seem to be arranged on a book-shelf in front of him, so that he finds one in a moment and takes it down. It's not so much a conversation as a very brilliant turn.[21]

But the marriage was already falling apart. It was a *mariage blanc*. Sonia had been in love with love as much as with Michael, and she desperately wanted a baby, but their honeymoon had made their differences and their expectations all too obvious from the start. Back home in England, Sonia had no understanding of the country life which meant so much to her husband, and she could talk to neither his estate workers nor the local gentry. Captain Pitt-Rivers, her father-in-law, made matters worse. Seeing her as a rival, when Sonia organised a pageant at Tollard Royal to benefit the churches on

Cranborne Chase the captain turned up with a horsewhip and threatened to make trouble. Before long Sonia took an overdose of drugs and was taken unconscious to Salisbury hospital. This was hushed up, but she began to drink heavily. Michael and she were rowing fiercely. At a dinner held for Ivy Compton-Burnett, a mutual friend, he fascinated the table with a venomous attack on the horrors of marriage. In the spring of 1961 Sonia took another overdose. She recovered again but left both Tollard Royal and her marriage and went to live in France. A couple of years later Raymond was an unwilling guest at a birthday dinner party held by Sonia for Deirdre Connolly in the house in Kensington Michael had bought her as part of the divorce settlement. As he was leaving he thanked Sonia for the dinner and added, 'Aren't you a lucky girl to have this lovely house?' Sonia was drunk as usual and blazed out: '*Lucky? – a house!*' The words were delivered with a shriek and she slammed the door angrily after him. She did not regret her words, and all she said was, 'After all, I've never liked Raymond.'[22]

11

Other People's Complexities

In the mid-1950s Jim and Alvilde's marriage, which was never completely easy, came under further strain. Alvilde refused to have any further sexual relations with her husband, and she also began an affair with Vita Sackville-West, two events which were presumably connected. There were ironies and complications. Twenty years had passed since Jim, a protégé of Harold Nicolson, had had an affair with Vita's husband. It was through Harold, and because of his friendship with Eddy, that Jim had come to know Vita well. 'Vita is adorable,' he wrote in his diary in June 1949 after a visit to Sissinghurst:

> I love her romantic disposition, her southern lethargy concealing
> unfathomable passions, her slow movements of grave dignity, her
> fund of human kindness, understanding and desire to disentangle
> other people's complexities for them. I love her deep plum voice
> and her chortle. We talked of love and religion. She told me that
> she had learnt only at twenty-five that her tastes were homosexual.
> It was sad that homosexual lovers were considered by the rest of the
> world to be slightly comical . . . The memory of this evening will
> be ineradicable.[1]

As well as seeing Vita as both a confidante and a mother figure – an improvement on the one who had given birth to him – he was half in love with her himself. It was Jim who had introduced Alvilde to Vita, and she had been a witness at their wedding. Vita had been taken with Alvilde from the start. They became friends and had interests in common, especially gardening. At the same time Alvilde became a source of information for Vita about Eddy, who visited Roquebrune several times a year. By the middle of the decade Vita and Alvilde were in love and writing to one another daily. And they became lovers at Sissinghurst in October 1955.

The affair lasted a couple of years until, over a matter of months early in 1958, and with a variety of excuses, Vita brought the affair to a close. This was typical of Vita. During the course of her life she moved through a series of passionate relationships, casting off one lover for the next when she became bored. On this occasion she resumed an old affair with a local artist called Edith Lamont. Harold detested Edith, but he tolerated Vita's lovers, as she had always accepted his. Alvilde was devastated by the ending of the affair. To make matters worse, in the midst of this emotional crisis, Alvilde's twenty-four-year-old daughter Clarissa had a whirlwind romance with a handsome, feckless and wholly unsuitable Old Etonian called Mickey Luke. Luke had once spent time in gaol for beating up his girlfriend. The girlfriend later became Rosamond Lehmann's daughter-in-law, so the Lees-Milnes felt they knew everything they needed to know about him already. Alvilde, who had once entertained hopes that Clarissa might marry Prince Rainier of Monaco, was appalled. Jim refused to attend the wedding, which took place in June that year. Having lost both Vita and Clarissa almost simultaneously, Alvilde became more possessive of Jim than ever.

In October Jim had dinner with Harold and two other guests at the Travellers Club. One of the guests was Harold's son Nigel, who together with his partner George Weidenfeld was about to publish Vladimir Nabokov's controversial novel *Lolita*. The other guest was a young man called John Kenworthy-Browne. Harold thought Kenworthy-Browne might be suitable for a post with the National Trust. He could take over various duties hitherto undertaken by

Eardley, who was about to retire, and by Rick Stewart-Jones. Rick had died the previous year at the age of forty-three of heart failure brought about by a mixture of overwork, heavy smoking and too much drinking. John was good-looking, passionately fond of architecture, intelligent, Roman Catholic, of a good social background and generally possessed all manner of qualities which Jim was bound to find attractive. He applied for the post and, helped by recommendations from Jim and other friends, was appointed in the second week in December. Jim had planned to go to Lombardy in January to write articles for the *Sunday Times*, and he invited John along with him. He also invited Eardley, but Eardley was aware that the relationship between the two was by now rather more than mere friendship. From now on in their correspondence Kenworthy-Browne was invariably referred to as either 'the Candy' or simply 'the C'. On 21 December 1958 Eardley wrote to Jim:

If the C is doing the trip, do think once more if you want me . . . I think that the cat will be pretty much out of the bag if you take him on that tour. And it's wonderful for him and very helpful and instructive as well as a hol. And if some say he's your boyfriend they will stop saying so quite soon and forget it. Personally I should think it to be an honour. But then . . .[2]

He added, 'I shall do everything I possibly can to make the C a success in his new job. He won't look young for long working with the N.T. As you know after two weeks people start muttering to themselves and after a year have to start painting or something to get rid of the frustrations and rages. The hair too soon falls . . .'[3]

A month later Eardley, who was invariably practical, wrote to Jim again:

Darling Honey Pie Pot, I think of you and the C and am sure that you are having a heavenly time tho' doubtless desperate at getting deeper in love – the bore of it is you are not *both* 27 years old! But don't be naughty with yourself – live and rejoice in the present & if later the present turns black with violet spots, it can be coped with as an object in itself, not all hitched up with the future & trailing the past.[4]

Although he was aware of it, Alvilde had done her best to keep her affair with Vita from Jim. He now hoped to keep his own affair discreet. Since Alvilde was in the habit of steaming open her husband's correspondence, it did not take long before she was aware of what was happening. She confronted Jim and there were terrible scenes. Jim told her that he was in love with John and intended to go on seeing him. As a result Alvilde decided to give up both her house in Roquebrune and her French residency rights and return to England in order to watch Jim's movements more closely. Consequently, he told her that if she was going to keep him under such close supervision he would leave her altogether. For the next couple of years the marriage just about survived by Jim and Alvilde avoiding one another as much as possible. As the new National Trust Representative for the Wessex and Severn Region, Kenworthy-Browne took up residence at Dyrham Park in Gloucestershire, his headquarters. Alvilde, meanwhile, took every opportunity to complain about her husband and his lover to everyone she could. Desmond's old school friend Jack Rathbone, who was now the National Trust Secretary, was a particular target for her woes and feared that a potential scandal might mean the good name of the National Trust being brought into disrepute. Alvilde stormed into his office and demanded that Kenworthy-Browne be sacked for interfering in her marriage. She also wrote letters to leading figures in the organisation. However, as far as the Trust was concerned John was doing his job satisfactorily and had done nothing with which they could find fault. Alvilde's complaining began to be counterproductive: instead of her grievances, it was her vindictiveness which was noticed and caused trouble, and her letters were ignored.

In August 1959 Jim wrote to Eardley that he was going to France to see Alvilde in September but for no more than the month:

> The C & I are as one, eternally I feel, so much so I feel calmer about him because I have a confidence in our relationship enduring. Hubris you warn me. Perhaps. And probably I shall get my congé soon. Who knows. If you can calm Jack Rathbone down and make light of my troubles with A I shall be grateful. And if he suggests the C being sacked from the N.T. I shall forestall it by leaving myself – at *once*.[5]

After a last, unhappy, summer at Roquebrune Jim and Alvilde took a holiday in Vienna, from where Jim wrote to Eardley about his plans for the future. If Alvilde was set on living in the country then he must have a small flat of his own in London where John could come whenever he wanted. He was adamant about this. Needless to say, the news was not well received. Jim continued: 'Life here since I came hasn't been too bad – ups and downs it is true – and I miss the C desperately. One is mad of course but one must accept every emotional invasion as it comes. It is no use fighting against madness. Henceforth I am going to be perfectly, brutally frank with A. I think she and I will suffer less thereby.'[6]

They had been to the hotel Fiorintina, which was the same as ever. Barbara Hutton[*] and her twenty-eight-year-old lover were there, so he was not the only one with a young lover. David Hicks, 'the expensive, decorating poul(e) de luxe' decorator was there and 'one or two c-teasing, charm-displaying-by-the-bathing-pool, American young others':

> The whole thing is like a sort of bad, ending in a wet – no, not ending, which is worse – dream, all frustrating, inhibiting,

---

[*] Barbara Woolworth Hutton (1912–1979). American retail heiress. Married seven times.

reminding one of one's lost youth and the impossibility of a friendly old one even faintly attractive in a dear old-fashioned way. No, one is very unappetising I am afraid. As the C said to me at 6.30 a.m. not so long ago as the eastern sun poured through the drawn aside curtains upon my supine form: 'You do look sweetly revolting.' As the words came out quite spontaneously, it made me pause to reflect. Dear, dear me. Why does one worry and mind? . . . It is so foolish. If there were no one in my life I believe I would not care. And when I am well and truly sacked I am going to turn over a new and final leaf and let myself go in a happy, carefree, revelling in my disgustingness way.[7]

Alvilde's house in France, La Meridiene, was sold, and she returned to England, all the while insisting that his infidelity with John was a gross betrayal and treachery. Friends regarded her intercepting and steaming open of Jim's letters as a joke. 'Perhaps Madam puts the letters into a sort of cauldron & stirs them for the dog's dinner? This one would add spice no doubt,' Eardley wrote in a letter from Dorset.[8] The mere sight of a postcard addressed to John or mention of his name caused anger.

In February 1961 Jim went down to Long Crichel in order to do some writing. To his pleasure and surprise he discovered that John had also been invited. No doubt because she had opened and then destroyed a letter addressed to Jim, Alvilde already had advance warning. She followed him in her car, and then made a scene outside the house, which she refused to enter. The following day Jim wrote to Freda Berkeley:

If you have any influence with Alvilde, do persuade her not to make herself wretched and everyone else when there is so little need. I came [to Long Crichel] to write. I did *not* suggest John coming here. Raymond when he heard I was coming invited him without my knowing. Anyway why should I make excuses all this time? I am fifty-two and have always been independent. I shall not change now, I fear. I am desperately sorry for Alvilde because she cannot be happy, but I have told her over and over again – if living with me is intolerable then I shall clear out. She must make up her mind and cease expecting me to act the part of Romeo . . . The attitude of tragedy queen she assumes is very distressing. I will always love A., but [her] constant nagging and demands do submerge my love from time to time. After last night I don't know how I feel except prostrated.[9]

Jim was back in Long Crichel in July. Raymond told Frances that he was working all day on a new book,* while Alvilde was buying a house near the Severn north of Bath which sounded 'elegant and well-suited . . . but goodness knows how that marriage can be expected to totter on'.[10] The house was called Alderley Grange and was near Wotton-under-Edge in Gloucestershire. There was a large walled garden. Since the garden was a wilderness and the house in a state of considerable disrepair, their rescue became both a joint venture and a new and mutual interest. The marriage survived or, at the very least, continued to 'totter on' for the time being. Alderley Grange was built and restored with Alvilde's money – Jim still had none of his own – but he was obliged to give up the flat in Thurloe Square he had occupied for fifteen years, and his wish to retain a small London flat of his own never came to anything. Instead he usually stayed in Eardley's flat in West Halkin Street.

The fact that Jim failed to keep a diary between September 1957 and February 1964 gives some idea as to the state of his marriage. He would have been extremely reluctant to record his daily activities and commit his feelings to paper when Alvilde was likely to read them. Eardley continued to be the recipient of Jim's unhappiness. After one

---

* *Earls of Creation*, a study of five eighteenth-century earls (Bathurst, Pembroke, Burlington, Oxford and Leicester) and the houses they built (Cirencester, Marble Hill, Chiswick, Wimpole and Holkham), was published by Hamish Hamilton in 1962.

exceptionally bad episode Jim wrote: 'I feel so shaken, so headachy and quivering that I can neither work nor speak. I shall have to have it out with her because I cannot bear it any more, this being treated like a chattel.'[11]

John eventually left the National Trust and went to work for Christie's auction house. He bought a house in Fulham, which meant that Jim also could stay with him whenever he was in London. They went to the cinema and theatre together, and a few times a year they managed to go away on holiday. In July 1971, ten years after the Long Crichel incident, Frances and Raymond were invited to Alderley Grange. Frances wrote in her diary:

> With Raymond I penetrated the world of the Lees-Milnes, neither of us feeling entirely at ease. Raymond, hunched and miserable in the queues at Paddington, said he would have turned tail had it not been for me. As we ate breakfast together on the Monday train home he asked touchingly, 'Did I disgrace myself? I really dislike staying with people who hate me . . .' But they don't, I protested in all honesty. 'Oh, yes, Alvilde does. You see we committed the ultimate sin and invited Jim to Crichel with his boyfriend, and Alvilde got in her car and drove across country and made a scene. She wouldn't come in.' She is a bristly Aberdeen terrier, someone *lors la loi*, one is never at ease with her . . . and yet and yet, I feel a sneaking sympathy for her. She and Jim are outwardly loving, 'darlings' flying back and forth, yet according to Raymond the affair with the boyfriend is still paramount. So Alvilde buries her spiky heart in the garden, which is a glorious success, proliferating up walls, cascading, abundant, making blue pools round the feet of trees. Surely some sort of feeling emerges in all this beauty? Yet any other gardener would have given me some flowers to take to London and I would have asked any other hostess to let me pick some.[12]

Ralph Partridge died of a heart attack on 1 December 1960 at Ham Spray House. He was sixty-six. When, twenty-five years later, Frances Partridge published *Everything to Lose*, her diaries covering the years from 1945 until Ralph's death, its final words were 'Now I am absolutely alone and forever'. Frances had lived in fear of the possibility of Ralph's death for four years, but she had been sustained – however irrationally – by hope. When the blow came it was crushing, anguish the like of which she said she had never suffered before. When, weeks later, she started to make entries in her diary again she wrote of her surprise that 'just because the blow has been so mortal, as if roughly, savagely cutting me in half and leaving me with one leg and one arm only, I am with what seems to me total illogicality under this menace struggling to survive . . . What earthly sense is there in this pitiful frantic struggle? The life force must be stronger than I knew.'[13] She did not regard suicide as wicked, but it was selfish and would cause great pain to many others. For Frances this would have meant first of all to Burgo, her son and only child. Virtually all adults learn sooner or later that there is a great deal of sadness in life, but 'most also know that it is not *all* sad, that in its very essence lies something glorious and splendid, that the stuff it is made of arouses constant wonder and interest, that even when one cannot stop crying, one must suddenly laugh'.[14]

Less than a year after Ralph's death Frances sold Ham Spray and started a new life in London. In November 1961 she moved into a first-floor flat in West Halkin Street in Belgravia, in the same street as Eardley Knollys, and from there she wrote:

> Yesterday for the first time my flat seemed to come alive and now I look round at what I've planned and constructed and wonder what it's really like. The hall with its rich dark Indian pattern wallpaper is still heaped with books and without a rug. The bedroom, soft peaceful grey and white, bow window, countrified pictures (landscapes, cats, owls), and the sitting room warm pink, mustard, green and purple, have emerged just as I meant, and now the

books, china and piano complete it. I asked Eardley what sort of room it seemed. 'Very scholarly,' he replied.[15]

In London, where she had many friends, Frances began to make a new life for herself, and in August 1963 Burgo and his wife Henrietta Garnett, the daughter of David ('Bunny') and Angelica Garnett, had a baby daughter they called Sophie, and this too seemed to promise another new interest for her. Then, suddenly, only a month after Sophie's birth, Burgo had a heart attack and died in the midst of making a telephone call. He had a heart condition which no one had known about, and even if it had been known, nothing could have been done. Frances was 'too stunned and shattered' to write anything in her diary bar a brief statement of the facts, adding, 'I have utterly lost heart: I want no more of this cruel life.'[16] From everyone she found kindness – although Rosamond Lehmann made an unfortunate and confused attempt to attract her to the spirit world. After a few weeks Henrietta and her baby daughter went to stay with her parents in France, while Frances prepared to go with Raymond on a pre-arranged trip to Apulia: 'I don't think I was even capable of realising at the time what a heroic act of friendship he showed me in going ahead with it.'[17] (Although she feared beforehand that he would expect her to wash his underpants.) Frances did all the driving, since Raymond could not drive, and he was also hopelessly bad at map reading:

> [He is] inclined to ask me (in a mild voice while others hoot) which I think is the way, not realising that the one thing the driver needs is to be firmly directed. However he is angelically good-tempered and never minds asking the way of strangers. Because we went astray more than once and tried to take a road which stopped suddenly with the cheerful notice *Pericolo di Morte*, it turned into quite a long day's drive.[18]

In October, only a few weeks after her return to England from

Italy, Frances went to Cooleville to stay with Eddy. Julian Jebb, who had once helped sort out Eddy's books, was also staying. Julian, who was thirty-one, had been living in Rome and teaching English. He was now a journalist. It was a comfort to find him there – 'three's company, two's none,' she wrote. Eddy was so oversensitive that she was always afraid of hurting him by saying or doing something he might take amiss. As for Julian, '"queer" though he obviously is . . . what to say? He is euphoric, friendly, very articulate; he launches into imitations, crows with delight; everything seems to be *SIMply* delightful, his world is full of *BRILLiantly* clever people and *MARvellous* books. But I like him very much.'[19]

She found Cooleville enormously comfortable in an old-fashioned way and the food delicious. A horse-faced breezy spinster came to dinner, then Frances went to bed where she slept soundly. The next day Frances, Eddy and Julian went to the Wexford Festival, and in the evening they played Scrabble. Eddy and Julian squabbled over the rules – 'claws beneath velvet pads'. The talk was chiefly about people, and there were lots of stories; it was superficial, but easy and often funny. Julian remarked *à propos* of imitating people, which he did brilliantly, that he could do Frances very easily and he did. 'I was astonished,' Frances wrote. 'It's part of one's view of one's hidden, anonymous identity that there's nothing to imitate.'[20] The following morning they sat reading in Eddy's new conservatory, both of them lying on chaises longues: 'Julian was supposed to be reading a book for review, but I looked up and saw his eyes fixed, wide-open and sad, over the top of his book. He is too vulnerable ever to be truly happy.'[21]

Julian's full name was Julian Alvery Marius Jebb. His father was a schoolmaster and journalist. His early life at his family house, Kingsland near Horsham in Sussex, was dominated by the presence of his grandfather, the writer Hilaire Belloc. He had disliked his grandfather intensely, as well as all his works and the peculiar 'upper-class morbidity' he stood for.[22] The ten thousand books in Belloc's library were mostly 'memoirs and boasting'. After Belloc's death

Julian's mother preserved everything: his false teeth were still in a cupboard beside his bed. On a visit home in 1961 eight years after his grandfather's death, Julian wrote: 'Anxiety splotches and bumps all over my face. Smell of H.B. – scent, cigars, pee – extraordinarily strong in here as I came to bed.'[23]

The family were half-French and strongly Catholic, and Julian was sent to Downside School in Somerset. One of his brothers became a Benedictine monk at Downside Abbey and subsequently headmaster at the school; his sister became a nun. From Downside he went to King's College, Cambridge, where he co-edited *Granta*, the student magazine, with Jonathan Gathorne-Hardy and performed in reviews with the Cambridge Footlights. Tristram Powell, a contemporary, recalled him as 'a diminutive figure in a vast khaki army surplus overcoat which almost swept the ground. As he passed, there was a glimpse of an elfin face of alabaster translucence and great sweetness of expression, though a little troubled, and doll-like eyes.'[24]

He looked about twelve. Julian loved the raunchiness, the camp and the sexual innuendo of the Cambridge Footlights Club dressing room. Even the hardiest rugger player called him darling.

As well as a would-be star, Julian was also a dedicated fan. While still an undergraduate he started to write letters to Rosamond Lehmann:

> I read The Echoing Grove* in April on a peculiar journey in a slow train from Carlisle to London surrounded by fat, ugly, dirty and noisily sleeping people. The effect was profounder than anything I had experienced. It was as if for the first time I had eaten fire or water – a new element existed for me, a fourth dimension perhaps. Only at the same time I was aware of a nightmare quality. I felt as

---

* Rosamond Lehmann, *The Echoing Grove* (1953); a story of two sisters, one conventional, one Bohemian, and the lives they lead.

if I had arrived at a theatre, entirely empty, to see only a third of a play. A completion with continuity.[25]

When he received a reply to his letter Julian wrote again:

I have written only one good thing called 'One Man Short' which was about going to a party, being asked at the last minute alone! There is pain in the title because I am v. small and have only 19 years to my credit, which the people in my party thought less funny than I. p.s. I have put your letter in my Missal and will pray for your intentions if you do not mind.[26]

Rosamond forwarded the correspondence to Frances with a note:

This is from an angelic gnome of 19, – of all 'old souls' the oldest I have encountered is this writer. Our correspondence started with a fan letter re The Echoing Grove which in its profound understanding of and melancholy insight into the human heart, its tone of 'all passion spent' I assumed to have been written by an elderly gentleman broken by life's wheel. The *next* letter was somewhat wild in tone, and spoke of coming often in his car outside no 70, Eaton Square was referred to as Rosamond Land. He is as I said Hilaire Belloc's grandson – wants to be a writer – and will be, I should think. Dadie thinks him brilliant though unstable, as his hand-writing would suggest . . . Send back sometime and *don't* let on I've joked, as it will get back to him through D. or someone and lacerate his feelings.[27]

On leaving Cambridge Jebb worked for the Catholic weekly the *Tablet* and for a literary agency. He then went to Germany, where he produced and acted in English-language plays for Radio Bremen, and at the beginning of the 1960s he went to Rome. His love affairs were unsatisfactory and fruitless; perhaps others found his neediness

(above) Frances Partridge and Mattei at Orta in Italy. *(Norman Coates)*

(right) Eardley Knollys. *(Norman Coates)*

Eardley Knollys and Duncan Grant in Eardley's studio. *(Norman Coates)*

Desmond by Duncan Grant. *(Private collection)*

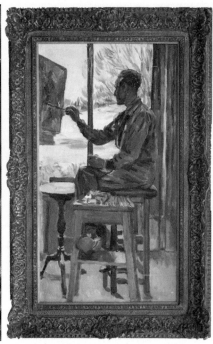

Eardley by Duncan Grant. *(Radev Collection/ Bridgeman Images © Estate of Duncan Grant. All rights reserved DACS 2020)*

(above) Raymond by Derek Hill.
(© Christie's Images/Bridgeman Images)

(left) Eddy by Ian Campbell-Gray, an Oxford friend, 1920. *(Radev Collection)*

Erotic drawings by
Duncan Grant.

Duncan Grant.

Brian Shawe-Taylor with his wife and sons.
(Private collection)

(left) Patrick Trevor-Roper at Harley Street, 1963.
(Private collection)

(above) Raymond Morgan and E.M. Forster.
(Norman Coates)

Julian Jebb with
Janetta Parladé in
Spain, 1962.
(Private collection)

Miss Rayner and her cows, 1970.
(Private collection)

Dadie Rylands, Raymond and Frances
Partridge playing croquet at Long
Crichel, 1970. *(Private collection)*

Sarawak
with Richard S.

Pat with Lindy and Sheridan
Guinness, July 1973. *(Private collection)*

Eardley and James
Lees-Milne.
(Norman Coates)

Derek Hill and Philip Hopkins, 1989. *(Private collection)*

Long Crichel House, south elevation. *(David Grandorge)*

exhausting. Although his upbringing and education seemed to point towards a career as a novelist, and he very much wanted to write and tried many times, Julian never got very far. He had a very real talent for observation but, as he was all too well aware, all his attempts at fiction were skewed by wishful thinking. In August 1961 he was in Klagenfurt in Austria and kept a diary:

> what at the moment I long to do, a short accurate account of an obsessive love affair between two totally unsuitable people. Queer, I suppose. Written pessimistic sympathy . . . I love them, want to tell the truth about them, know the delicacy and confidence with which I would have to treat them, do not doubt my ability to invent their behaviour truthfully – but still see the icy fact of my passion for their invention and existence to be self-reflection. They seem like subtly unrelated dream figures, manipulated by me unknowingly into a pattern which is gradually more destructive to their truth – figments. Figments.[28]

The story of two men called Mathew and Hans never got past the second chapter.

Back in England, Julian rented a top-floor flat up eighty-nine stairs in Warrington Crescent in Maida Vale. A single large studio bed-sitting room was crammed with furniture, and at one end there was a big Victorian baroque mirror. Every surface was piled with old newspapers, magazines and final reminder bills: he referred to this as his rising tide of squalor. In winter the flat was very cold and the roof leaked so badly that he kept the place warm by leaving the gas oven on day and night and keeping the door open.

In 1967 Julian joined the BBC arts department as an assistant producer, where he co-produced a series of literary programmes. He became part of what Melvyn Bragg described as a 'small gang' who were given the run of the airwaves when BBC2 was new, young and utterly careless about ratings and the jargon current among television producers. All of them were eager to become professionals, and the world of the arts was a jungle through which they could hack their way as they wanted. The channel was largely ignored, and so, Bragg wrote, 'you could put a few pals together and have a damn good time making the programmes. Julian came and saw this and wanted a place at the table.'[29] As part of its mission to promote the arts and put writers on the screen, BBC2 broadcast a programme called *Take It or Leave It*, a quotation guessing game devised by Brigid Brophy. Through Julian's contacts and friendships a number of writers appeared on the screen for the first time – the participants included Cyril Connolly, A.S. Byatt, Philip Toynbee, Mary McCarthy, Anthony Burgess, John Bayley, Iris Murdoch and Elizabeth Bowen ('Will I look a hag?' she worried). No marks were awarded, and no bells were rung – there was only plenty of conversation. Unfortunately, *Take It or Leave It* was a failure, either because it was too simple or too highbrow, but it was replaced by *Read All About It*. This was chaired by Bragg himself, and books were discussed by a wider range of people – sportsmen and starlets who were known to the public rather than mere writers.

Julian was also writing, and an interview with Evelyn Waugh was published by the *Paris Review*. As well as conducting the first-ever studio interview with the painter Francis Bacon, Julian produced a number of interview-based documentaries. His subjects included Christopher Isherwood, John Osborne, Patricia Highsmith and Anthony Powell. He also made a number of longer, mostly literary documentaries. Julian both thrived and suffered in this world. In 1968, just before making a programme about Tennyson, he went to Tramores in Spain in order to stay with Janetta Jackson. Janetta had first been taken to Spain by her mother in 1936, but finding themselves caught up in the Civil War they returned to England, and Janetta went to Ham Spray to stay with Frances and Ralph. They became almost her surrogate parents and they remained very close. Later Janetta worked on *Horizon* with Cyril Connolly. Although now living in Spain, she had become a close friend of Julian's. He wrote to Frances from the room in which she usually slept when she went to stay with Janetta in Spain. 'Tennyson manuscripts and books already stacked up,' he wrote:

> There had been no sign of Janetta on the quay, and no telegram. But there magically she was, quite alone and beaming. We went to a cool, grand, noisy bar and talked, or rather *I* talked. Torrential stuff poured out about last month, the anxieties, the adventures, the pills (I am *stuffed* with black and green calmers called Librium), Cyril [Connolly], my feelings of impending crisis, my visits to the doctor, my non-sex life – everything. Poor Janetta! She listened marvellously, connected, was looking lovely – smooth, calm, voluptuous, thinner. Goodness, one does love her![30]

The most celebrated of Julian Jebb's documentaries, *A Night's Darkness, A Day's Sail*, was about Virginia Woolf, which he made the following year. In the programme the words of people who had known Woolf or been part of the Bloomsbury group were interwoven with readings from her novel *To the Lighthouse*. Among the contributors were Raymond Mortimer (who thought Virginia looked like 'a seventeenth century abbess'); and David Garnett ('a Botticelli dancer'). Lord David Cecil described how the Bloomsbury group had certain mannerisms of voice and phrasing: 'a rather breathless way of talking and a very solemn face. That was the thing I noticed. And that was rather alarming because when they shook hands with you they didn't smile, they just handed the hand, and if you didn't know them, this grave look and this limp handshake was not welcoming.' Elizabeth Bowen (who thought Virginia looked like 'the wife of a very distinguished soldier') concluded her contribution with a late memory of Virginia Woolf mending a torn curtain and then suddenly rocking back on her heels in the spring sunshine and hooting with laughter.

The longest contribution of all was given by Louie Mayer, the housekeeper to the Woolfs, about the last day of Virginia Woolf's life. It was nearly lunch time when they discovered she was missing. Leonard Woolf must have looked on the table and seen two notes lying there.

One was for him with Leonard on it, and the other was for Mrs Bell, Vanessa Bell. And he picked up his and read it and rushed down and said, 'Oh Louie, where is Mrs Woolf – which way has Mrs Woolf gone? I think she may have committed suicide.' And of course I took fright and I too rushed up the garden but I couldn't see anything. And he said, 'No, I suppose she probably went towards the river.' And he just ran off towards the river and I thought what's the best next thing to do so I ran and told the gardener and the gardener rushed up to the local police station and said would the policeman come. And they both went to the river and they found her walking stick there. And it was about over a fortnight, I think, before we really discovered – some boys found it on the bank.[31]

Frances went to the Ealing Studios to see a preview of the film. 'It quite carried me away,' she said, 'very moving, and very good too.'

A Night's Darkness, A Day's Sail was probably the high point of Julian's career.

12

Far, Far Away from Reality

If Eddy's departure from Long Crichel was upsetting for everyone, a few years later the unexpected arrival of a young Bulgarian called Mattei Radev unwittingly caused even more of an upheaval.

Mattei Radev became a highly respected picture-frame maker, but he arrived in Britain as a stowaway. Born in Bulgaria in November 1927, Mattei came from a family of shopkeepers who had originally lived in Macedonia and changed their name from Raphael to Radev. The family owned vineyards around a village called Brestovitsa, near Plovdiv, the second-largest city and the cultural capital of Bulgaria, as well as the heart of the vine-growing country. After the creation of the People's Republic in 1946 the Radevs' property was confiscated by the Communist Party. One cousin was shot and another imprisoned for criticising the Party. Mattei was desperate to escape, and a friend agreed to go with him. They arrived at the border on a public holiday and managed to avoid the border guards who were drunk. They escaped into Turkey and then travelled overland to Istanbul. For nearly three months they stayed in a Red Crescent Hostel and watched the ships as the passed through the Sea of Marmara, waiting for a boat which would take them to England. At last one night in April 1950 Mattei and his friend sighted a British cargo ship, the merchant vessel *The Preston*. They paid a boatman to row them out, but the friend was caught almost immediately. For four days Mattei managed to hide in a lifeboat, surviving on lemons, some bread and a little chocolate. When he was finally discovered he claimed British protection; from then on he worked his passage, remaining on board the ship until it reached port in Glasgow.

Once he had docked, Mattei was taken by the police for detention in Barlinnie Prison. Barlinnie was the largest, and grimmest, gaol in Scotland and still had an execution block where prisoners were kept before they were hanged. After the necessary formalities, Mattei's release must have seemed to him like a second escape. Once out of prison, he travelled to London, where he found lodgings at Arlington House in Camden. Arlington House, which had 1,140 small rooms, 140 staff and sufficient space for a thousand men, was one of a chain of hostels founded by the Victorian philanthropist Lord Rowton. In *Down and Out in Paris and London* George Orwell praised the Rowton houses as the best lodging houses available. In 1932, when Orwell was writing, the charge was a shilling for a cubicle and the use of the excellent bathrooms. For half a crown one could pay for a 'special', which was practically hotel accommodation. His only objection was the strict discipline. There were rules against cardplaying and cooking. Alcohol was strictly forbidden, and there was a humiliating system of fines and punishments, including a fine for bed-wetting. Residents had to be out of bed and downstairs by 9 a.m. – anyone who lingered for three mornings in a row was obliged to leave. This Victorian disciplinary regime carried on until the 1980s. However, most of the men worked and paid their own rent.

While Mattei was living in Arlington House he found a job as an orderly at the Whittington Hospital in the Upper Holloway Road. The Whittington was an amalgamation of three local Victorian hospitals which served the boroughs of Islington and Haringey, and it was also a teaching hospital for the University College London medical students. One of the consultants at the Whittington was Patrick Trevor-Roper, and the young Radev, with his thick, dark hair and striking good looks, caught his eye. At the time Trevor-Roper was helping to find accommodation for hospital staff, so he introduced Mattei to a friend, Robert Wellington, who was the manager of the Zwemmer Gallery, an annexe of the Zwemmer bookshop on the Charing Cross Road. Wellington lived in St Andrew's Place, a Crown Estate house among the Nash terraces of Regent's Park, and rented out rooms. He offered Mattei the use of an attic bedroom, which was also occupied by the house water tank so that whenever a lavatory was flushed it could be heard in his room. This Regent's Park mansion was quite close to his former digs in Camden Town, but the people he now began to encounter were a world away from his companions in Arlington House. Mattei lived in St Andrew's Place for nine years.

During the early period of his new life, Mattei took various jobs. His employers included Nicholas Sekers, a former refugee from Hungary who had become a fabric manufacturer in West Cumberland. He also tried the fashion designer Sir Hardy Amies until the day Amies frankly told him, 'I don't think this is for you.' Finally, the artist Robert Medley proposed that he frame some of his paintings. This suggestion led to an apprenticeship with Robert Savage, the owner of a framers' workshop and gallery opposite the Brompton Oratory.

Meanwhile, Wellington set about trying to educate the young Bulgarian on how to conduct himself in British society. Desmond Shawe-Taylor and Jack Rathbone also lived in St Andrew's Place and a young artist friend who visited Wellington had the impression that all the other rooms in the house were occupied by men wearing smoking-jackets. Mattei's education too included instructions on how to dress properly. When he once appeared on a weekday wearing green corduroy trousers Wellington told him to go and change. Mattei protested. Wellington slapped him. Mattei changed his trousers, having learnt that in British society corduroy trousers must only be worn at the weekends – or at least when in Wellington's company. Robert Wellington's next-door neighbour was the grandly eccentric actress Margaret Rutherford. When she noticed that they shared the same initials she suggested that Mattei anglicise his name to 'Matthew

Radford'. He declined to do so, but she continued to call him 'Mr Radford' whenever she saw him. Wellington had a large circle of friends, and he held parties in his house. It was at one of his parties in 1957 that Mattei Radev first met Eardley Knollys and Eddy Sackville-West.

By the late 1950s Eardley had lost all enthusiasm for working for the National Trust. As the Trust grew larger and more professional, it also became more bureaucratic and a less enjoyable institution to work for. These were sentiments Jim understood and shared. When Eardley came into an inheritance he had less financial need to continue working, and in 1957 he gave his notice, although he agreed to stay for another year. 'It seems to me as if N. Trusteries have come to an end,' Eardley wrote to Jim at the end of January 1959. 'I think the powers that be have decided that I'm a back number and don't count.'[1] When Paul Hyslop was sent to make a report on the temples at Stourhead – work which he would have expected to be entrusted with – 'instead of going blue & shrieking with fury I sit back & think how nice to let them get on with their cat's cradle'.[2]

Eardley intended to devote the rest of his life to painting. He also continued to buy and sell pictures, a legacy of his years with the Storran Gallery, which he greatly enjoyed. More important than anything, however, Eardley was by now head over heels in love with Mattei Radev. The difference in ages between the two, twenty-five years, was slightly greater than that between Jim and John Kenworthy-Browne, but Eardley was just as besotted. At the end of January 1959, after a short holiday in Paris, just as besotted with Mattei – whom he invariably referred to as 'my golly wog' – Eardley wrote to Jim. His excitement was effusive:

Well, I too have been having the divinest five days in gay Paree with my funny golly wog. Oh he is such a pet, I chortle & chuckle & giggle like a school girl every time he speaks. He teases & jokes all day long with me & is so quick & witty I can't keep up. Is that not an extraordinary description (true) of that rather hostile silent reserved fellow of three years ago? I suppose love colours all but even so the things he mispronounces & says all wrong seem to be so funny. We came in & he said, over *eau minerale*, that he wanted the 'fuzzy' kind & then 'you know, the fussy kind'. He is absolutely adorable to be with, travel with, stay with. We had very nice rooms at the Hotel d'Angleterre, utterly quiet, and the honeymoon atmosphere never ceased. Of course he's hopeless in some ways, ring up or take the initiative. But what lovely qualities. *Integrity* my dear of a quite exceptional degree & apparently the most exceptional devotion (though of course retaining other loves in London & one does not know how much he cares for them & always there lurks Boulogne dock in the back of the mind & one's own advanced years etc etc). Meanwhile however & in the present it was absolutely continuous joy & how lucky & undeserving of such pleasure one is. I feel I haven't worked or earned or given anything that life should be so kind to me. Really.

So you see my pet you are not the only old sentimentaliser & we'll blub on one another's shoulders if necessary later on.[3]

The unexpected arrival of Mattei in his life made Eardley become bored and dissatisfied with the company at Long Crichel. After his return from Paris he stayed in his flat in Belgravia for two weeks with a temperature and feeling vaguely unwell, a tedium broken only when visited by Mattei 'with *flowers*'.[4] In February he wrote to Jim saying that he did not want to go back to Crichel. He dreaded seeing Raymond again, because he did not like him any more: 'the more he likes me the less I like him'.[5] He wanted to set up house in London with Mattei, who could make frames while he painted: 'But I am cursed my dear by lovely Crichel, [a] glorious studio and three dearest friends. Isn't it just lovely & just awful?'[6] However, by the time summer came Eardley was back in Dorset and getting along like mad with his painting, 'but I feel solitary as I hardly speak the same language as my old pals here. Oh for some jokes (not cackles at others' discomforture [*sic*]) & some lightness & youth! Long C is indeed an ivory tower, far, far away from reality . . . Yes I wish we lived together. You and Golly are the ones I want to be with.'[7] Jim answered: 'I hate the smart world. I hate the queer world too, and the Pats, Desmonds and Jacks have a horrid side. I love you however. If you ever leave West Halkers shall we share something? Perhaps it would not work. Then there is the Golly-C mix-up.'[8]

Whatever the emotional connection between the two, Eardley's sexual connection with Mattei barely existed – although everyone assumed it did. They did not sleep together because Mattei refused to. He regarded himself as strongly masculine, and he did not want the kind of relationship which Kenworthy-Browne, as the younger, compliant partner, shared with Jim. This did not prevent Mattei from looking elsewhere for sexual gratification, and his promiscuity made Eardley feel jealous:

> How often that [after two weeks'] separation one looks to see if one is still Number One. Not that M. ever admits such a thing and cleverly keeps one on tenterhooks while never admitting the physical unfaithfulness – not that I seriously ever tax him – One is *so lucky* to have anything in that line & it is such bliss to be with someone lively & young & affectionate & keen & noticing & interested & creative (a terrible contrast to those old centipede crabs I live with).[9]

In later letters Eardley admitted to Jim how much he missed having sexual contact with anyone, but his bonds with Mattei were cemented in other ways. In 1960 the highly temperamental Robert Savage sacked Mattei from his job in his framing workshop for no significant reason, so Eardley lent him the money to set up his own picture-framing business in Fitzrovia. The area was home to many furniture makers, craftsmen and other framers, and it was also close to the trade which West End galleries brought. For all his faults, Savage had trained Mattei well. The new business attracted customers and it thrived. But in private matters, when eventually competition to be Mattei's 'Number One' arrived, it came not from a man younger than Eardley but from someone considerably older.

In March 1960 Raymond received a letter from Sir Michael Adeane, the Queen's private secretary, on Buckingham Palace writing paper. It was headed 'private and confidential':

Dear Mortimer,

Encouraged by Harold Nicolson I am writing to ask your advice on a matter of some importance to the Queen.

Her Majesty takes a very great personal interest in the Order of Merit, which is in her own gift & not in that of the Government and she regards it – as I think others do – as the highest distinction that we possess.

At present many of the members are very old and there will unfortunately soon be other vacancies to the ones in hand at present (2). The Queen is anxious that one at any rate of these – not necessarily one of the two we now have but one of the vacancies we are likely to have in the next year – should go to an eminent literary figure. At present, as Who's Who shows, there are plenty of soldiers, sailors, airmen, & scientists but the Order is a bit thin in Literature and the Arts. The question is who should get it & this is where I should be extremely grateful for your advice.

We had thought that Edith Sitwell might be considered, but I don't think she would be considered by everyone as having made a sufficiently serious or lasting contribution to poetry. Other names that have been suggested are those of Auden & William Empson & people have written at one time or another to propose Somerset Maugham & E.M. Forster. I doubt however whether the last two are quite in this class.

I am extremely ignorant in these matters myself but I realise how difficult it is to reach any decision which will give anything like general satisfaction. However I believe the best thing to do is to go for pure merit, disregarding any irrelevant disqualification. Then, when the Queen comes to consider the list she can regard or disregard the disqualifications as she wishes. For example, I believe that Auden went off to the U.S.A. at the outbreak of the last war. If so some people might hold it against him & it might be that the Queen might decide on these grounds that the order should go to someone else. Or she might not.

Your advice on these names – or on any others that might occur to you – would be very deeply appreciated & I make an apology for asking it in view of the importance for the Queen of keeping up the standards of her order.

Yours sincerely

Michael Adeane

The Order of Merit is restricted to twenty-four members from Commonwealth realms, together with honorary members from beyond. By 1959, the year of Adeane's letter, no author had received the order since Walter de la Mare in 1953, and de la Mare had died three years later. T.S. Eliot was a member, but he was the only writer, and he was a poet – there had been no novelists since Thomas Hardy, who had died in 1928, and Henry James who had predeceased him. In his reply Raymond made various comments and suggestions to Adeane: Auden, he thought, was the best living poet after Eliot, but he considered him to be 'an American rather than an Englishman living abroad'; Edith Sitwell, with whom he had been on friendly terms for many years, 'may be said to have cowed the critics'. Her DBE was appropriate but sufficient. Raymond proposed other names, including Kenneth Clark – 'I think that nobody has ever written better about painting' – and A.J. Ayer, the philosopher – 'there is no writer alive for whose intellect I have greater respect'. Raymond's clear choice, however, was E.M. Forster: 'Among men I should without hesitation suggest E.M. Forster. I have known and liked him for many years, but I hope that this has not coloured my judgment.

Most good judges, would, I believe, agree that he enjoys unsurpassed prestige among the young as well as the old, and that he is greatly admired also in the United States.'[10]

Forster had been offered, and turned down, a knighthood ten years earlier ('I seem to be a Great Man', he said without enthusiasm to J.R. Ackerley[11]) but had agreed to be made a Companion of Honour in 1953, and over his lifetime he also received eight honorary degrees. He had been nominated sixteen times for the Nobel Prize for Literature. Such was his authority that during the war Forster's broadcasts were listened to by huge audiences when he argued for the importance of the individual, for freedom, for tolerance – as well as for friendship. Famously, in 1939, in an essay entitled 'What I believe', he had written, 'I hate the idea of causes, and if I had to choose between betraying my country and betraying my friend, I hope I should have the guts to betray my country.'[12] Opinions such as these and phrases like 'Only connect' were signs of the influence Forster had during his lifetime. Although he had not published a novel since *A Passage to India* in 1924, Forster still wrote reviews and critical articles and made broadcasts, and in the post-war world his opinions, as a public intellectual and literary figure, remained considerable. His writings set a standard for civilised, liberal values.

Because of Eardley, Mattei had become a frequent Long Crichel visitor. The coincidence of the fact that Mattei and he shared the same birthday – 13 November – gave Eddy the opportunity to joke each year: 'You and I, born on the same day – me, an English aristocrat, and you a peasant from Bulgaria!' One weekend in early 1960 when Eardley and Mattei were both staying at Long Crichel Forster was also a guest. He often visited. He was particularly close to Raymond and Frances Partridge, both of whom he had known a long time and were also 'Bloomsbury' people. When he left at the end of the afternoon Forster picked up a pen which did not belong to him and asked for Mattei's address so that he could send it to him. The pen was not Mattei's – it had only been a pretext for contacting him – but this letter was to be the first of many: over the course of the next decade he was to write Mattei 120 more.

Mattei Radev became the last love of Forster's life. He was both an exotic foreigner and of a lower social class: exotic foreigners and working men were the type whom, over the course of Forster's life, he had always thought of as sexually exciting. Towards the end of the year Forster was a witness for the defence in the case brought by the Crown in the obscenity trial which the publication of *Lady Chatterley's Lover* caused. Lawrence's novel became notorious for its sexual content, but it is a novel with many aspects. Mellors, the gamekeeper in *Lady Chatterley's Lover*, and Alec Scudder, the gamekeeper in Forster's then unpublished novel *Maurice*, represent social as well as sexual congress: they are – at least supposedly – evidence that class prejudice can have a kind of reconciliation through sexuality.

The affection between Forster and Mattei, if presumably not the sexual attraction, was mutual. Nearly fifty years apart in age, they were complete opposites, but Mattei was also fascinated by the older man. If Mattei seemed exotic to Forster, then, in a country where corduroy trousers could only be worn at weekends, in his own way Forster must have seemed equally exotic to Mattei. Frances Partridge said that Forster lacked all visual taste, both in the way he furnished his rooms in Cambridge and in his clothes:

> he always chose to dress in almost aggressively dim grey clothes, woolly cardigans and cloth caps that would have merged into the London fog. I think this was because . . . Morgan felt much more affinity with the lower than the upper classes, and completely lacked ambition, envy and snobbishness. Starting with his mother and his aunts he spent much of his youth among middle-aged and elderly ladies – the prototypes of Mrs Moore in *A Passage to India* – and to such safe backgrounds he often returned after some bold adventure in a rajah's palace, where a very different side of his nature was expressed in his wearing a turban and Indian dress.[13]

Despite what Frances called his 'prevailing expression . . . of gentle amusement', Forster was as likely to send notes of reproach or rebuke when displeased, as well as notes of gratitude when satisfied. Mattei regularly received both: 'Dear Mattei, That is a very nice letter, except for a sentence which you missed out. The sentence in question is "I am coming on April the 10th". Do you think you could take up your pen and write it now?' Mattei, if less demanding, was also equally capable of hurting by retreating into silence and elusiveness. In contrast to all the letters from Forster which Mattei kept, in Forster's own archive there is only a single postcard from Mattei dating from 1964, and two letters from the following year:

Postcard, Luxor, 13 September 1964. Picture of wine-pressing and bird-snaring, Thebes.

Dear Morgan, I am enjoying this trip very much. The Nil [*sic*] under moonlight is wonderful. The sights to see are enormous. I am in Egypt for 3 days.[14]

Letter, 10 Ogle Street, 20 March 1965.

I was looking at a tree today and noticed that the stronger branches were supporting the weaker, and these in their turn were giving strength to others still weaker. The same as stronger rock should support a lighter one. Then I thought that in the unanimated world this must be a law – The stronger supporting the weaker in the animated world the opposite is true. The big animals destroy the smaller ones, stronger nations subordinating weaker ones; Then I thought that the very same tree would not allow another smaller one to grow nearby; and that religions teach people of mercy, goodness, charity and so on – defying some of the laws of Nature! Then I got confused and must stop.

How are you? Love Mattei[15]

227

Letter, Athlone Ward, Middlesex Hospital, Mortimer Street, 24 June 1965.

Now the cause of my trouble the doctor told me was aspirin. He said I must not take aspirin because my stomach cannot take it . . . So the cause of my trouble was caused because on Monday I took one tablet of Alkaselzer [*sic*] which made my stomach bleed. I am reading *Cider with Rosie* – reading all day long.[16]

Morgan Forster was finally awarded the Order of Merit on his ninetieth birthday, on New Year's Day 1969. Mattei's friendship with Forster lasted until his death eighteen months later.

In May 1962 Eddy's father, the 4th Lord Sackville, died at the age of ninety-one, and Eddy succeeded to his title. Eddy told Jim that in the ten days since his father's death he had written over a hundred letters, thanking people for their condolences. In November the new Lord Sackville took his seat in the House of Lords, but he never chose to speak in a debate. Eddy not only disliked people who argued with him, he also disliked the sound of his own voice – and he avoided any kind of responsibility whenever he could. Death seemed to interest him, however. It was just another fascinating aspect of ill-health. In January 1964 *The Times* asked him to write an obituary for Raymond Mortimer, a 'ghoulish business' he told Leonard Woolf. He was writing at Long Crichel while Raymond was sitting – very much alive – in another room. Despite his genuine ill-health and his hypochondria, Eddy always assumed that he would live as long as his father.

In July 1965 he spent a few days holidaying in the west of Ireland with a friend called Father Christopher Pemberton, who, before his ordination as a Catholic priest, had previously worked for the BBC as an announcer on the Third Programme, which was where Eddy and he had met. Eddy and Pemberton returned to Cooleville together. That evening Eddy had an asthma attack, and he then told Pemberton that he was going to the lavatory. When he failed to return, and Pemberton found the door locked, he fetched a ladder which he propped up outside the lavatory window and climbed in. He found Eddy's body lying on the floor, dead. The doctor's certificate stated 'Acute asthma cardiac failure'. At the time there were various versions of the events which led to Eddy's death, and the story put about by some of Eddy's friends was that he had collapsed and died while listening to his favourite gramophone record, an altogether more seemly concoction than the actual truth.[17]

Rather than be laid to rest in the family vault at Withyham, among the velvet palls and silver coroneted coffins of his eighteenth-century Sackville ancestors – which was what he had told Jim and Desmond twenty years earlier – Eddy had arranged for burial at the local cemetery outside Clogheen. This was as a considerable surprise to the village, but Eddy had become devoted to its inhabitants. His body was laid out in his bedroom in the mantle he wore as a Knight of Malta, and the villagers trooped through to pay their last respects. After the service the funeral procession walked the mile to the cemetery on foot. The mourners included Desmond and Eardley, who had come over from England. At the graveside it was discovered that a kindly neighbour had lined the grave with red roses. The mourners then returned to Cooleville House for lunch. A requiem Mass for Eddy was also held at the Jesuit church in Farm Street at the end of July. Evelyn Waugh, Jim Lees-Milne, Eardley Knollys, Raymond Mortimer, Paul Hyslop and Rosamond Lehmann all attended. The obituary in *The Times* – written by David Cecil – said that Eddy's life might best be summed up by the word 'Dilettante', in its original sense: a man who devoted himself to the arts.

Before the death was confirmed, Julian Jebb phoned Frances to tell her that he had heard a rumour that Eddy had died. 'I have ever since felt increasing sadness – waste – loss – a hole in the world,' she wrote.[18] Eardley, who had been in France, visited Frances on his way to the funeral, looking 'lean, brown and handsome . . . I saw no great signs of grief or regret in him. He seemed indeed alight with some inner jubilation.'[19] Eddy had died just after Mattei had been taken ill with aspirin poisoning. When he arrived in Paris and found a message of 'Grande Urgence' Eardley assumed it must be Mattei, and for two hours he believed that it was. Afterwards he felt only relief. Raymond, however, was almost in tears and obviously 'cut up'. He told Frances that he felt as if 'half his brain had been shot away'. Eddy had been his oldest friend by far, but now Raymond looked 'shrunken, pitiful, crushed'. 'I was so sure he would outlive me. I don't feel I should live much longer,' he said.[20]

Eddy's will had consequences for the remaining Crichel Boys. Cooleville was sold to an American. A twelve-year-old cousin, Teresa Sackville-West, received a legacy of £70,000 and some furniture. Diana, Eddy's sister, was left £10,000. Eardley and Desmond were appointed his executors and trustees, and they, together with Raymond, received £1,000 each. Raymond, and others, had been expecting substantial legacies, perhaps not fully realising that Eddy's sizeable income came from family capital. None of Eddy's staff was left anything. Embarrassed, Eardley, Desmond and Raymond felt obliged to invent small legacies. All Eddy's books were bequeathed to Raymond, although Raymond had more than enough books already. Desmond was left Eddy's piano and all the gramophone records, despite the fact that he had a considerable library of records of his own and had no need of more. Eardley, however, benefitted considerably from Eddy's death. As an art dealer Eardley had over the years acquired a valuable collection of contemporary paintings. Now, thanks to Eddy, he had been gifted a second collection of twentieth-century art which was worth thousands. It was quite possible that Eddy made his will on the assumption that everything would remain as it always had been, but instead Eddy, who all his life tried to spread goodwill, had now in his death achieved the opposite. Raymond, Desmond and Eardley chose to make life tolerable between them by agreeing that he had been ill-advised by his lawyers.

In fact, the resentment felt by Raymond and Desmond against Eardley simmered.* John Banting, Eddy's old and rather hapless friend, received an annuity of £150, for which he must have been deeply grateful – one of the few who was.

Long before Eddy's death and its aftermath, Frances had noticed how the denizens of Long Crichel sometimes got on each other's nerves. They reminded her of old married couples:

> I've been at Crichel since Thursday, all four present. Desmond arrived breathlessly for lunch on Friday looking like a black-beetle in a leather coat and a turtle-neck sweater. This produced an audible groan from Raymond and a very strict po-faced speech later on from Eardley. Why do they mind so much something that is purely superficial and unimportant, and to my eyes rather endearing? . . . Another bit of inter-Crichel criticism: 'Raymond is extraordinary,' Eardley said to me, 'he's just like a little boy. He came into the drawing room yesterday and said: "I've had a sleep and done an hour's work and now I'm going to have a bath." Or else he says: "I've been reading for two hours and now I'm going to bed."' I do notice, now he mentions it this slightly eccentric habit of Raymond's. Old age? Eddy shows this in snoozing off for quite long periods, a look of sad boredom on his tilted face, and perhaps an occasional tiny snore.[21]

Eventually, Eardley decided that he could not take any more. A few days before Eddy died Eardley wrote to him to say that he wished to withdraw from the partnership. Raymond and Desmond were upset. Eardley told Jim that they regarded him as a 'rotter'. Jim wrote back: 'Dearest Rotter, Of course you will be held up to public

---

* Eardley was also made Eddy's literary executor. His archives can be found in the British Library, New York Central Library and at Knole. However, many of his letters – from Graham Greene, Edith Sitwell, André Gide, Benjamin Britten, etc. – were subsequently sold on behalf of the Charleston Trust and dispersed.

obliquy [*sic*] as responsible for ruining the valuable lives of RM and DST. Every drawing room in London will ring with the word Rotter. So, dear, you had better get used to the epithet at once. Anyway you will be a Rotter with me, who am the greatest arch Rotter of our generation.'[22]

The bequests and lawyers and the winding up of Eddy's estate inevitably suffered from delays and complications. Frances complained how quickly the loss of a loved and lovable human being was 'translated and degraded into material terms'.[23] Eardley had already said to her that he could not possibly afford to stay at Long Crichel, and now Raymond told her that much as he wanted to stay on there was no question of his being able to afford it, although he hated the idea of selling up and living in Canonbury permanently. 'In plaintive tones' he told Frances that Eddy had promised to look after him in his old age if he became too tired and ill to work, but there was nothing about this in Eddy's will. Eddy was sixty-four when he died; Raymond was now seventy. For her own part Frances feared the imminent 'closing of the happy, brilliant, charming Crichel episode sorely'.[24] These conversations took place barely a fortnight after Eddy's death.

A month later Frances was back at Long Crichel. The house was full of dramatic tension. Eardley, Raymond and Desmond were joined by Jack Rathbone, Desmond's old friend and housemate. Rathbone was thoroughly enjoying his role 'as Confidant in this Racine play', and spent his time taking everyone for long walks in order to talk the matter through.[25] After dinner on Saturday (Jack was with Desmond next door) Eardley said to Frances, 'To be honest, Eddy died for me ten years ago.' He was being honest, but he had cold-heartedly withdrawn his affection from someone of whom he had once been deeply fond. The following morning Frances went to sit outside in the sun, and Desmond soon came and sat down beside her. He asked if there was any chance that she would join the Crichel *ménage*. He seemed to her so distressed that she could hardly bear to refuse him, but she felt that the strain of living with three other people would be too great – especially if one of them was not Ralph, and Ralph had been dead for five years now. Jack thought Desmond's history was at the root of his agitation – his father's murder, his mother's eccentricity and the death of his sister meant that he had been deprived of a proper family life. Crichel represented this to him. In particular Frances felt she could not live with Raymond – they were too alike, both too 'categorical'.[26] However, she found him more confident than he had been a month earlier. She asked him if he thought of giving up Canonbury and living full time at Long Crichel. 'If you and Eardley, or Dadie were to be here I might; but I'm only prepared to live with old chums,' he said.[27]

Meanwhile, Mattei's business prospered. He took on assistants of his own, and in time he opened a second workshop, in Bourlet Close off Riding House Street, not far from the first one. In 1966 he paid Eardley back for his generosity by buying a small house in Hampshire called The Slade. The house had been a hunting lodge on a country estate, and it was somewhere they could live together. Eardley arrived back at Long Crichel starry-eyed with excitement. Raymond was far from pleased. Frances wrote:

> After hearing about it Raymond went up to his bath, but returned to dinner in a much worse state – preoccupied, self-centred, impatient . . . At dinner he was pitiful, had forgotten to brush his hair, interrupted Eardley's and my remarks with impatient strings of 'Yes, Yes, Yes', burst into thunderous blimpish disapproval of the Labour Party, of Harold Nicolson's bad spelling and all 'young reviewers who didn't read three or four books round every book they reviewed' (as he did for his dull piece about the Zulus last week), and was inclined to contradict everything anyone said in a very dictatorial fashion. I encouraged him to go to bed, sat talking to Eardley for a while and then went up early myself – and brooded.[28]

In the end Pat Trevor-Roper offered 'most quixotically' to share the Long Crichel expenses for a year, though he said he would come down for only five or six weekends or a fortnight in the summer. Raymond was delighted. A legal document was drawn up in which Eardley was deemed to have given his notice of retirement from the Long Crichel partnership on 1 February 1966 and Pat to have started his partnership on 1 July. Pat had been told by his secretary that Eardley did not like him; Eardley said that it was obvious Pat knew by the way that he looked at him so nervously. Raymond continued to wonder whether it was prudent for Eardley to wish to keep so close to Mattei. Nevertheless, Pat moved in, and before long everything at Long Crichel returned to normal.

13

Pat's Room

Pat was a breath of fresh air. He was a warm, friendly and outgoing man, both amused and amusing. Pat – he was also known as 'TR' – was much less reserved than his brother Hugh, but they were close, and they shared an independent-minded, almost anarchic attitude to life. Hugh was bookish and retiring, typical, as Pat would have defined it, of the 'myopic individual', but he had been a great influence on Pat's early life. 'Everyone says he is charming and very unlike me,' Hugh said of his brother. 'I agree with both propositions separately, but don't like them put in such emphatic juxtaposition,' said Hugh about his brother. 'He is a very good eye surgeon, musical, easy-going, and of a political naïveté which leaves me speechless.'[1] And in a letter he wrote: 'he only sends postcards, very brief and almost illegible; I don't think I've ever had a letter from him in my life.'[2]

The brothers' childhood had been dismal, lacking in kindness and encouragement from their parents. As little boys the only affection they ever knew was when they cuddled one another in bed. Expressions of emotion were discouraged, and if they asked their parents questions, they were given 'curiosity killed the cat' for an answer. The unexplained rules of adult behaviour seemed bewildering. When Hugh once innocently remarked to his mother that he worried a great deal about how babies were born she ran out of the room in horror. They also noticed that other people's parents were nicer to them than their own:

perhaps for obscure adult reasons parents merely pretended not to like their own children. Having spent their childhood being mystified, both Pat and Hugh developed a thirst for truth, openness and honesty: there must be rational answers to problems if one found the right place to look. Truth was simple; it was people who complicated things.

After a grim prep school, Pat went to Charterhouse, where he was a senior classics scholar. In 1934 he matriculated as an exhibitioner at Clare College, Cambridge but diverted into medicine in order to join his father's profession. In his third year he read Natural Sciences with Anatomy and then qualified at the medical school at Westminster Hospital. He decided during wartime to specialise in eye surgery. One night he was forced to flee through the streets in his pyjamas after his flat had been bombed. Taking refuge in the hospital air-raid shelter he occupied a mattress beside that of Dr E.F. King, a celebrated eye surgeon. King told Trevor-Roper that he was not clever enough to succeed in some branches of medicine, 'but you'll get to the soul of a person through his eyes'. From 1943 to 1945 Pat served in the New Zealand Medical Corps with the Central Mediterranean Services. Although wounded during the Italian campaign, he was one of the first Allied soldiers to step off a landing craft on to St Mark's Square in Venice.

Pat was temperamentally a busy man. He combined his work at the Westminster Hospital with consultancies at Moorfields Eye Hospital and the King Edward VII Hospital for Officers. Devoted to the cause of better access to ophthalmic medicine at home and abroad – particularly in African countries – he was a founder member of the International Academy of Ophthalmology. He was also a vice-president of the Ophthalmology Society of the United Kingdom and he edited its journal *Transactions* from 1949 to 1988. In the 1960s he campaigned against what he called the 'venal manipulations' of drug companies who organised spurious conferences for doctors at expensive holiday resorts where speakers would endorse the companies' new products. Twenty years later he fought successfully for the repeal of laws which prevented the sale of cheap spectacles, against the resistance of the opticians' lobby; once their monopoly had been broken cheap reading glasses that could be bought over the counter without prescription. In the United Kingdom he helped set up the London Eye Bank, where he instituted a technique of injecting dimethyl sulfoxide into stored retinas in order to increase the shelf life of the transplanted organs. On behalf of the Royal Commonwealth Society for the Blind he planned and founded eye hospitals in Ethiopia and Nigeria during periods of civil war and directed the establishment of mobile eye-treatment units in Yemen and Sierra Leone. He was also a trustee of the Medical Foundation for the Care of Victims of Torture.

Among his private passions were historic architecture and the preservation of old buildings. In 1952 he saw that Plas Teg in Flintshire, the seventeenth-century ancestral home of his own family, the Trevors, was about to be destroyed. The owner had died, but his cousin, who was the heir, had been killed during the war and the house had fallen into disrepair. Pat begged Jim Lees-Milne to help him to save it. They rushed up to north Wales, where they managed to persuade the auctioneer, who had acquired the house in order to pull it down, to sell it to Pat for £1,000. He spent a great deal more on its restoration then eventually sold it on again. Pat also helped found both Save Britain's Heritage and the Spitalfields Historic Buildings Trust, which among its campaigns rescued and renovated Christ Church, Nicholas Hawksmoor's masterpiece in Spitalfields. Pat's London house near Regent's Park was used as the office for the Thirties Society, later to be the Twentieth Century Society, of which he was again a founder member.

The Regent's Park house, to the north of Harley Street, was large, and his thriving professional practice – which made all his other achievements possible – was contained in its consulting rooms. His private patients, as well as personal friends, included Benjamin Britten, Angus Wilson, Francis Bacon and Nancy Mitford. It was said that some of his patients came for a check-up not out of necessity but for the excellence of the conversation. A number of art dealers paid in pictures in lieu of private fees, which both gratified Pat's enthusiasm for art and helped increase his picture collection. However, one client who was dissatisfied was the wife of the Prime Minister Alec Douglas-Home. She thought the spectacles which he had prescribed for her husband, and which he had worn on television, were unflattering and had made a bad impression on the voters. In her opinion it was Pat's fault that her husband had so narrowly lost the 1964 general election. Another client was Clementine Churchill. She willed that her corneas be used for grafting. When the time eventually came Pat did the surgery.

At the end of 1964 Pat was visited by the twenty-four-year-old Bruce Chatwin. A decade earlier Chatwin had suffered damage to one of his eyes during a rugby match at Marlborough, his school. The problem had since recurred and was not confined to his eyesight – he had a multiplicity of symptoms, including 'fatigue, discomfort and a vague subjective unease'. Pat said that Bruce did not so much halluci-nate as fantasise: 'When I look upward I feel brown clouds.' Pat discovered a latent squint, and the effort of trying to pull it straight had caused the stress. He ascribed Bruce's condition to pressure from his boss, Peter Wilson, the Chairman of Sotheby's, and the result of 'a bright, sensitive and rather neurotic young man trying to cut a dash'.[3] Pat recommended that he should give up such concentrated work – with which he was disillusioned – and get away from the office. Bruce told him that he would like to go away and write, which was apparently the first time he had vouchsafed such an ambition. Pat said to Bruce that if he could afford it, he should take six months off and travel. He also told Bruce about his eye hospital in Addis Ababa, which was 'staffed by hopeless Bulgarians', and that he himself went every year to Anglophone Africa. Just a few weeks later, in February 1965, Bruce set off for a long period of recuperation in the Sudan.[4]

It was later said of Bruce Chatwin that he was never fully confident in his sexuality and that his life was a flight from this reality, whether he went to Edinburgh, Patagonia or Australia. Pat Trevor-Roper could not have been more different. He was totally at ease with himself and comfortable in his own skin. From the evidence of his photograph albums the holiday companions he seemed to enjoy the most were parties of young men – in the pictures they are generally wearing swimming trunks, or less. Along with the visual arts, travel was an obsession for Pat. Hugh once claimed – not wholly in jest – that the only countries his brother had never visited were Angola and Paraguay. 'Pat was due to leave for Kurdistan yesterday, but I am thankful to say has given up the plan, because of the changed situation there,' Raymond told Dadie in March 1975. On holiday his travel companions included Ann Fleming, the widow of Ian Fleming. She wrote in a letter to Paddy Leigh Fermor:

> Just returned from a week in Morocco with Patrick Trevor Roper. Forty-eight hours in Rabat then belted down to Marrakesh; had we gone over the Atlas we would have belted too much, so we lotused there. I fear he should have had a younger, less timorous companion: there was a lot of screaming to stop the car to explore fields pale orange with marigolds besides patches of dark purple linaria. So last Sunday morning he was swimming in the Atlantic at El Dadija, and me in unheated empty swimming pool.[5]

Pat toyed with the idea of building a swimming pool near Eardley's old studio at Long Crichel. However, he wanted something like a natural pond, while Desmond and Raymond wanted something more conventional and sensible. As a result nothing at all ever got started.

Pat's bedroom has never been changed. The room, which Pat took over from Eardley, is at the south-west corner of the house and directly over the drawing room. It has two inside and two outside walls, and two windows. In the summertime there is sun in the room

239

for much of the day. The south-facing window re-fashioned by Gerry Wellington looks onto the croquet lawn and rises from floor level, giving the unexpected impression that one can get out of bed in the morning and walk straight outside into mid-air. The west window looks across the garden towards the churchyard and church. According to Frances, one evening after 'a noisy, all-shouting-at-once argument' about God broke out, Pat sat on the fence regarding his religious beliefs.[6] Pat was the only Crichel Boy to attend regular service at the parish church, and he also gave money to the church for its upkeep.

In one corner of the room – as in other bedrooms in the house – there is a small, triangular washbasin. These bedroom basins, which were installed by Miss Duncan before the war, are all in slightly different arrangements, and the sink in Pat's room is behind glazed doors, like the doors of a china cabinet. The room is painted in different shades of blue. The walls are a soft blue-grey, and much of the furniture is the same blue-grey, with details picked out in gold. There is a bed with a chaise longue at its foot, a wardrobe, a large, red, comfortable armchair, a built-in corner wall cupboard, a low chair with a decoratively carved back and a table in front of the window overlooking the church. On top of the chest of drawers there is a 'Self-Recording Barometer' manufactured by Sharman D. Neill Ltd of Belfast and a mother-of-pearl writing box for stationery and postcards.

On the mantelpiece above the grate Pat placed a small Shakespeare bust and a few Victorian ornaments, as well as a wooden Buddha and a small metal plaque from a Thailand Ophthalmic Society conference. There are also postcards – one of them has a picture of the Emperor Franz Josef of Austria – and there is a photograph of an old boyfriend at a dinner party. Above the fireplace hangs a dark, mid-nineteenth-century landscape, with two small shadowy figures in the bottom left-hand corner. Among the other pictures in the room there is a collage portrait of Queen Victoria by Roger Fry.

There are three bookcases, as well as three shelves attached to the wall which hold *Baedeker Guides* to northern Italy, southern Italy and Switzerland, and a French Blue Guide (*Rome et ses Environs*). Among the books are novels by Robin Maugham, the nephew of Somerset Maugham, a Cambridge contemporary and friend; some of the Maughams have handwritten dedications to Pat. A *Queer Reader* and *The Penguin Book of Gay Short Stories* stand among books about ophthalmology and the eye. When the Japanese writer Yukio Mishima came to London it was Pat who was asked to take him on a tour of the city's gay bars, clubs and decadent night spots.

There are also books on travel and conservation; the Second World War – especially on Italy, where Pat saw active service; *Transactions of the Ancient Monument Society*; the *Almanach de Gotha*; and a few books by his brother Hugh. Also, *And So to Bed, An Album Compiled from his BBC Feature* by Edward Sackville-West, inscribed 'For Eardley with best love from Eddy, October '47'. It was as if in Eardley's rush to leave the house as soon as possible this book had been left behind almost deliberately. The author was dead, and everything had changed.

Folded between the pages of *The Golden Echo*, the first volume of the autobiography of David Garnett, is a letter to Pat from its author:

> You will find Noel Olivier Richards whom you knew at the Westminster Hospital & who was the nearest I had to a sister & no doubt many other friends, which will encourage you to read the books. The second volume is about the first world war & the years I spent working as an agricultural labourer living with Vanessa & Duncan. I hope I shall collect the bifocals on Monday & fly to France on Tuesday. Thank you again for being not only such a skilful surgeon but also the person you are.

Pat either wrote or edited eight books of his own, mostly in his professional field, but in 1954 he wrote a preface to a book on four eighteenth-century studies of court music by a writer called Alan Yorke-Long, 'an outstanding and unforgettable person – six feet two inches in height and proportionately broad', who two years earlier had died of cancer when he was only twenty-eight.[7] Eddy and Desmond had helped Pat tidy up his manuscripts. Pat's other books included *A Textbook for Diploma Students* (1955); *Lecture Notes in Ophthalmology* (1960), which went into seven editions and was translated into five languages; *Ophthalmology* (Pocket Consultant Series, 1981); and he contributed to *Diseases of the Cornea* (1962). Pat also wrote frequently to the correspondence pages of the *British Medical Journal* or contributed a 'Personal View'. He delighted in the arcane. His letter to the *BMJ* of 16 January 1971 on the association of sex with blindness was typical:

the myth of the evil eye (primarily as the destroyer of fertility) still permeates our society, and the ghost of St. Lucy [the patron saint of Ophthalmologists] is always waiting in the wings . . . I was reminded of this when I read the Bowman lecture given by Henry Power, the great pioneer of corneal grafting (and vice-president of the Ophthalmological Society of the United Kingdom), in which he described how amblyopia, retinal haemorrhages, trachoma, neuroretinitis (though 'only in young ladies'), total blindness, not to mention agoraphobia and other bizarre symptoms were all attributable to masturbation. Admittedly this was in 1888 . . .

The book by which Pat became widely known to the general public was *The World Through Blunted Sight: An Inquiry into the Influence of Defective Vision on Art and Character*. Published in 1970, its first edition was dedicated to Raymond and Desmond.* In the preface he wrote:

---

* Later editions were dedicated to Herman Pasma Chan, PTR's partner from the 1970s.

Throughout these pages I have sought to trace the influence of altered vision on the personality of man; and, by reflecting on some writers and painters whose sight was impaired, to harness the nature of this impediment to the pattern of their artistry. It is always rash for a scientist to venture from the solid shores of his exact science into such speculative waters; and, if I have seemed to flounder among too many unrelated disciplines, let me plead that, by constantly retreating behind the theories and experiments of others, I have tried to let these speak for themselves, and only rarely presumed to arbitrate. I am conscious, too, that I may have digressed more than a little on the way. Perhaps this also may be excused, for the marches of our subject are ill-defined, and there are some tantalizing pastures just off-course, into which it was a constant temptation to stray.[8]

In fact, the author of *The World Through Blunted Sight* constantly gives in to temptation and wanders into all manner of tantalising pastures. Desmond used to parody Pat's idiosyncratic manner when speaking, and of his beginning a sentence with the word 'That'. Pat's book is very much like an illustrated lecture, and it can be difficult to plot any argument other than to trace 'the influence of altered vision on the personality of man'. Some of the illustrations are startling, such as the picture of Wyndham Lewis's brain showing a pituitary tumour pressing on the optic nerve 'which can still be inspected in the pathological museum at Westminster Medical School', and *The World Through Blunted Sight* is full of fascinating anecdotes and quotations. During the course of its six chapters from 'The Unfocused Image' to 'Total Blindness', Trevor-Roper considers El Greco's astigmatism, Dürer's squint, Turner's cataracts and Renoir's myopia. Discussing the Impressionists, he writes:

we may be tempted to wonder how different the world of art might have been if all these famous painters had been forced to wear glasses constantly. We might even agree with Mr Cross, the Vicar of Chew Magna in Somersetshire, who once declared, 'The newly invented optick glasses are immoral since they pervert the natural sight, and make things appear in an unnatural and false light,' or with the epitaph in S. Maria Maggiore in Florence which says: 'Here lies Salvino d'Armato of the Armati of Florence, Inventor of spectacles: may God forgive him his sins. AD1317'.[9]

And, as a closing reflection in the appendix at the very end of the book, Pat adds:

The English, with their nonconformist consciences, and in contrast to the Latins, are said to be largely scotophiliac, preferring their intercourse in the darkness. One recalls the curious finding that when the women attending a provincial hospital were questioned why they had brought their child for circumcision – was it because their husbands were circumcised – a quarter of them did not know the answer, as they had never seen their husbands naked.[10]

The first impression Frances had of Pat was that she liked him very much – 'a quick, eager, clever man with a passion for facts and information'[11] – although an amusing account of 'an all-bugger weekend at Crichel, six of them'[12] from Julian made her think again. Julian told her he was quite shocked by the amount of anti-women talk there had been, particularly from Pat, who said that female minds were inferior and that women didn't deserve a better education. Pat, however, had many women friends and probably enjoyed being provocative. Inevitably, because the circles in which they moved intersected, Frances and Pat met frequently, and she mentioned him often in her diaries, even if her feelings were sometimes ambiguous:

Arriving in London on a warm, scented and golden autumn day – euphoria. Why? I travelled up from Crichel with Pat (he drove

244

me at a steady ninety miles an hour, but much too well to alarm me, into Salisbury), thence by train. Here is someone I liked and was drawn to and interested by at first meeting, but a sort of wooden barrier erected itself from the feeling that he despised women (hearing so, in fact, from Julian). Well perhaps he does; but now I feel he has become a friend. He has quick sympathy and the power to grasp other people's thoughts.[13]

While they stood on the platform at Salisbury station waiting for the London train Pat talked to Frances about his father, the doctor, who was now over eighty years old; although Pat's father was sincerely grieving for his wife, who had recently died, he had also just taken a mistress.

On an outing to Badbury Rings Frances badly gashed her shin on some barbed wire. Back home at Long Crichel she asked Pat for a piece of Elastoplast. He gave her all he could find, but it was much too small for 'the large messy crescent of bleeding, distorted flesh which was revealed'.[14] There was, she said, something comical about all this. It turned out that there was neither more Elastoplast, and no other dressings or antiseptic ointment in the house. Back in London Frances's own doctor gave her anti-tetanus and antibiotic injections. 'Of course he's absolutely brilliant at his own line but fairly hopeless at every other branch of medicine,' said the doctor who knew Pat well.[15]

Pat was interested in the history of the house at Long Crichel in a way that none of the others had ever been, which was why it was Pat who answered her letter and continued the correspondence when, out of the blue, St Barbe Hill wrote and sent photographs c/o the Old Rectory. Pat also made a list of the principal past employees. The list started with the Deverells. Mrs Deverell's cooking might have been excellent, but she was personally erratic. When she threw herself into a stream to try and drown herself the effect was tragicomic – and the unfortunate obvious comparison with Virginia Woolf was decidedly more comic than tragic. In September 1955, even before Eddy had bought Cooleville, Eardley wrote to Eddy about the Deverells' recent behaviour:

> The Devs, though up and down and at the moment better have been very cross and bad-tempered I have thought and it has just occurred to me that possibly they have heard talk of your Irish projects and imagine that you are leaving here for ever without having told them. If my surmise is right do put them in the picture. Otherwise I can't think why they have been so ratty but anyhow they are going to have a week off before you come back and we do our best to please them![16]

However, when they returned from their holiday, the Deverells gave their notice. Eddy told a friend that they were at 'sixes and sevens'.[17] (The friend sent him some pâté as a consolation.) As 1955 ended with the imminent departure of the Deverells, Eddy finalised his arrangements for the purchase of Cooleville and filed his last 'Gramophone Notes' to the *New Statesman*. The Deverells moved into a caravan park at Whitchurch near Blandford. Eddy continued to pay them a regular pension of £150 a year. This ended with his death, which caused considerable consternation until Eddy's executors and the Sackville estate managed to find funds to prolong the allowance. Nevertheless, Deverell continued with his complaints: 'Just a note to let you know I have to go into Weymouth General Hospital for another operation. I think it has been brought about because I am run-down and don't get enough to eat. I only have one meal a day as I can't afford more. I will let you know when the bed is open for me.'[18]

Desmond reported to Frances that, with great trepidation, a new couple had been engaged at vast expense: 'So pray for us and for yourselves during your next Crichel visit.'[19] The new couple were called Joseph and Edwige Hillier. The former was no longer a butler but a 'house parlourman' and Mrs Hillier a 'housekeeper'. In 26

January 1960 they were witnesses to Eddy's will. Raymond wrote to Eddy to tell him that Hillier was also in hospital for an operation

> but Mrs H says she can manage with Mrs Andrews coming in a little earlier. Eardley and I have bought a Hoover washing machine because Mrs H pines to do the laundry and the village woman is getting very old and dilatory. It costs £64 and I hope you approve and will send me a cheque for a quarter of this amount. It ought to pay for itself in about a year, as laundry costs 30s a week. How wonderful to have a servant who asks to do more work.[20]

After five years, in June 1961, the Hilliers also gave notice – he was drinking, 'and your drink too,' Jim told Eardley:

> I am sorry but thought last time I was there that they were both too hysterical. The real trouble is that he has not enough to do. Men servants indoors always go to pot if they are English; not so rapidly if foreigners who never rest and work all the day in the garden or garage somewhere and hate leisure except to go to bed and f... from time to time. We have got a Spanish couple coming to Alderley who have to come to us because we have got their permit, and must by law apparently stay three months, so not until October shall we be skivvy-hunting again.[21]

Desmond enjoyed recording things. From the beginning of October 1961 he began to log the monthly household expenses in an account book. That month the food total came to £53 6s 11d, the largest amount – £26 18s 1d – being spent at Durden's, the grocer. Two shops – Coward's and Hunt's – supplied the fish; meat came from Peaple the butcher, the milk from Harrison and bread from G.W. Green, the baker. Despite the fact that a gardener was employed to look after the six acres of land owned by Long Crichel House, the kitchen garden had only old and unproductive apple trees, and, according to Desmond's bookkeeping, 'veg' to the value of £4 6s still had to be bought. Occasionally there were exceptional deliveries, such as one for cigarettes. Raymond was a heavy smoker. The downstairs lavatory, which had sheet music for wallpaper, invariably had some of Raymond's cigarette butts floating in the lavatory pan – despite all the little notes on the walls informing the visitor as to what could and could not be flushed away.

Household supplies arrived at the house in regular deliveries from the shops, carried in little vans which wound their way through the villages and the back lanes of east Dorset. In other ways Long Crichel became more inaccessible. The nearest station, at Blandford Forum on the Somerset and Dorset Railway, which ran from Bath to Bournemouth, closed to passengers in the wake of the Beeching Report in 1966, a century after it had opened. It briefly stayed open for freight, but the tracks were lifted three years later.* Inaccessibility and general social changes made it harder to attract staff willing to live in. Pat's list includes three names – Shiers, Winter, Robertson – who between them account for six years after the departure of Mr and Mrs Hillier, none of them having wanted to stay for long.

In October 1967 Raymond reported to Dadie Rylands that they had just engaged a cook for Long Crichel, 'a near lady aged 59 in trousers'.[22] She was bringing not only three dogs but two pet Jersey cows. He fancied that the comfortable accommodation they could offer the cows was her reason for accepting the job. Meanwhile, he said, the Italian man servant they were employing was growing a little calmer: he had been telling him how to make a béchamel sauce. General gossip and expressions of anxiety about the servant problem was, in Raymond's letters, every bit as important as who had attended the latest Long Crichel dinner party:

---

* Blandford Forum was one of several stations mourned by the musical duo Flanders and Swann in 'The Slow Train', their lament for the imminent closure of stations throughout the United Kingdom: 'No more will I go to Blandford Forum and Mortehoe on the slow train from Midsomer Norton and Mumby Road . . .'

Our dear gardener here is in hospital, whether for two days or an epoch is not known yet. How we could replace him I can't imagine. Our servant in Canonbury seems on the verge of a nervous breakdown. How stupid it is to depend on increasingly unobtainable servants! But how could I start cooking at 73? (Raymond to Dadie, 29 July 1968)

[Miss Rayner is] well-satisfied with the oil-heated Aga, an improvement on solid fuel. (Raymond to Dadie, December 1968)

A burglar seized some silver of Pat's and a fine clock of Desmond's from LC, but seems to have taken nothing of mine except an old silver salad cruet (and a silver candle stick, one of a pair) – which Desmond believes perhaps rightly to be modern and his own . . . Poor Des had a retina detached, luckily before Pat left, who put it right with only one week in hospital. He is remaining at Long Crichel with the consent of the cowherdress for the next fortnight. (Raymond to Dadie, 24 March 1969)

We practically engaged a new lady . . . A sort of female Hitler Jugend Aryan type – wearing black jackboots (no spurs that I could see), hot pants, leather jacket (wet variety) and too-raven black hair. Fortunately current housekeeper agreed to stay 'until her next bout of depression whenever that might be'. (Jim to Rosamond, 5 April 1971)

Miss Rayner has given us notice, but I have high hopes about a man I'm expecting to see today, elderly but not alarmed by the rural isolation. (Raymond to Dadie, 26 August 1971)

Of course the man servant I engaged has bailed out without even looking at Long Crichel. (27 September 1971)

Thank you for your letter. I'm hoping to hear that you will soon want a room in this two-fork, one-gable private hotel, without any private bathrooms or bidets or showers or loos.

And also at Long Crichel. The three of us have just engaged a cook, who came at her suggestion for last weekend to see the place and let us try her cooking. She is elegant, good-looking, thin, I should think a well-preserved fifty with a married son at Worcester, almost a lady – and has been a successful hairdresser and teacher of hairdressing in Cape Town. She is interested in cooking, and has what I consider the right ideas about it. Mystery – why does she want to bury herself at Long Crichel with nobody to talk to except us and Mrs Andrews [the housekeeper]. She says she likes being alone and always has, and that she hates hairdressing. (Raymond to Dadie, 11 October 1971)

Mrs Hughes continues to be a smiling super-treasure, but in Canonbury we have a glum unskilled temporary cook. (Raymond to Dadie, 6 February 1972)

You have an open invitation to Long Crichel (except in February when it will be cookless). (Raymond to Dadie, 30 November 1973)

Dinner with Desmond: He had a row with Raymond (he called it the 'first in a lifetime' though it certainly wasn't), about the servant problem at Crichel. I see both sides as usual. I suppose Des must have got very excited because Raymond said suddenly, 'I think you'd better go to bed.' Desmond (getting scarlet in the face at the mere memory) shouted: 'Raymond, you *can't* talk to me like that – you really *can't.*' (Frances to Dadie, 15 August 1975)

Mrs Hughes has had a stroke 'very slight' says optimist Des but Raymond says he can't tell till after the weekend whether our much looked-forward-to weekend is on or off . . . Raymond says she is very lethargic as a result of taking anti-high blood pressure pills. I can't imagine why she's not being doing so for years – she talks about it enough. But I fear she's a hysteric. I've taken such pills for *years* regularly with nothing but good results. (Frances to Dadie, Thursday, July 1976)

We have had a horrid blow. A fortnight ago Mrs Hughes had a heart attack, was taken to Salisbury Hospital, seemed to be recovering then died. I had become quite fond of her, more so than Pat or Desmond. (Raymond to Dadie, 16 December 1976)

[The mother and daughter are] well-educated, not genteel in the bad sense, or hardly, and seems sensible as well as amiable. Cooking not quite what we would like, but will probably improve. In London Paul and I have a married woman of Hungarian, probably Jewish, origin who used to work in a circus with a CHIMPANZEE. (Raymond to Dadie, 7 January 1978)

In 1979 Mrs Best arrived. Mrs Best lived in Moor Crichel, and she had previously been cook at Crichel House. 'Dear Mr Shawe-Taylor,' she wrote at the end of January, 'I am not certain what date you wanted me to come for a short trial. Perhaps you would let me know either by letter or a phone message via Cmdr Marten. I hope you seriously consider me for the post of housekeeper as I am sure my daughters and me would be very happy at Long Crichel House.' Mrs Best came with her two daughters, and she stayed for years. She was aggressive and could be quite scary. Depending on one's tastes, her cooking was found to be satisfactory, excellent or just 'beige'. She also installed a microwave oven so that her leftover food could be reheated. This was a novelty in itself, since it meant that, in theory at least, her employers could now cook or, rather, reheat food for themselves: they had never been greatly encouraged, or particularly welcomed, to enter into the kitchen before. On one occasion, when Cyril Connolly and Janetta Jackson came to stay, they were invited by Michael Pitt-Rivers for drinks. They went under strict instructions that they must return in time for dinner at Long Crichel. Instead, Cyril had disloyally entertained Pitt-Rivers and his guests, who included Lord David Cecil, with impersonations of his Long Crichel hosts – and carried on drinking, which meant they got later and later. Meanwhile, Mrs Best's meal became colder and colder, and everyone at Long Crichel grew more and more anxious and cross. Cyril and Janetta, who was driving, eventually turned up hours late. This was long remembered. Cyril had broken an absolute house rule. Meals had to be served on time – and Mrs Best was in charge.

Inevitably there were times when there was no one available to do the cooking, which meant that either family or guests – like Frances – had to step in to do the cooking. Raymond believed in fine cooking. In fact everything he knew of kitchen and domestic matters he had picked up second-hand from his former cook who every week used to take the bus along Oxford Street to Selfridge's food hall. Desmond was less interested but wanted to be well fed. Pat was not interested at all in food and hurried his meals. This was considered annoying and very bad form.

14

Through a Vodka Glass Darkly

After his unhappy school years and his hospital service during the First World War, Raymond had been irresistibly drawn to the European south and had taken every chance to explore the galleries, the landscapes and the restaurants of France, Italy and Spain. Raymond saw himself as a European. In 1935 he wrote the preface to *The Spirit of London*, a book by an Austrian–Jewish writer called Paul Cohen-Portheim. Despite his wartime internment, Cohen-Portheim, who died in 1932, had great affection for Great Britain and her citizens. 'In itself it is a small thing to be at home equally on the Zattere and Kufürstendamm, in the Rue de Lappe, and in Islington,' Raymond wrote. 'But it is upon the spread of an attitude to Europe like his that the continuance of civilisation depends.' It was what Cohen-Portheim believed and so did he. Later Raymond's enthusiasm for travel took him to the Orient, and after the Second World War he was bowled over (a favourite expression) by the colours of India and Ceylon. In 1952 he wrote to Kenneth Clark from Madras:

I've been intoxicated by India ... The Matisse brilliance of the clothes in the North; & here, in the South, sombre complicated colours, puce, maroon, ochre, bottle-green, indigo. And the Ceylon landscapes are gorgeous. I long to [bring?] some of our painters here: they would surely open their eyes to the visible world. If one lives in the Euston Road,* there is hardly a colour to look at.[1]

A lifelong curiosity about people, places and things took Raymond to Indochina and Burma and the Mayan jungles of Central America in search of the ruins of the past. Raymond's photograph albums were different from Pat's. Instead of pictures of boys in swimming trunks, his albums were filled with photographs of his sight seeing expeditions.

In September 1966 Raymond went to Russia. In another letter to Kenneth Clark he said that the last time he went to Russia forty years earlier was at a very bad moment; now that he was going back he was thrilled at the prospect of seeing much that he had missed. Raymond was one of a party which included Frances, who had never been to Russia before. Frances was full of enthusiasm – 'swamped by excited anticipation and sense of adventure'[2] – whereas Raymond, when he started a journal a couple of days after the party arrived, already sounded weary: 'Once again – and I fear probably the last time on an arduous journey. The preparations have produced too much anxiety. What do I expect? From forty years ago I remember the queer *coup d'oeil*, but nothing about the food oddly . . . Food will be dull & meals andante molto . . . Water hot but no heating (or plugs).' Frances was delighted by her breakfast of fruit juice, water, sweet buns, toast, strawberry jam and excellent, if milkless, tea. She made no complaints about the heating or the lack of plugs, and she said she thought that the rooms were magnificent. Despite his complaints, and although the north always meant less to him than the sunlit Mediterranean, seven years later, at the age of 78, Raymond sailed around the Northern Cape as far as the Arctic frontiers of Norway and Russia.

---

* A reference to the School of Drawing and Painting in London. The school was founded in 1937 but closed at the outbreak of war in 1939; the 'Euston Road School' was known for representational rather than avant-garde art.

Despite a basic mutual affection Raymond and Desmond did not always get on well. Frances said that Raymond kept drawing her attention to 'the heavy weather Desmond makes over every little task', 'his passion for keeping waiting', 'his appalling hair-do' (Desmond was more or less bald). On the other hand, Desmond complained that at Long Crichel, even in the finest weather, 'Raymond never went out of doors but spent twenty-four hours stewing, sighing and smoking over his review all morning, snoozing in the smoke-filled room all afternoon and all night. The smell of stale smoke in his room was appalling. Wouldn't it be a good thing if he sometimes took a little walk?'[3]

At the beginning of July 1971 Raymond, Dadie and Frances discussed going together on an expedition to Italy in September. Unfortunately, Desmond suggested to Frances that he would like to join them. Raymond wrote to Dadie:

> I was dismayed because he is so excitable and fussy and prone to keep one waiting. Nor did I presume that you would welcome the notion. Was I mistaken about that? In any case I summed up my courage and told him I was embarrassed and apologetic, but could not face travelling with two such powerful personalities as you and himself. I'm afraid that he must have been hurt, but he took it very well, saying he didn't realise that I had found you difficult in Brazil. Of course I didn't. There is no-one I enjoy travelling with so intensely. But I muttered something about your being sometimes rather temperamental, and found that the least painful form of evasion that I could think up. If you should be anxious for him to come I suppose I ought to face it. But four is less good for travel in my view than three, and I knew from Pat that he would keep us waiting almost every day in hotel halls. 'Oh dear,' as Fanny says, it is seldom tactful to propose joining a trip arranged by friends; but Desmond likes his friends so much, especially you that it would never occur to him that he could be thought trying or *de trop*.[4]

Frances wrote about what she called 'this painful situation' in her diary: Desmond had no idea that his 'violent excitability' made him an impossible travelling companion. Raymond spoke to him after breakfast: 'Of course poor Desmond was hurt and spoke to me later about it. I tried to pour unguents on the wound as far as possible, including a suggestion that he and I took a trip some time, to show that by me at least he wasn't unwanted.'⁵ Desmond had other eccentricities. While staying in a village in northern Spain with Frances, Ralph and Janetta he sunbathed naked on a patch of dried grass behind the gates in front of the house. Crowds of ragged and barefoot village boys used to gather and stare in wonder at the distinguished critic's pale, sun-creamed body – which was doubtless what he was hoping for.

On holiday Raymond's faults, as Frances saw them, were his insistence on always getting his way and his habit of distributing what he called 'pearls of wisdom'. In 1972 Raymond, Frances and Dadie had a fortnight's holiday in Italy, a journey which started in Rome and finished in Milan. They spent the time exploring the cities, visiting churches and art galleries, and eating, drinking and bickering among themselves. In Verona Dadie – who was like a scout master, always charging ahead – was interested in more than just art galleries: 'After dinner he wanted to walk to the Piazza again (Dadie's third visit today). He is excited by the handsome young men with their renaissance hair and elegant clothes and figures, gets carried away and waves and beckons at them embarrassingly, murmuring they are "very pretty".'⁶ By Bergamo the journey was coming to an end. Arriving late in the art gallery they were faced with an astonishing collection: Botticelli, Bellini, Antonello da Messina, Lorenzo Monaco, Titian, Tintoretto, Velásquez, Guardi, Raphael, Perugino. Frances was so excited that she told Raymond she could not bear being constantly interrupted by his constant lectures on what she was looking at. Afterwards she said she felt ashamed and guilty – making the excuse that she was feeling unwell. Exactly a week later Frances was back home in West Halkin

Street. 'I think and ponder about the structure of Raymond's character and the strange way his mind works,' she wrote.[7]

In 1977 Raymond, who had already been appointed CBE and made an officer of the French *Légion d'honneur*, was awarded the prize of the Académie française. Frances accompanied him to France for what she called 'Raymond's coronation in Paris'. 'Dear fellow he was terribly nervous,' she told Dadie:

> & it was hard cheese that owing to the too long speech of his friend Maurice Druon[*] & the fact that the eminent audience (mostly over 90, propped on crutches & sticks, & all of them Academicians or Monsieur de or Ministre de this or that) were standing & couldn't do so forever, owing to this Raymond had to substitute a shorter ad lib speech for the one he had taken a fortnight to write. In frog of course.[8]

Raymond's health and memory were beginning to fail, as he acknowledged in a letter written in November 1978, a year after the Paris trip: 'The beastly truth is that I have become a very fond foolish old man . . . But I lose everything, forget engagements as well as the names of my oldest friends, drop things, tumble over and wake up feeling tired.'[9] Playing bridge was now almost his only recreation. That past summer he had felt too feeble to play croquet, a game he had loved and played ruthlessly. Nowadays he hardly ever went to a play or to see an opera or a film. It was an effort to do anything except read – which he fancied he did as fast as ever. Twelve months later Raymond was in Bart's Hospital suffering from kidney failure. His brain was now working on 'only one cylinder,' he said.[10] 'Bad news of Raymond again,' Jim wrote in his diary. 'He is bedridden and said to be sinking.'[11] And on Thursday, 9 January 1980 Raymond died.

---

[*] French novelist (1918–2009) who during the war broadcast for the BBC and was later a war correspondent. In 1947 he translated ESW's *The Rescue* into French as *Ithaque deliveree*.

That Sunday Jim wrote in his diary at greater length:

Dear old Raymond died this week. Expected and not to be mourned for: he was eighty-five and exceedingly unhappy. The last day he did not speak at all, and the following morning he was found dead in his bed. I grew very attached to him. There was something paternal about him and sweet. At first I was scared of him for he was censorious and picked one up, demanding explanations of one's idiotic remarks. He was solely a critic and not creative, with a lynx eye for the syntactical faults of other writers better than himself, as I have discovered from H[arold]. N[icolson].'s papers. He quite properly held my writings in contempt and latterly would not even review my books. This made A. cross, and hurt me a bit. But I bear no resentment whatever. There is to be no memorial service at his request. In a way this makes me sad, for he seems to disappear in a puff of wind. Will he be remembered by posterity? Only by specialising scholars. Yet for fifty years he was a famous and feared reviewer. He knew every literary person of his own and the ensuing generation. He was received at every party of note, and was revered by everyone with aspirations, either social or literary.[12]

Shortly after Raymond's death Paul Hyslop lent Jim, who was writing Harold Nicolson's biography, two packets of his love letters to Raymond. 'No doubt he did love R. I have never read any of Harold's letters so uninhibited,' Jim wrote. 'As much lust letters as love letters, and curiously not as quotable as Harold's to Vita.'[13] In September 1980, only nine months after Raymond's death, an extract from Jim's book relating to the Nicolson–Mortimer affair was published in *The Times*. Jim was not pleased, but his publisher told him it would be good publicity.

Desmond's obituary of Raymond for the *Sunday Times* concentrated on Raymond's great passions – for books and for travel:

He was the most bookish of men – it was a word he often used in print and in speech: the most deeply distressed if chance or unwonted lack of foresight left him deprived of a book during the briefest wait or journey. On the other hand he was not what is called a bibliophile; and not quite, in the old-fashioned sense of the term, a man of letters.

Notwithstanding his acute visual sense, he did not care *greatly* for books as physical objects; and a few ashes from his perpetual cigarette would often find their way into the gully between the pages. Books innumerable passed through his hands (he was scrupulous in returning those that he had borrowed to the London Library of which he was a life-long pillar), and books innumerable filled his disordered shelves in Canonbury, as well as the Dorset rectory that I happily shared with him and various other friends after the Second World War. But he hadn't what you would call a library: he had no set either there or in London, that was likely to be quite complete, even of cherished authors like Balzac or Colette or Henry James. There might even be a Jane Austen missing.

To this rule one exception must be made. Although Raymond could face with equanimity gaps in the run of an author's works that would drive a collector-bookman frantic, he would sink into instant gloom if deprived of the encyclopedias, dictionaries and works of reference that were his daily bread. For there were two ruling passions in his life: intellectual curiosity, and love of the visible world . . . Moreover [this] range was uncommonly wide: a fact that helped to make him one of those rare and desirable literary critics capable of tackling books on all manner of subjects.[14]

Desmond had more to say about how much Raymond enjoyed dining out and staying in beautiful houses, as well as the intellectual seriousness of Bloomsbury and Montparnasse; then how in later life he enjoyed 'the comings and goings of his friends, and of *their* friends, in the quiet of rural Dorset'. The obituary ended with a mention of his customary

> pre-dinner bath: a ritual to which he was as devoted as any ancient Roman. (If he had written that sentence, he would have been down on his knees to discover whether the Romans *did* take their baths before dinner.) His best ideas, he used to say, came to him in the bath, from which he would descend, refreshed, renewed and ready for anything that might be proposed by the youngest of new visitors, or the oldest of old friends.[15]

In his will Raymond made a few bequests, including a legacy of £100 to Mrs Andrews the housekeeper. He left his drawings by Matisse and Cocteau to Monroe Wheeler of Hay-meadows, Rosemont, New Jersey. To Desmond, Raymond bequeathed all his personal chattels still in Long Crichel House. All his 'property real and personal situate in any part of the world' was left to Paul Hyslop, his friend and companion for more than forty years. He failed, however, to appoint a literary executor. Essentially Raymond was a modest man, and in all probability he assumed that after his death no one would want to read his writings again and they would not be republished. Eight years before he died Dadie asked him about his literary archive. He replied that Paul had been instructed to hand over his papers to Dadie in order that they might be deposited in the archives at King's College, Cambridge. 'Your continuing willingness to undertake the Herculean task [of sorting my papers] touches me profoundly,' he wrote, 'though I should love to have a selection [of reviews] printed the prospect provokes silly nervosity.'[16]

In the days before his death Raymond wrote to Dadie to say that his letters from E.M. Forster were 'in a hell of a muddle all mixed up with unpaid bills'.[17] His handwriting, which was once neat and tidy, now sprawled over the page. A selection of Raymond's papers was later sold through Heywood Hill's bookshop in Curzon Street for

£500. The description in the catalogue – stray fragments of a literary life – reads:

> 152 Mortimer (Raymond) Collection of 15 MS notebooks and four photograph albums 1905 – c1950. 12 limp-bound exercise books, one in wrappers, a ring-binder, a 1928 appointments diary: over 1200pp. Most of the material is early, including work-books from Oxford (essays on prose-style, the representation of minorities, Matthew Arnold, Shakespeare, Bunyan, the metaphysicals), juvenile poems (copied into a book by his aunt) and fiction: the MS of a large part of a novel, other stories, 'The Lion's Den' (published in the London Mercury and selected for The Best Short Stories of 1924). Diaries include an extensive account of a visit to Italy (?1920: over 100pp) and a short journal from Paris in the Second World War (c15pp, mostly notes: Vercors, Aragon, Duff Cooper &c). Later material includes drafts for book reviews and a fat ring-binder full of notes on suicide, madness, drunkenness, masochism. All four albums date from the period 1905 – 1918, many of the photographs being of the hospital where Mortimer worked in the war.

Also for sale for between £10 and £50 were a number of his books. Most of the remainder of Raymond's papers was eventually sold to Princeton University, New York.

The television documentary which Julian Jebb had been preparing on Tennyson was filmed, in part, on the Isle of Wight with John Betjeman. (Julian also went with Betjeman to Australia.) 'On John's last night [on the island] we have a celebration dinner,' Julian wrote in his diary. 'John and I do a parody of Woman's Hour. Box cameras flash and the best from the White Hart cellars is produced. We talk about the pleasures of filming and all the crew agree that it is among the five chief pleasures of the world.'[18] From 1976 onwards Julian co-produced *Arena Cinema*, which was presented by Gavin Millar, and there were several full-length documentaries for the BBC programme *Omnibus*, featuring Christopher Isherwood, John Osborne, Patricia Highsmith and Anthony Powell among others. He was also doing written journalism, but aside from *A Night's Darkness, A Day's Sail*, there were two documentaries that stood out in Julian's career: one with Barry Humphries as Dame Edna Everage, *La Dame aux Gladiolas*, and the other a family portrait of the Mitford sisters. The Mitford programme included conversations about childhood and the sisters' father Lord Redesdale; it also featured Julian, together with Diana Mosley and Deborah Devonshire, talking about the war and about the Mitford voice, and there was some archive film of Nancy, who had died in 1973:

Nancy: Well, I enjoyed it very much, I'm ashamed to say, an awful thing to say, but it was very lively in London in the war, everybody was in a good temper, nice, jolly.

Diana: But then she was a fire-watcher and she learnt what to do and she gave up two nights a week for fire-watching in Curzon Street. And then somebody said, 'Would she lecture to the new fire-watchers?' and she said, 'Yes, I would,' so she gave up another night to lecture. When she had done it about three times the lady who ran it all said, 'Would you mind giving up the lectures?' and she said, 'No, not in the least, but could you tell me why?' 'Well,' she said, 'it's your voice, your accent irritates people so much that they would like to put you on the bonfire.'

Julian: Have you ever suffered from the Mitford voice?

Diana: No, never. You see, I have never been a public speaker, and I've never been in public life. No doubt if I had I would have suffered, but it has just been my private sorrow to have the Mitford voice.

Julian: (to Deborah) Weren't you so keen about it yourself?

Deborah: We are saddled with it, aren't we? It's awful. Living in the North of England it's even sillier than it is living anywhere else.

Julian: But you don't personally mind it much, do you?

Deborah: I'm afraid I do, yes, but I can't change it, I'm too old.

Julian: What do you think it sounds like to other people?

Deborah: Ridiculous! (LAUGHS) And you can see them thinking it.[19]

Barry Humphries first met Julian in the late 1960s, and they made three television programmes together. The first was about the late-nineteenth-century Anglo–Australian artist Charles Conder, who had died at the age of forty from syphilis – Humphries was passionately interested in him and collected his works. The second film was made in Dieppe in 1977 and took as its subject artists and writers – Walter Sickert, Aubrey Beardsley, Oscar Wilde and Ernest Dowson – who had congregated there at the turn of the twentieth century. Julian had something of the spirit of *fin de siècle* himself. Then, in the late 1970s, Julian and Barry Humphries made Dame Edna Everage's television extravaganza *La Dame aux Gladiolas*, an in-depth interview with the self-styled Australian mega-star, filmed at the Dorchester. The conversation was reverentially conducted by Julian, while Edna munched the contents of a large box of 'Nivea Creams'. These films were particularly successful and duly praised. However, a visit to New York to interview Peter Cook and Dudley Moore ended in some confusion, and after this Julian's career began to flag. The damaging effects of pills and alcohol took its toll on his work. Humphries once managed to persuade him to attend a meeting of Alcoholics Anonymous, in the hope that, as Humphries said, something 'might penetrate the solid carapace of his Denial'.[20] However, he was too busy giving the group the benefit of his voluble advice to listen very carefully to the words of the others, and the experiment failed.

Julian's consumption of pills made Eddy's hypochondria seem a very modest affair. In March 1979, while in bed with flu at the flat in Pelham Crescent to which he had moved, he wrote to Desmond. Although typed, Julian's letter is full of corrections and interpolations within parentheses added by hand. Visually striking, the letter also demonstrates just how much at home he was in the quite literally intoxicating world of pharmaceuticals and self-medication:

The amusements of being ill: first: THE DOCTOR CAME TO VISIT. Not since I was thirteen in Sussex in 1949 has a medico done that service. A quiet, slightly self-conscious, large-eyed Cornishman of about my age (45 next week) came with an old bag, a pin-striped suit and sat on the bed . . . Since then I have had the Manhattan Skyline of pills: two large *Redoxon* stand in for the tallest of all twin buildings (those ones which King Kong, Superman and many others are scaling or having a dance up all the time – don't know their name). Then comes Emp. Stat. Build. In the form of *Tuinol* (strong sleepers*), jostling in the bedside city beside *Penicillin* (spelling?) is the old friend, the Pierre of pills, *Mogadon*. A rather unsightly piece of modern sculpture by *Benovate* (an *Ecsma* artist [*sic*]) is to be found in the twisted tube in the Central Park of the Bedside Table, China town, So-Ho are rather vaguely represented by Distalgesics, (painkillers, worth a visit. Guide advised**) stocky, brown-glass bottles. Way, way, below, in the carpet of the bedroom – Hudson, swim, deliciously the magic *Perrier Water* (44p. per bott. take care when purchasing this popular site as charges vary greatly according to area). The air of my Manhattan is a trifle less bracing than the true one but just as exciting, just as odd. And of course left out the Museum of Modern Art/Guggenheim: the AntiBiotic, Tetrocyclin (spelling) orange discs glowing in the tube. Of course some people can't see the

point of modern art, if you know what I mean, and *I*, for one –
well, personally I don't mind the stuff, it's the side effects, really,
isn't it?[21]

Well-wishing friends had brought him flowers: 'tulips curling in
all directions towards the light' and 'jonquils with a scent so powerful
that they batter through the 'flu and drug infested nose to knock you
back with pleasure'.[22]

Julian always had a self-destructive streak. During his time at
Cambridge and soon after, he managed to run through two
substantial legacies, each of about £16,000, at a remarkable speed.
He lost and he broke things, often presents he had been given by
friends. He deliberately forgot to pay bills. The American writer
David Plante recorded in his diary: 'Julian said he had to go to court
for not having paid his bills, but he couldn't, he simply couldn't, open
brown envelopes with narrow windows in them that show his name
and address.'[23] And he set on fire his last but one dwelling, a basement
flat, losing all the letters he had accumulated from the many friends
whom he valued more than anything.

By now he was starting to drink before lunch – usually vodka
washed down with white wine – and almost every night he took
sleeping pills. Julian twice admitted himself to the Arnold Ward, a
gloomy addiction unit at St Bernard's Hospital in Ealing. In 1983 he
made diary notes on his stay:

> Thursday night. Exhausted. Terrified of not sleeping. Dread return
> to depressive symptoms. Retiring into self. I noticed I cannot 'help'
> or talk to anyone without a false grin, let alone give any vivid
> account of anything. Terror, mainly of severe delayed reactions. Of
> being a weeping paranoid zombie.
>
> As I wrote those lines the door opened without knocking and
> there was the apparently stern, not very bright, do-everything-by-the-
> book nurse bringing me – oh, true-drug-joy, a second Heminevrin.

It was the sudden having of the dose which was the last straw. Why not use the ones which break up so one does not have the jolt?

I don't see how you can possibly de-intox . . .

Monday. It seems quite inconceivably impossible that I've only been here a week. And only in 'Arnold' for two of the worst days of my life. My appetite is reduced to nothing, my concentration flamboyantly . . .[24]

One evening there was a fancy-dress party at St Bernard's. There was a competition for the best costume, which Julian won by dressing in yellow and doing a tap dance on the table. When asked what he had gone as, he replied that he was the spirit of Lucozade. Despite the hospital gloom, Julian continued to receive visitors – including Lady Diana Cooper and Antonia Fraser, and the Baths sent messages. There were so many upper-class visitors that the sister in charge told them that she was not running a buffet service for the aristocracy but a drying-out ward. Six weeks after his treatment he was drinking again – reality being too awful. 'He couldn't face it except through a vodka glass darkly or "Heavenly Hemmies" (Heminevrin) lightly – any flight from uneventful reality,' a friend he had made in hospital said of him.[25]

For a long time Julian was protected at the BBC by Melvin Bragg, but Bragg – who later felt that he too was one of those who had behaved too harshly – moved on, and career-driven younger men were promoted over Julian and given the work he used to do. His contributions were rubbished, and his suggestions were disregarded. He made proposals for making films about Dadie Rylands and Rosamond Lehmann, but they never happened – and would never have happened with Julian in charge. His last film was about Anita Brookner, whose novel *Hotel du Lac* he had correctly predicted would win the Booker Prize, but the programme was cut to pieces in the editing. The callousness of his treatment, which was made worse by his drinking and drug-taking, made him uncharacteristically embittered and aggressive. The BBC had hitherto been happy to retain someone with a wide-ranging knowledge of the arts, but such was the nature of the change in the climate of the organisation that he was unable to survive. Julian was essentially an amateur in an age of professionals. Tristram Powell, his Cambridge friend, who was now a director and screenwriter, later suggested that he could only have continued to exist in television as an eccentric literary guru on a late-night arts show.

At the beginning of November 1984 Powell and Kate Meynell, a friend from the BBC, went round to Julian's second-floor flat in Ladbroke Grove. He had not been seen in the office for two days, nor had he answered his telephone. They were accompanied by two policemen, and one of them kicked the door down. One of the policemen came down the stairs, his head bowed. Julian had taken an overdose of Heminevrin, 'the delicious nearby assurance of death'.[26] He had often talked about suicide near the end. The weekend he died he was supposed to go down to Long Crichel. Desmond had written to Frances to make the arrangements:

> Dearest Fanny, Many thanks for your happy postcard from Skye. I'm looking forward to seeing you – also Dadie and Julian on Friday 26th, & shall be at LC from now until then. So far I've only been able to get in touch with JJ (very euphoric over choice of Booker prizewinner, and shocked that I hadn't been watching the finals on TV!); and he says he could catch the 3.10 that day from Waterloo. If that would suit you as well, I'll try [to see] if Dadie can manage the same train; if not we'll think again. If you get this in time, perhaps you could give me a ring during the weekend.
>
> Much love from Desmond.[27]

In the top right-hand corner of the letter, Frances added a note in red ink: 'Julian didn't come but killed himself.'

On 22 November Desmond wrote Frances another letter: 'I continue to feel devastated & curiously diminished – almost lonely – after Julian's suicide. Even faintly guilty, at not making it clearer how much we all loved him, faults & all.' Afterwards Desmond always said that Julian was the friend he missed the most.

In 1993 Tristram and Georgina Powell edited a memoir called *A Dedicated Fan*. It included Julian's interviews with Evelyn Waugh and Elizabeth Bowen, as well as unpublished journals and memoirs written by friends. Among the contributors were Patrick Leigh Fermor, Antonia Fraser, V.S. Naipaul, A.S. Byatt, Thom Gunn, Jonathan Gathorne-Hardy, Barry Humphries and Paul Theroux. It also included Germaine Greer. She was furious. She had been 'summoned' to a wake, but she wouldn't go – she had not the stomach for it. It was as if by his last action 'you show us that you don't care'. Melvyn Bragg was more forgiving. Julian – who could look absurdly young – had been told that 'he must have a portrait in his attic'. These words now struck a chord with Bragg: 'The chilly attic was what too few of us saw. I wish I had realised about it fully and gone and knocked on its door, if only to thank him for the kindness he showed me and the pleasures he introduced me to.'[28]

Frances gave the editors the entry from her diary from October 1963, written during her stay with Eddy at Cooleville. Julian had also been there, playing Scrabble and doing imitations: 'I suddenly realised with a pang that he is too vulnerable to be happy.'[29]

15

Loves and Muddles

In 1981 the artist Derek Hill made over his house and gallery in County Galway to the Irish state. Like Long Crichel House, St Columb's was a former rectory, but it was even more remote. Hill received few visitors, and his health was not as good as it had been. As well as the house he gave a significant part of his art collection, including works by, among others, Pablo Picasso, Stanley Spencer, Auguste Renoir, Jack Butler Yeats, Edwin Landseer, Morandi, Graham Sutherland, Oskar Kokoschka and, of course, some of his own. There were also items of Islamic and Japanese art. But he was a collector still and did not give everything away.

Raymond told Desmond and Pat not to let Derek join the Long Crichel ménage, predicting that he would cause them trouble. However after Raymond's death they invited him anyway to help pay the bills. Derek had first stayed at Long Crichel in 1946, and he already knew the place well. He had known Eddy since the 1930s when Eddy, along with Arthur Waley, had taught him to ski. He had also known Raymond for many years. During the war, when Derek registered as a conscientious objector and worked on farms to help with the food shortages, he became interested in edible fungi. Raymond suggested he might like to write on the subject as the *New Statesman*'s 'Fungus Correspondent'. He was hoping for short, chatty pieces like dinner-table conversation, a style which unfortunately Derek could not achieve, and the commission did not last long.

Although not as intellectually vital as other Crichel denizens, he was friendly, pleasant company, Billy Bunter-ish in both his geniality and build. Unlike Eddy, Eardley, Desmond, Raymond and Pat, Derek came as a lodger rather than a co-owner. This sometimes caused problems. Because in his eyes, he was a guest, he felt that he did not have to take on the duties and responsibilities shared by Pat and Desmond, who were the owners of the house. Pat, sarcastically, used to refer to him as a paying guest. And he never got on with the cook Mrs Best: he did not like her, and the feelings were no doubt reciprocated. The problem with Derek was that he had always enjoyed a somewhat itinerant existence; rather than his home, Long Crichel was only yet another of the houses in which he could live from time to time and leave some of his possessions. He still owned a small hut on Tory Island off the Irish coast, where he did much of his painting, and he shared a small house in Hollybush Hill in Hampstead with his brother. However, he lent Long Crichel some of his pictures, including a Sickert, and Eardley's old studio, which Eardley had wanted Desmond to burn down after finding that it could not be moved to his new house, now came into use again as somewhere to paint.

Derek was born in Southampton in December 1916 in the midst of the First World War. The family money came both from shipping coal from Newcastle to Southampton and from a cloth-making business in Frome in Somerset. His father was a businessman, but he was also a well-known cricketer who captained Hampshire for sixteen years and played with W.G. Grace for England. His mother was from a Quaker family, and Derek imbued his pacifism from her. He said that she demanded more affection than anyone he had ever met which led to him finding it difficult to show affection himself. At thirteen he was sent to Marlborough College, his father's old school, but he was unathletic and unpopular, and he was beaten a great deal.

The ballet critic Richard Buckle recalled Derek from their school days together:

> He was tall with the long lustreless brown hair and brown eyes. His features did not quite belong to each other. The big square head and strong chin were at variance with the delicate upswung Modigliani nose admired by the older athletes, and the little petulant mouth which turned down at the corners when he was left out of some gaiety or if someone tried to steal a credit for his work. He was a funny mimic and a story teller.[1]

Derek was saved by his artistic talent, for which he won a school drawing prize, and his parents allowed him to leave school when he was only sixteen in order to pursue a career in art. In the autumn of 1933 Derek went to Munich to study stage design at the Münchener Lehrwerkstätten (Munich educational workshops), a former Bauhaus institution. One of his teachers was Kurt Schwitters, whose lessons included experiments with texture, colour, tone and composition. In Munich he also became friends with Unity Mitford, who had come to Munich to meet Adolf Hitler and meanwhile enrolled at a language college. Derek and Unity used to meet every week and go for expeditions and picnics, and they frequented the Café Heck, which sold marvellous chocolate cakes piled with whipped cream. 'We were children really,' he said years later. 'Unity was fanatical but ignorant: she thought exactly what she was supposed to think and whatever the Nazis wanted her to believe.' Once, when Derek was in the elegant Carlton Teeraum, Hitler arrived so he rushed out and telephoned Unity. She came over in a taxi but left her camera in the car in her excitement. Her hands trembled so much she could not lift the cup of hot chocolate Derek ordered. 'I shall never forget you for this,' she told Derek. 'It's the greatest thing that has ever happened to me.'

After he left Munich Derek continued his studies in Paris and Vienna until the *Anschluss* put an end to the production of *Agamemnon* on which he was working. By the time he was nineteen he was in Moscow, where he lived for two months in the Hotel Novo Moscovskaya opposite St Basil's Cathedral. He had been offered an introduction to Alexander Tairov, who, along with Vsevolod Meyerhold, were the two great figures of Russian theatre during a brief golden age in Russian drama. As well as attending rehearsals and meeting designers, he went to see about sixty theatrical productions before travelling east on a nine-day train journey across Siberia to Vladivostok. Not long after leaving Moscow, the Stalinist purges began. Tairov survived the Terror, but his Chamber Theatre was condemned for its 'Aesthetism and Formalism' and the actors sent to Siberia. Meyerhold was tortured by the NKVD, the Soviet secret police, and executed by firing squad in 1940. He too had been accused of 'Formalism', a catch-all insult for so-called elitist art which did not conform to the canons of Socialist Realism officially imposed in 1934.[2] His wife was also murdered.

Although Derek's monthly allowance from his parents was only £25, it was enough to live on. From Vladivostok he sailed to Japan, where tourists were so rare that he was interviewed by the newspapers. Afterwards he went to China, visiting Peking and Shanghai. He then worked on a boat as a steward travelling from Shanghai to Saigon: his duties included looking after elderly English ladies who were seasick.

He also visited Bali, where he loved the dancers; the six weeks he spent on the island he called one of the great experiences of his life. Eventually, he sailed home from Colombo on the P&O liner *Strathnaver*. The ship was crowded with maharajahs and nabobs from India and Ceylon on their way to Europe for the coronation of King George VI in 1937.

Back in London Derek did more theatre design, including a ballet for Frederick Ashton at Sadler's Wells, until going to Paris in early 1939 to continue his theatre studies. However, Edward Molyneux, a leading Paris couturier – and former lover of Harold Nicolson – had seen one of Derek's early paintings and heard that he was in Paris. One morning he went round to Derek's flat and told him he had to give up stage design and study art instead. Derek agreed. Every morning Molyneux's chauffeur went to Derek's flat then drove him to wherever he wanted to go in Paris to paint. When he finished a picture, Derek took it to Molyneux's apartment on the Quai d'Orsay in order to compare it with the pictures in his collection. The paintings Molyneux owned had been assembled from the fortune he had made from his fashionable and wealthy clientele, and included works by Manet, Monet, Corot, Renoir, Degas, Courbet, Van Gogh and Cézanne. Derek claimed these were the pictures which taught him to paint.* Molyneux, who had originally intended to be an artist himself, and Derek went on painting trips. He gave Derek an easel, but he had to teach himself how to handle oil paints and never had any formal training as an artist.

The war brought Derek back to England and to a life as a farmhand, which was very different from the one he had been living for some years. He worked at several farms, including one near Romsey, where he was sometimes fed on squirrels and rooks. He had to rise at 6.30: 'I have to milk cows, clean out stalls and pick maggots out of sheep; next week I hear I shall have to cut off a certain tender part of pigs, which will be terrible for me and the pigs!'[3] When he found time off from his work as a farmhand, Derek kept in touch with the world to which he wanted to belong. In 1940 his paintings were included in a show called '9 Painters' at the Reid and Lefevre Gallery. Among other artists showing were Vanessa Bell and her son Quentin, Duncan Grant, and Helen Lessore, the wife of Stanley Spencer. The works Derek exhibited were painted in France or earlier. A picture called *La Seine à Bougeville, Sous la Passerelle des Arts* was purchased by Sir Edward Marsh, a former private secretary to Winston Churchill and a significant patron of the arts. Three years later, in February 1943, Derek had his first one-man show at the

---

*Molyneux's collection was eventually acquired by the National Gallery of Art in Washington.

Nicholson Gallery in St James's Place, where his buyers included Noël Coward. With the major museums and galleries closed, the public was starved of art, but the commercial galleries were still open and exhibiting. Although taxes were at record heights, life in wartime seemed so provisional one might as well spend money on a picture as on anything else.

In October 1945 Derek went to Ireland for the first time. He found the country congenial in both social and artistic terms, and for six months he lived in a cottage on Achill Island off the coast of County Mayo: 'The inspiration and revelation at Achill and in Connemara was the light – the wonderful washed light – and I discovered the scenery I love above all. I painted landscapes and a lot of sea pictures, enjoying the sensation of having nothing in front of me except the Atlantic.'[4] He was keen that friends should visit him. He kept in touch with Eardley, but rather than write letters he sent early twentieth-century picture postcards: a stuffed gorilla, lovers standing in the sea kissing, a buxom young woman sitting at a table looking pensive. In March 1947 he sent Eardley a picture of Achill:

> I loved your conversation even though the audible disappointment when it was Derek not Graham pained a little. However I *have* started painting again so who knows? I am glad Eddy likes the frame. This is where the cottage is so hurry over soon when you return from Paris. Early June? Do bring the Sutherlands as ever since I saw Achill I *long* for Graham to paint it. I sent a fresh lot of steak the other day so hope it arrives. D.[5]

At the time Graham Sutherland was probably the most highly regarded young British landscape painter, and Derek was doubtless keen to keep up with him.

In 1949 Derek was invited to paint a portrait of Henry McIlhenny, an American art collector, at Glenveagh Castle, his home in County Donegal. He had first met McIlhenny in Rome in the 1930s. He was a big figure in the local society, such as it was, and throughout the summer he held sophisticated and enjoyable house parties at Glenveagh. Afterwards McIlhenny urged Derek to find a property of his own close by. St Columb's, with its twenty acres of lakeside land which had formerly been the rector's glebe, had belonged to a Church of Ireland benefice near the village of Churchill two miles away. It overlooked Lough Garten and had been in use as a fishing hotel, but in 1951 it was on the market for £1,000. Despite its remoteness and the reservations of his family, Derek decided to buy the house. Not only was it pretty and unspoilt, best of all it was surrounded by magnificent scenery which offered considerable opportunities for painting. Derek's brother John, a professional decorator, helped with the interior. Derek and he had discovered and bought rolls of original William Morris wallpapers, which were being used as drawer-lining paper in an Edinburgh hotel. Islamic objects, colours, textiles and designs were also important. (Derek knew about Islamic architecture and published collaborative studies in the 1960s and '70s.)

Around this time Derek was offered a post in Rome. In 1952 he spent a week at the British School in Rome, and the following summer he was invited to become their art director for a few months of the year. He was given a studio and a room, his keep, and a petrol allowance. He was free to work when he wanted but, in return for various considerations, was to be prepared to take some students with him when he went out to paint. Derek would also introduce them to some Roman artists and give them a certain amount of direction. His initial involvement lasted two years, during the winters from 1953, although this period was extended, and he remained on the faculty until 1963.

Jim stayed with Derek when he was writing and researching *Roman Mornings*, a collection of essays about eight Roman monuments which particularly appealed to him. Then, in August 1971, Jim went to stay with Derek at St Columb's. After a flight from Bristol, there was a two and a half hour drive from Belfast Airport.

Jim, who liked neither Ireland nor the Irish, was unimpressed: 'Derek's house is set in a relentlessly green salad bowl. One felt like a slug at the bottom trying ineffectually to climb out of it.' But he admitted that it was also 'as pretty as can be, a sort of real rectory with a real rector'. Peter Montgomery, an old Eton friend, was also staying but, 'like all Irishmen', he drank too much.[6] The boiler had burst, and there was no hot water, so they had to take baths in a cottage a hundred yards away. After his bath Jim lay on the floor in his dressing-gown before going to bed. Meanwhile, Derek and Peter Montgomery were deep in discussion about the alleged refinements of sexual practices current among the old English aristocracy and the best people of the New World: 'Some were so nauseating and others so comical the mind boggled,' he wrote.[7] Jim thought Henry McIlhenny, with his 20,000 acres and twenty miles of fencing, 'a friendly, absurd cosmopolitan-society, American, millionaire queen. But he was shrewd, philanthropical, and a genuine connoisseur of the arts, with good taste. He laughed at Derek's oversensitivity while Derek cried with vexation over Henry's overbearing proximity – the comparatively poor man at the gate.'[8]

A few years later, in August 1974, Raymond also went to stay, but by then what came to be known as the Troubles had started, and the problems relating to the situation of St Columb's were even greater than before. He wrote to Dadie: 'I went last Wednesday to stay with Derek Hill in County Donegal for five nights. He took me for long expeditions to see his friends and the beauties of the landscape which indeed are stunning. Crossing the border by road entailed queuing for an hour while our soldiery searched vehicles for explosives, which are easily carried [across] the hundred miles of unfenced frontier. Frisking of one's private parts at the airport, and no hand luggage allowed.'[9] They were on the way to a party being held by the Marquess of Dufferin and Ava, and his wife, at Clandeboye in County Down, a young and fashionable couple and patrons of the arts. 'I felt like a dry stick of Bombay duck,' Raymond said.

Derek's finest paintings are probably his landscapes. One can see in the pictures he painted in France, Italy and Turkey, but most of all in Donegal and Tory Island, the lessons he learnt from the Manets, Cézannes and Courbets he first saw in Edward Molyneux's collection. His palette generally included browns, greens, greys, ochres and mauve. The critic John Berger admired Derek's Irish paintings, and he wrote a brief introduction for an exhibition of eighteen works which Derek held at the Ulster Museum in Belfast, 'Paintings of Tory Island: 1958–1959'. However, Berger had a completely different opinion of Derek's portraits. When in 1961 Bryan Robertson, the director of the Whitechapel Gallery, prepared to curate a large retrospective of Derek's work, Berger readily agreed to write another introduction but changed his mind once he saw them: 'such painting was not fitted for today's truth, and he could not go back on that'.[10] Derek told Eddy that he was so hurt he might have to give up painting altogether, but he must not repeat this. Of course, Eddy being a natural gossip immediately told Clementine Beit. She in turn wrote to Derek and told him to pull himself together and have a little pride and dignity about it all. In fact, the exhibition turned out to be a success – it also became the first show in which Derek became noticed as a portrait painter, and after this there was a demand for his work. Within the wide social circles in which he worked there were plenty of people who could ask him to paint their portraits and Derek did four or five a year. That he did not accept commissions in the strictest sense was a matter of pride to him, but he would occasionally ask someone if they would like a portrait without having any obligation to buy. His pictures were generally of members of the Establishment who were well known: the writers, musicians, politicians and aristocrats of what might be called 'the Anthony Powell world', where the British upper classes and the artistic intelligentsia coincided. His subjects included Arthur Rubinstein; Lords Hailsham, Mountbatten, Drogheda, Zuckerman, and Longford; Isaiah Berlin; Anthony Eden; John Betjeman; Frederick Ashton; Kenneth Clark; Steven Runciman;

Osbert Lancaster; Erskine Childers; and the Duke of Buccleuch. His last major portrait was of Alec Guinness, 'so delightful, but so difficult because his genius depends on the anonymity of his face'. For the most part his sitters were men. 'Of course people are quite sensitive about the way a picture turns out: the way they look,' he told Grey Gowrie. 'Likeness is quite a subjective thing, and not everyone agrees about it. Women are especially sensitive, which is why I've painted fewer women.'[11] When Deborah Devonshire hung Derek's painting of her in the shop at Chatsworth Derek was furious. A portrait of the writer L.P. Hartley was so disliked by some of his women friends that Hartley hung a little curtain over the picture which could be drawn when they came to visit him. Derek's picture of the explorer and writer Wilfred Thesiger, which he regarded as one of his best, had an even less fortunate fate. Thesiger and his mother stayed with Derek in Donegal, and Derek painted three pictures. The mother, having chosen the one she liked the best, hung it in her bedroom. When she died Derek asked Thesiger about the painting. After a long correspondence it transpired that he had asked his brother, a former director of Colnaghi's to get rid of it. The last letter he received from Thesiger's brother read: 'I gave it to a student at the Byam Shaw School . . . so that the frame should not be wasted.'[12]

On 1 January 1972 Jim began the New Year reflecting that it was thirty years to the day since he had begun his first diary. After having made scarcely any entries between 1953 and 1969, he started once more in July 1971. Now, he said, he would continue writing for another six months. In fact, he continued writing more or less for the rest of his life. The previous evening he had been reading Winifred Gérin's biography of Emily Brontë, and he was struck by Emily's knowledge of passion, presumably without having experienced it. The desires were there, and although they had been unrealised they were no less poignant – indeed, they were more so: 'It is unfulfilled love which intensifies passion.'[13] A week later, lying in bed, he started to read his 1942 diary. What he discovered was the long-forgotten 'priggish young man' who wrote them:

> How immature I was then in spite of my 33 years, how censorious and absurd. I have forgotten so much that happened to me. Yet I find it difficult not to believe, irrationally perhaps, that all the experiences of my past life, good and bad, the thoughts thought and the things (not deeds) done have not been to some purpose to be gleaned in a later time. In other words I cannot believe that all the million things that have happened to me are for nothing, and will be wasted. There must be an accumulation of my stored knowledge and experience for somebody's purpose hereafter, if only it will be sifted by the Almighty.[14]

The pages had originally been dashed off in longhand, shorthand or typed, and he began to edit or prune them by about a third. After a delay he showed them to Rosamond, an old and loyal friend whose literary judgement he trusted; she was both impressed and encouraging. When he showed the diaries to Norah Smallwood at Chatto & Windus, she and her colleagues were 'mad about' them and accepted them immediately. Not before, as he told Rosamond, he had lost his nerve and taken them back from Chatto, then, on recovering it, returning them again. 'I think they're drivel,' he said. He was given an advance of £1,500, and eventually, in the summer of 1975, his diaries for 1942 and 1943 were published as *Ancestral Voices*. The reception for the book among both friends and reviewers was enthusiastic. In his review in the *Listener*, entitled 'Lordly England', Anthony Quinton praised the author's frankness, his portrayal of the characters who inhabited the distinguished houses of England – 'the good old souls', the eccentrics, 'the Waugh-like monsters of selfishness' – and his evocation of the feel of life in wartime England:

His candour is very considerable. He says that he has excised 'accounts of his and his friends' indiscretions. But quite a lot of agreeably indiscreet material remains, and the reader is not too hard put to discern what was going on in the private realms of the diarist's life. Two specific forms of sincerity serve to vouch for the genuineness of the whole. 'Admiring my slender limbs through the clear water I thought what a pity they aren't somebody else's.' Most people, no doubt, harbour such thoughts; but it takes real grit to let them be released in printed form to the general public. Secondly, Mr Lees-Milne has not drawn a veil over his less successful pieces of historical prophecy. In April 1942, he wrote: 'I foresee a renewal of the German onslaught when the mud has gone and terrible Russian defeat.' The battle of Stalingrad began in September 1942 . . .

The bit of England that this book depicts, from its pleasingly unusual angle, is above all that of Cyril Connolly's *Horizon*, with its articles by hyphenated gentlemen-aesthetes, its editorial pleas for American food parcels, its tightly knit intellectual élite all known to each other from school and university.[15]

Desmond wrote to Jim from Long Crichel. He said he found *Ancestral Voices* 'fascinating, funny, original, extraordinary'; 'for it *is* extraordinary that you write so well straight off the reel'. However, it seemed odd that he constantly described himself as misanthropic: 'It isn't at all the impression that comes through either in life, or even from the book. On the contrary, you seem passionately interested in dozens of people – and not just in a coldly analytical way, but affectionately and appreciatively . . . if it is [not] so, you put on a lifelong act of amazing duplicity, and even succeed in carrying it through (which I should have thought impossible) in a detailed diary.'[16]

Not everyone was pleased. The heirs of some of the houses where Jim had been received were unhappy with his unflattering comments about their relations. Hugh, Duke of Grafton, a former colleague at the National Trust, was shocked by what he saw as a breach of confidences and good taste. Since Jim was sometimes writing about people who were still alive – donors and potential donors – there was some truth in this. Despite their obvious interest and their importance to the Trust's history, the books were banned in the National Trust's own shops, although eventually they relented and agreed to sell it. The criticism depressed him, but by the end of November 1977 he was busy with the follow-up to *Ancestral Voices. Prophesying Peace,* which covers the years 1944 to 1945, was published in 1975. He feared that the book, which used a painting of Jim by Derek as a frontispiece, was inferior to its predecessor, but David Higham, his agent, compared him to Samuel Pepys.

After *Prophesying Peace*, the following two volumes also covered two years and were published at two-year intervals: *Caves of Ice* (1946–1947) in 1983, and *Midway on the Waves* (1948–1949) in 1985. *A Mingled Measure* appeared after a long gap in 1994, and this included the years when so little was written. Jim finished editing *Through Wood and Dale* (1975–1978) just before his death; it was published posthumously in 1998. Each volume in turn was given a title taken from Samuel Taylor Coleridge's poem 'Kubla Khan'. In 1992 Jim was 'outed' as gay by Alan Clark, who, announcing that he was publishing his own diaries, added that his would make a contrast to the outstanding diarists of the mid-century – Chips Channon, Harold Nicolson, James Lees-Milne – all of whom were homosexuals. Displeased, Jim sent Clark a postcard reminding him that he was in fact still alive. Clark's reply was charming but evaded, 'as one would expect', the matter which had led Jim to write.

Jim and Alvilde left Alderley Grange in 1974. They felt that they could no longer afford to keep the house going – and there was the perennial servant problem. Worst of all, the Labour Party had won the general election and the couple's first instinct was panic: 'We are finished. We may as well pack up. We have left it too late. We were warned we had three months to clear out of England.'[17] But instead of emigrating they moved to a maisonette in Bath. The maisonette included a library which had once been part of a house owned by William Beckford, the novelist, collector and, in the early nineteenth century, reputedly the richest commoner in England. After a few months they rented a house in the village of Badminton, but Jim kept the library. The rest of the premises was rented to officers in the naval establishment in Bath, and Jim commuted daily to his library in order to write. His later years were remarkably productive.

Among Jim's papers there is an undated typed letter from Eardley at the top of which he has written 'Not a very nice letter'. It begins with an account of a 'flaming row' between Jack Rathbone and Desmond then continues:

> Well I am very understanding of the promiscuity of your chum. Why should we never be shocked or disapprove of anything??? Of course the reason of the disapproval is misunderstood and one is taken for an old prude. The fact is, I think, anyhow for myself that fucking always has a meaning other than mere lust [and] has to be satisfied when one is young and randy, to over-indulge it means you kill the joys of bed-with-LOVE, or at least damage that possibility. And the more you go on the less that side of it exists for you until you become a buggery old queer with no experience of real love at all. But then I've never felt that being queer is different from anyone else, and the above remarks can apply precisely as well to someone hetero and promiscuous. I do entirely understand your reactions. But you must rejoice in all the rest, your being so fascinated by him, and his obviously delighting in you and your company.[18]

After twenty years, Alvilde had come to accept the presence of John Kenworthy-Browne in Jim's life. Jim still spent time with John and stayed with him in London, and he fretted and became jealous in his absence – yet when he was with him he frequently became irritated. As a man who was now in his seventies, he had to accept that his middle-aged lover had a life of his own which he could not intrude upon. Indeed, in a letter to Rosamond about his 'symptoms of senility', he wrote that one of the signs was 'A revulsion from the very idea of physical love. I find the whole thing not so much disgusting as fatuous. How can people be bothered to do it? Oh how awful the whole thing is – getting old, I mean. Yet I do adore my friends in a "nice" way. And I adore you.'[19]

Then, one afternoon in February 1979, he had lunch at Brooks's club with a young man called Michael Bloch who had written to him about Harold Nicolson and the barrister and writer Philip Guedalla, whose life he was proposing to write. Bloch was 'suave and dark, with large luminous eyes like Brian Howard's, but not chi-chi like Brian. Quietly spoken so that I strained to hear and very intelligent.' Unfortunately, Alvilde called punctually at 2.30 p.m. to drive Jim home, so the meeting had to be cut short, but he had promised to introduce Bloch to Rosamond, whom, like Julian Jebb many years earlier, 'he pines to know'.[20] Shortly afterwards, they all went out for dinner, which was a success. Rosamond liked his intelligence and positive views.

Michael Bloch – Jim called him 'Misha' – was a twenty-five-year-old post graduate student at St John's College, Cambridge. He was of Polish–Jewish descent, the son of a factory owner in Northern Ireland, and he had been educated at the local grammar school. He knew little about, and had little interest in, art and architecture. Writing years later, Bloch wondered what Jim had seen in him. He thought that perhaps, like Jim, he was a bit of a fantasist, lost in a world of dreams, and he felt himself to be an outsider. In fact, as Jim told Rosamond, 'Of course he is 100% un-English and this is what fascinates me.'[21] But they had been attracted to one another immediately: presumably they just got on. And Jim was ready to fall in love again. Soon they began to meet frequently, and Jim became depressed that they did not see one another more often. It was only after Jim's death that Bloch discovered from his papers the exquisite intensity of Jim's passion. Rosamond became Jim's confidante, as Eardley had been during his earlier relationship with John Kenworthy-Browne.

Now Misha. Yes, I am smitten. I had hoped, indeed rejoiced that I was immune for ever more from beastly 'in love'. I have suffered so much from it in the past. But here it is again. Yes, I suspect I shall suffer pain. I always do. 'How self-pitying he is,' you are saying to yourself through a little veil of tears; at least I hope there is just a little veil. But you see, I have to keep my head. He could easily be my grandson, and he has his own loves and muddles, which is natural and right, and talks to me about them. I may be very silly, but I truly believe we have struck up a rather beautiful (don't retch – do you remember how once I spelt it 'reach' and you put your blue pencil through it?) relationship. Horace Walpole and Madame du Deffand you will say). Well, there is something in that analogy.* I make no demands I need hardly say, I just worship from a distance. I don't at all agree with John [Betjeman] that he is mad. Nothing could be further from the truth. But he may be emotionally a-quiver. I don't mean about me, for of course he isn't. He reminds me of Jamesey Pope-Hennessey,† with none of Jamesey's bitchiness, more than anyone else I've ever known well. He is extremely intelligent, and writes the best letters I have ever received. I am sure he will become a first-rate writer. What he has lent me of his to read, part of his biography of his gt. gt. uncle Jan Bloch, the Polish Jew author of a remarkable book on Peace and War (I had never heard of until a week ago) and a chapter he has already written on Guedalla are

---

* Madame du Deffand (1697–1780) was a patron of the arts, known for her wit and intelligence; corresponded with Horace Walpole (1717–1797), antiquarian, politician and writer, between 1766 and 1780.

† James Pope-Hennessy (b. 1917, murdered 1974), biographer, and intimate friend of JLM.

excellent . . . Yes, I loved my weekend at Cambridge. It was really only 24 hours because I had a boring lunch near here with the High Sheriff which I couldn't chuck, so when that was done with, I motored on to Cambridge, and got there at 7 o'clock. We just talked until 2 in the morning. Then I was taken to a guest room in St. John's College where I slept till 9, went to breakfast with him, and talked till I left at 5 . . .[22]

'How long am I to suffer?' Jim wrote in July 1979. 'The last spell endured 15 years at least, and is not entirely over today. Does this mean I shall be eighty-five before I have recovered from this one. In other words, are all my remaining years to be spent aching, waiting for the post, the telephone call, the mild jealousies, the angst?'[23] He put off telling Alvilde about Michael as long as he could, and correspondence from both Rosamond and Michael was conducted via Jim's Bath address in order to prevent her from seeing the letters. He told Rosamond that he feared Bloch's would provoke comments such as:

'What, another letter from that boy? What can he possibly have to say to you that I am not allowed to know?' Or 'I suppose he is a male tart too,' which is not the sort of remark that I relish. Anyway she has been better just lately, and only drops a very few snide remarks. It is awful to tell you this, for I do love her dearly. Only she will not understand that some people are endowed with an inexhaustible supply of love. Love isn't measurable. Because I love one person, that doesn't mean that I consequently must love another person less. And I do love M. It is not what most people would call a love affair. It really is almost platonic, and so I think it should remain.[24]

Inevitably, however, Alvilde found out and was unhappy. Unable to hide her dislike and jealousy, she sent Michael Bloch a letter threatening dire consequences if he did not leave Jim alone. Michael consulted Rosamond, and she dictated a reply, telling Alvilde he was not behaving in a way which could harm their marriage and saw no reason for it not to continue. In July 1980 Alvilde invited him to Badminton and apologised. She told him she had almost lost Jim twenty years before and 'couldn't bear to go through that again'.[25] But when Alvilde discovered Rosamond's role in writing the letter, she never spoke again to a friend she had known for years.

In February 1980 Michael Bloch went to Paris to work for Maître Suzanne Blum, the Duchess of Windsor's lawyer, a woman who, despite being in her eighties, was still formidable. The job was only intended to be for six months but lasted almost a decade. Thereafter the relationship between Jim and Michael was mostly conducted by letters, and they met only occasionally. Jim was sometimes calm and easy, sometimes overwhelmed by passion. ('In some dreadful way I almost wish he would die so I could therefore possess him totally. At times I feel I am going mad.'[26])Time and distance greatly helped, however. Alvilde once even wrote to Michael asking if he could help suggest an idea for Jim's next book.

In March 1984 Jim told Rosamond about a visit he had made to the Edward VII Hospital to see Eardley. He found him 'sitting in a chair with his back to the window, transformed into a very old man, hollow cheeks, sunken eyes, waxen complexion; teeth too large for his tiny head and hands too large for the rest of him. He was very low, I failed abysmally to bring solace, and left depressed.'[27] Eardley improved and recuperated at a convalescent home in Brighton. Eventually he recovered, and sometimes Jim and he still travelled together – to Switzerland, Scotland, Spain and elsewhere, but they were no longer as close as they had been. When Jim wrote to Eardley to tell him that he had sold his papers to the Beinecke Library at Yale University, Eardley was furious and demanded that he withdraw his letters to Jim. It was too late, but Jim made it a condition of the sale that his papers were not to be made public until after his death.* Eardley continued to paint avidly, and in the 1970s and '80s a number of exhibitions of his paintings were held in various galleries. The pictures were mostly priced in the low thousands, and he had a limited success. Since leaving Long Crichel, he had lived at The Slade, the house near Basingstoke which Mattei had bought for him (its actual name, Slade Hill House, was never used). Mattei too tried his hand at painting but had no great natural talent and was never more than a Sunday painter. Guests who sat down to lunch at The Slade were as likely to be the Sitwells as the cleaning lady – or both together. Then after lunch Eardley and Mattei would retire together to the studio 'to do a spot of painting', but each might be found shortly afterwards fast asleep in an easy chair.

In September 1991, while Jim was having lunch at home with Alvilde and friends, Mattei rang to say that Eardley had died. He had phoned The Slade from London but had no reply. When he went round and let himself in with his spare keys, he found Eardley slumped half on the floor and half on the bed with his blue eyes open. The doctor said that he must have died instantly. The following day, a Sunday, Jim attended church. Afterwards he wrote:

Eardley hated churches; would seldom visit one, even to sightsee. Hated religion, a subject we never discussed. The other was his health. And how beastly I was when he stayed last month. Walking down the Centre Walk, I strode ahead, deigning to turn my head from time to time. He was without doubt my best friend these fifty years, for we met at the National Trust towards the end of 1941. All those wartime and postwar years when we visited properties together, laughing, gossiping; he was forever patient and tolerant, someone I could always turn to in moments of near-desperation; and we went abroad together year after year. Latterly a change in

---

* EK's papers were also subsequently sold to Yale University after his death.

us both, no doubt. Old age and bad temper. Yet he wrote to me how much he enjoyed his visit. After Communion this morning, while the Vicar was talking of his summer at Lake Como, I kept saying, 'Yes, how interesting', my thoughts concentrated on E.[28]

The funeral was in the 'dehydrated, ice-cold chapel' at Putney Vale Cemetery. There were hymns which Eardley would have hated. Jim added: 'How sad I feel. I already miss E. There is no one who possesses my entire confidence now.'[29] Not long afterwards he lunched with Mattei at Brooks's: 'Sweet as always, but broken-hearted. For him, Eardley was England.'[30]

16

Olive Green Leaves on Ivory Skin

In 1978, three years after Jim Lees-Milne, Frances published the first volume of the diaries which she had kept for much of her life. *A Pacifist's War* was an account of wartime life, but it was also a celebration of both her love for her husband Ralph and of their shared and deeply seated belief in pacifism. The book was well received. It was followed in 1981 by *Memories*, which was a mixture of both biography and her pre-war diaries. *Everything to Lose* in 1985 covered Frances's diaries of the years from the end of the war to Ralph's death in 1960 and included accounts of her first visits to Long Crichel. After this, five further volumes were published, although Frances sometimes seemed unaware that what she was making public was also hurting people dear to her, her abstract desire for 'truth' having prevailed over everything. In *Beneath a Waning Moon* Jim described his physical resemblance to that of Frances: 'My face is corrugated like Aunt Jean's used to be, Auden's was, and Fanny Partridge's is. As though the skin has been scratched with a strigil. I never imagined this would happen to me. I really am extremely ugly . . .'[1] He also recorded his feelings about her writings:

I find Fanny Partridge's diary riveting, especially as I know most of those she consorted with. Many references to Eardley, who I think comes out best among her friends of the 1960s. She is a very good writer . . . But the more I read the less I care for Fanny. Her prejudices come through the vitriol – anti-God, anti-royalty, anti-upper class (though I sympathise with her contempt for the idle, vain and snobbish like Helen Dashwood). We were both amused to read how much she disliked staying with us at Alderley.[2]

With typical self-deprecation, Jim also said that she made his own diaries seem 'adolescent and low-brow'.[3]

Throughout the 1960s and onwards there was a revival of interest in the Bloomsbury group. In 1961 Michael Holroyd was commissioned to write a biography of Lytton Strachey. The first volume, *Lytton Strachey: A Critical Biography, The Unknown Years 1880–1910*, was published six years later in 1967, and the second volume, *The Years of Achievement, 1910–1932*, appeared the following year. In 1972 Quentin Bell, the son of Vanessa and Clive Bell, published *Virginia Woolf: A Biography* in two volumes. Quentin Bell's publisher was the Hogarth Press, the company founded by his uncle and aunt, Leonard and Virginia Woolf, and called after their house in Richmond in Surrey. It was as if a dam had burst and everyone was suddenly infatuated with the group who 'lived in squares, painted in circles and loved in triangles', and led open and ambi-sexual lives.[4] Over the following years more and more collected writings, biographies, and Bloomsbury-connected studies appeared. There were also television documentaries like Julian's *A Night's Darkness, A Day's Sail*.

Lytton Strachey had died in 1932 and Virginia Woolf nine years later, but many friends and relations who belonged to, or were close to, the Bloomsbury circles were still alive. Among them were Frances, David 'Bunny' Garnett and Duncan Grant. Garnett's first wife, Ray Marshall, was an elder sister of Frances. After her death in 1940, he married for a second time; Angelica Bell, his second wife, was the daughter of Vanessa Bell and Duncan Grant. (Grant and Garnett had, for a time, also been lovers.) After the Garnett marriage ended, Bunny Garnett went to Provence and spent the rest of his life there. In 1970, with the help of Eardley, Duncan Grant went to live in the basement of 3 Park Square

West, Pat Trevor-Roper's London home. Pat suggested that Duncan might prefer to pay him with a painting or drawing each year instead of rent. The large and well-proportioned basement room was without any outlook, but its ample skylight filled the room on fine days with a beautiful light. In December 1971 Frances went to visit Duncan's new flat. 'He has made it very attractive with lovely pictures,' she wrote. 'Besides Pat we only had the unprepossessing "Don" (poet Paul Roche*) and "my new friend David Pape", a dark intelligent Canadian. I asked Eardley what was supposed to be the point of Don? "He has the most beautiful figure in the world."'[5] Roche was a former priest and both a poet and translator from Latin and Greek. Duncan had encountered him in Piccadilly. Although married with children, he became Duncan's model, companion and occasional sexual partner. Aside from the pictures he painted for exhibition and sale, Duncan drew scores of small erotic sketches inspired either by a model or by body-building magazines.

This new, sometimes almost fanatical, interest caused the 'Bloomsbury-hounds', as Frances called them, to come sniffing at her door. Invariably they had already made up their minds about what these people they had never known were 'really' like anyway. Frances had inherited Dora Carrington's copyrights, which gave her considerable sway, and in 1968 she fought a battle with the BBC who had commissioned Ken Russell to make a film about Lytton Strachey based on Holroyd's biography. She wondered why she had cared so deeply. The answer was Ralph: she could not bear the idea that her late husband might appear in some sort of dramatisation.

Even in her lifetime versions of Carrington appear in novels by Aldous Huxley (*Crome Yellow*), Wyndham Lewis (*The Apes of God*) and an all but forgotten novelist called Gilbert Cannan† (*Mendel*).

---

* Paul Roche also looked after Duncan Grant at the end of his life and was with him when he died.

† Gilbert Cannan was a friend of Mark Gertler, and the novel is an account of the unsatisfactory relationship between Mendel (a Jewish art student) and Greta Morrison (a young woman from Victorian Bedford).

D.H. Lawrence used her in both *Women in Love*, in which she appears as 'the actual harlot of adultery', and as a model for Ethel Cane, an American heiress, in his short story 'None of That'. Lawrence described her as 'blonde, with thick straight hair, and she was one of the very first to wear it short, like a Florentine page-boy. Her skin was white, and her eyes very blue, and she was not thin. At first there seemed something childish about her – do you know that look, rather round cheeks and clear eyes so false innocent? Her eyes were warm and naïve and innocent but full of light . . . Oh, she was extraordinary!'[6]

Ethel becomes sexually attracted to a brutish but successful toreador. She is raped by his bull-ring assistants and she kills herself.

In 1936, four years after Carrington's actual death, Rosamond Lehmann's novel *The Weather in the Streets* appeared. Anna Cory, an artist and photographer, is in love with Simon, who is homosexual. Simon dies. Anna goes through his papers and gives away his clothes. She also makes a wreath, an episode which virtually duplicates Carrington's diary entry for Friday, 22 January 1932: 'Ralph brought me some bay leaves, and I made a wreath . . . I went in and put it around Lytton's head. He looked so beautiful. The olive green leaves against his ivory skin. I kissed his eyes and his ice-cold lips.'[7]

Carrington visited Rosamond the day before she killed herself. Afterwards, Rosamond said she had noticed a kind of euphoria about her – 'a transcendent mental clarity that came with knowing the end of her suffering was in sight'. Anna's final words about Simon, 'he looked so triumphant', could equally well have been used by the real woman about her lover.[8]

After having seen off Ken Russell and the BBC, Frances discovered before long that another playwright called Peter Luke had a play – as yet unnamed – with the theatrical impresarios. Peter Ambrose Cyprian Luke was the brother of Mickey Luke, the husband of Alvilde Lees-Milne's daughter Clarissa (Clarissa and Mickey Luke had four children but parted). An old Etonian of Hungarian descent, Peter Luke hoped to be an artist, but after two years in art school the war broke out, and he joined the Rifle Brigade. In 1958 he had been taken on by ABC Weekend Television as a story editor for *Armchair Theatre*, a well-regarded series of single contemporary television plays. Subsequently he became an editor, director and writer of drama for the BBC. In 1967 a play Luke had written nine years earlier, based on a 1904 novel by Frederick Rolfe called *Hadrian VII*, opened at the Birmingham Repertory Theatre near New Street Station. Even in such a restricted space, the play was a triumph, and it opened at the Mermaid Theatre in London in April of the following year. Alec McCowen's performance as a failed candidate for the priesthood who finds himself raised from indigent obscurity to the Chair of St Peter, all told in an atmosphere of purple vestments and incense, completely enthralled the critics. In 1969 *Hadrian VII* transferred to Broadway, where it ran for almost a year. The play was an international triumph, and after this the playwright was free to write whatever he liked or, indeed, write nothing at all. Unfortunately, when Luke got around to writing something new for the stage, he chose as his subject matter the Bloomsbury Group, with the prospective title of *Poor Virginia* or *Poor Lytton*. Egged on by others, Frances decided to put up a fight.

It was eighteen months before Frances heard about the play again. In April 1973 Dadie sent her a copy of *Bloomsbury*, as it was now called. She wrote back saying that it was not as bad as she had feared, and if they were prepared to alter some causes of offence, such as an imaginary three-in-a-bed scene and an equally imaginary Christian deathbed, it might be possible to come to a civilised agreement:

> Of course I'd *much* rather they didn't put the bloody thing on, & so would you & Alix,* Noel Carrington,† etc I feel sure, but I don't think that can be helped . . .

---

* Alix Strachey, widow of James Strachey, Lytton Strachey's brother, and inheritor of Lytton Strachey's copyrights.

† Dora Carrington's brother.

Virginia. I see no copyright infringement, but it seems to me her speeches are so grotesquely unlike her style. She would never have said (Act III. 14) You shit! You bloody bugger! It hardly fits her remark to Vita (Holroyd p. 704) 'I should mind it to the end of my days if he died . . . he seems perfectly calm & cheerful & likes to argue about truth & beauty – you must admit this is admirable (when he was at death's door).

Ralph is of course the figure I find most 'distasteful'. Putting feelings in my pocket & attempting detachment, I think he would *never* have said, & I would like altered if possible:

Act 1 Sc. 4 p29 'I'm Major Partridge.' Who would? Surely a gent (so-called) says 'My name's Partridge.' His rank can generally be observed and commented on by his pips – as the author wants to make the point, nor p30 'absolutely top hole!'

p 31 'bally well'

Christ![9]

The following March Frances heard that 'Peter Luke's bloody play' was going to come on after all. Dadie arranged that Daniel Massey, the actor who was to play Lytton, should come and see her. Frances was furious with Dadie for going over to the other side: 'Now he writes that they "will talk to you about the double (treble) bed scene which he wants to treat very lightly . . . " Meanwhile all my fume and fret has returned, and my desire to decamp from the country and life.'[10]

Daniel Massey was a friend of Julian, and when he arrived a couple of weeks later he turned out to be quite charming. This did not prevent Frances from losing her temper and saying that she thought *Bloomsbury* a hopelessly bad play, silly and piffling, and that everyone she had shown it to thought the same. Massey had read what Dadie had told him and said to Frances that he had fallen in love with 'all these people' but could not see that the play did not represent them. After more amiable but outspoken talking, Frances said that if no changes were made, she must wash her hands of the play and hope it was a flop: 'All this was combined with jokes and laughter.'[11]

Janetta and Raymond went to the first previews of *Bloomsbury* at the beginning of July. Their opinions were, from Frances's point of view, reassuringly damning. They both thought it 'awful, futile and vulgar'.[12] However, the audience laughed. Janetta thought Virginia the worst, ranting and raving, Carrington, hopeless, Ralph 'terribly unattractive, Lytton much the best'. 'Did you ever feel you'd like to leave?' Frances asked. 'Oh *yes*, and Raymond and I talked and got ticked off. The dreaded author and his wife were there and I longed for them to have a curtain call so we could shout *Boo*, but of course there wasn't.'[13]

Raymond told Dadie that he was 'nauseated' by *Bloomsbury*: 'Massey I thought gave the only interesting performance, but failed to convey any touch of Lytton's charm, and of course had to speak the most grotesquely uncharacteristic lines. Virginia a raving lunatic talking like a character in Noel Coward, Carrington with an accent I presume comes from Liverpool . . . The dear public believe that they are being treated to a slice of history. No shape, no sense of the passage of time, just a charade, improvised as it were after too much drink.' But Pat had enjoyed it, and Raymond feared it might last for a month or two longer.[14] In fact, the play lasted for an even shorter time than Raymond anticipated. On 4 August 1974, just a month after *Bloomsbury* opened, Frances recorded in her diary that 'The great joy of the weekend, a joy whose savagery has quite surprised me, was seeing the words "Last two weeks" in the advertisements for the Bloomsbury play . . . I wake up each morning thinking with vicious delight of Peter Luke's disappointment, the intensity of which is I suppose a measure of how much I have minded it.'[15]

In 1985 Luke brought a play about Marie Stopes, the passionate advocate of birth control, to the Wyndham Theatre. It starred Joan Plowright, but, like several other plays by Luke, it too sank without trace. In the end only *Hadrian VII*, a pipe-dream fantasy about a pope who never was, remained as Luke's lasting achievement of the theatre.

In June 1987 Desmond was visited at Long Crichel by a man called Michael De-la-Noy. He had come with a 'cautious blessing' from Eardley. De-la-Noy was writing a biography of Eddy Sackville-West, and Eardley, Eddy's literary executor, had given him permission to do so. Frances was also staying at Long Crichel that weekend, and Desmond told Paddy Leigh Fermor they both thought De-la-Noy 'a faintly queer fish, but not so bad . . . Perhaps only a queer fish would tackle the task, Eddy being a difficult & not obviously repaying subject – hard to catch his curious personality & frequent funniness, both intentional and not.'[16]

De-la-Noy had started to write to or visit Eddy's friends. These friends included Leigh Fermor, who recalled Eddy's extreme speed in driving and 'the way he would be totally overcome with laughter – in an armchair, his knees would go up to his chin, arms clasped round them in total collapse . . . My overall memory: total charm, amusement and far-ranging talk, and tremendous kindness; and total civilization, sometimes slipping over into debilitating sensitiveness.'[17]

Michael De-la-Noy, the 'faintly queer fish', was born Michael Delanoy Walker. In 1967 he had been appointed by Michael Ramsay, the Archbishop of Canterbury, the first-ever press officer to be employed at Lambeth Palace. Three years later, two frank but sympathetic articles in the magazines *Forum* and *New Society* about a bisexual transvestite Army colonel living in Earls Court proved too liberal for the Church of England and brought about De-la-Noy's dismissal. After a period as Director of the Albany Trust* and Secretary of the Homosexual Law Reform Society, he decided to

---

* A counselling organisation founded at the Albany in Piccadilly in 1958 for homosexual men and women and other sexual minorities.

write full time. Since his middle name was clearly more distinctive, he dropped his surname Walker, hyphenated Delanoy and adopted it as his nom-de-plume when he began to write.* In all he wrote twenty books, including biographies of Edward Elgar, Scott of the Antarctic, Michael Ramsay, Denton Welch and the Queen Mother, his most successful book. However, it was the overlap between the Establishment and the gay demi-monde which was De-la-Noy's natural territory, hence his interest in a life of Eddy. On its publication in October 1988 the reviews for *Eddy: The Life of Edward Sackville-West* were mixed. John Bayley's article in the *London Review of Books* was written in combination with assessments of two other very different authors: C.S. Lewis and J.B. Priestley. However, whereas Bayley found the portraits of neither Lewis nor Priestley wholly convincing, De-la-Noy's 'well-compiled and elegantly narrated' *Eddy* was totally credible, 'revealing all, as a neurotic nobleman should . . . there is neither mystery nor evasion in the brisk, sad, undeviating and rather gallant life. Sackville-West called his biography of De Quincey – not, it must be said, a very scholarly one – *A Flame in Sunlight*, and in a sense the quotation fits him too.'[18]

Among Desmond's papers there is an undated letter from Frances, probably written in the 1970s, thanking her hosts for a weekend at Long Crichel:

> Dear all, I never leave Crichel without more gratitude and affection than a mere funny postcard can express. And Easter weekend, for all its mixed weather, was especially delectable, the high spots left in my mind being Desmond rushing to the piano to play Rigoletto in the style of Britten, Pat's memorable wail about sitting 'shaggy and disreputable in his vest' & Raymond's equally remarkable

---

* A friend mischievously put it about that De-la-Noy was really Delaney; to add insult to injury another friend started calling him 'Shelagh' after the author of *A Taste of Honey*. De-la-Noy was apoplectic.

fantasizing about the same vest as painted by Magritte. Lovely! I was delighted to see the elusive Julian again, and the Berkeleys and the Cecils.[19]

For Pat, who walked around the house in bare feet, his toenails uncut, general appearance was low on his priorities. Jim once collected Pat after he had given a lecture in Bath to take him to the railway station. They first of all stopped at his hotel to pick up what he called his luggage – this turned out to be no larger than a sponge bag. He was wearing filthy old trousers, a dirty red pullover and an open shirt; presumably these were the same clothes in which he had addressed several hundred distinguished doctors and nurses the day before. Jim, who always took great pride in his clothes, wondered what his audience must have thought of this scruffy, red-faced, rather 'niffy' man who was also an international authority in his field.

In the 1980s Pat became involved with the Terrence Higgins Trust, a charity which had been named after one of the first men to have died of an AIDS-related illness. The Trust met in Pat's London house, and he served as a trustee. It took three years after the disease had first been observed before the press took an interest in the story, but when they did, the newspapers revelled in the outrage over a genuine medical crisis. The disease had first been seen in the USA, where it had initially been called GRID – Gay-Related Immune Deficiency – and although this had soon been changed to the more neutral, and accurate, Acquired Immune Deficiency Syndrome – almost overnight it became known as 'the Gay Plague'. One journalist claimed that AIDS sold more papers than bingo. Suddenly 'cesspit of their own making' headlines were everywhere: 'Pubs ban on gays in AIDS panic' (*Sun*); 'Aids is the wrath of God, says vicar' (*Sun*); 'Storm over AIDS priest cover-up by hospital' (*Daily Express*); 'Gays put Mrs Mopp in a sweat over AIDS: "Work in your gloves" order to theatre cleaner' (*Sun*); 'Victims of Gay Plague long to die; torment haunts final sad weeks' (*News of the World*).[20]

For fear of a backlash, no action was taken by the Conservative government on the recommendations of the Wolfenden Report regarding homosexual reform. Labour friends told Jack Wolfenden they would have done the same. In 1960 an Opposition motion to implement the recommendations of the report was heavily defeated. In 1965 a Conservative peer, Lord Arran, once again set the business in action in the House of Lords and, in 1967, on the initiative of the Labour MP Leo Abse, the Commons did the same. In the summer of 1967 the Sexual Offences Act came into effect, almost ten years after the Wolfenden Committee reported. By then the atmosphere had changed. According to a *Daily Mail* survey, two thirds of the public no longer believed homosexual behaviour should be criminal-ised – although 93 per cent still believed that homosexuals were in need of medical or psychiatric treatment. The Act decriminalised sex between two men in private (this only applied to England and Wales and did not cover the Merchant Navy or the Armed Services). It was a sort of gesture of tolerance, offered on condition of good behav-iour.[21] But the moral drawn by the press from the arrival of AIDS seemed to be that, as had long been supposed, gay men could not be trusted to control their own behaviour. In 1987 Margaret Thatcher, who in the 1960s had consistently voted for laws promoting homo-sexual toleration, told the Conservative Party Conference that children were being cheated of a sound start in life by being told that they had 'an inalienable right to be gay'. The following year, Clause 28 of the Local Government Act passed into law. From then on libraries, schools and council-run museums and galleries were forbid-den from 'promoting homosexuality' as a 'pretended' family unit.[22]

Among the friends of Pat, Jim, Desmond and Derek who died with AIDS were Ian McCallum, the curator of the American Museum near Bath; Rory Cameron, a horticulturalist; Sheridan Dufferin, the last Marquess of Dufferin and Ava; and Gervase Jackson-Stops, the Architectural Adviser to the National Trust for more than twenty years, and his partner Ian Kirby, a garden designer

– together they had rescued and restored the Horton Menagerie, a semi-ruined folly in Northamptonshire.*

The publisher Sebastian Walker also died. Sebastian and Pat had a brief affair – he was one of Pat's boys in swimming-trunks – and Pat introduced him to Long Crichel. Although the affair did not last, Sebastian continued to come frequently for weekends. He would help with the cooking, a personal passion, and one which generally involved a great deal of cream. Meanwhile, Desmond, who could not cook to save himself, hovered around the kitchen giving everyone else instructions on what to do. There were also visits with Sebastian to Lord David Cecil and his family at Cranbourne and to Cecil Beaton at Reddish House in Wiltshire. He was also introduced to Lennox and Freda Berkeley and Freda became one of his closest friends. Back in London, Sebastian and Desmond went to concerts together.

Highly intelligent and a great partygiver, 'Seb', or 'Sebby', was almost self-consciously boyish, using words like 'crumbs' and 'golly'. Before he left Oxford, he had an interview to enter the security branch of the Foreign Office. He was asked, 'Have you anything else to tell us?' 'Yes, I'm homosexual.' 'That doesn't matter so long as you can keep it under control.' Sebastian replied, 'I have no desire whatever to keep it under control.' That was the end of Sebastian's diplomatic career.[23] Instead, for a short time Sebastian worked in industry with his family firm before going to work for the Jonathan Cape/Bodley Head/Chatto & Windus publishing consortium, becoming their sales manager. From 1977 to 1979 he became Chatto & Windus's director of children's books. He noticed that there was a gap in the market for children's books, and especially for books for babies and small children. In 1978, at the age of thirty-five, he set up Walker Publishing with a loan from his bank of £20,000. The company, which began in his back bedroom, offered top-quality

---

* In August 1989, Margaret Thatcher visited the Mildmay Hospital privately to meet AIDS patients. Afterwards she sent 'a small cheque to help with fund-raising' for £1,000 from her personal resources.

paper and colour printing. Sebastian also paid his authors and illustrators more than his competitors, who complained about his poaching. In a very short time his business became a major concern, children's publishing was revolutionised and Sebastian himself became very wealthy.

Jim never cared for Sebastian and objected to his referring to duchesses he did not know by their Christian names, but in June 1976 Alvilde invited Sebastian and his Australian boyfriend Donald Richards, whom Jim thought 'extremely pretty', to stay. (Richards had in fact told a friend in Australia that he was living with an English aristocrat called 'Sebastian Sackville-West'.) They had been through a mock wedding together. 'They live together in a nice house in Islington in blatant sin, making no bones at all about their relations,' Jim wrote. 'In fact a bit too much the other way. They say things like this: "Unfortunately, being gay, we got no wedding presents two years ago." This actually said at dinner to Alvilde. Really I like their frankness, but not the flamboyance.'[24] However, according to Nicholas Shakespeare, Chatwin's biographer, Donald was a 'sexy, whorey, homosexual who jumped into bed immediately'. He was unfaithful to Sebastian and had an affair with Bruce Chatwin. 'Bruce quite liked tarty men and he justified them if they could also read Rilke and know that Kafka wasn't a deodorant.'[25] Richards was the younger of the two but more experienced than Chatwin. Sebastian eventually threw Donald out, and in time Bruce also grew bored with him and paid for Donald to go back to Australia, where he died of AIDS in 1990.

From Islington Sebastian moved to a substantial flat in Holland Park Road, where he held large parties. Despite this, Sebastian was essentially a solitary figure. He had an insatiable need for love, and his insecurity was at the centre of everything he did, but if one tried to get too close, his shutters came down. Although naturally indiscreet, he realised that for the bachelor founder of a successful children's publishing house to be known to be dying of a sexually transmitted disease would not be good for business. While he was still able to, he decided to save the firm, and so in May 1990 Sebastian gave away 51 per cent of his company to a discretionary trust for the benefit of the staff, as well as authors and illustrators. After he was told that he would eventually suffer from deterioration of the brain, he refused further treatment, and Sebby died in June the following year. Pictures and sculpture from his art collection, on which he had spent some of his fortune, were sold a few months afterwards by Sotheby's.

When Jim recorded in his diary that Bruce Chatwin also had AIDS, he added that Derek, who was rather proprietary of him, naively denied that this was the case. He insisted to Pat that Bruce 'caught a mysterious disease from bathing in the South Seas too close to a whale, or some such nonsense'.[26] Bruce's parents and brother only learnt that he was gay six months before his death in January 1989. 'He had a very original mind, and was one of the most physically attractive mortals. I used to tell him he looked like a fallen angel,' Jim wrote:

I was stimulated by him when we went for long, rapid-striding walks around Alderley. Once we walked from Badminton to his house in Ozleworth, down Worcester Drive, past Oldfield, till we passed the Bath–Stroud Road by Tresham, he never halting in stride or talk. But I was irritated by his false cackle. He was a great self-pusher and publicity seeker, and terrible show off. I recall one evening when Bruce and I dined alone at Alderley. He and I sat before the fire drinking and talking late into the night. I wondered whether to ask him to stay the night, and decided not. Just as well, perhaps. He was very beguiling, stretched on the rug in a cock-teasing attitude. He was, with all his intense vanity, discreet. Yet on this occasion he admitted that he would never decline to sleep with any male or female if pressed, but only once. Nonce with me.[27]

Desmond's health also began to decline. He was getting older. Jim noticed that he had spent nearly a fortnight reading a book about Verdi. He would pick it up, then put it down again, finding an excuse not to read it, yet all the while protesting that it was interesting and important. It would be another two weeks before he started writing his review. This was the same condition into which Raymond also fell in old age. He continued to drive but would lose his way and arrive at his destination hours late. During the summer of 1995, he sat out 'sunning himself like an old lizard or inveigling anyone who was half-willing into a game of croquet'. In November Desmond died of a heart attack. After a brisk walk he had been relaxing in a very hot bath, where he was found by Mrs Best. 'He was painfully aware of the clouding over of his brain, it was not a bad end,' as Pat wrote to Paddy Leigh Fermor in a letter. Pat also invited Leigh Fermor to Desmond's memorial service – 'the junket' – at St Martin-in-the-Fields and 'the modest beano afterwards'.[28]

In his diary, Jim wrote:

I am sad over Desmond's death. Though it is just as well, as Freda [Berkeley] says, for he was going the same way as Lennox, and derived no pleasure from life. Des, so abounding in enthusiasms, so excitable, so fussy about a newspaper being crumpled instead of carefully folded, so very, very clever, so affectionate, sometimes in his enthusiasm laying his head on one's shoulder. I feel sure he knew more about music than any man has ever done, and his programme notes summed up every piece in exquisite prose and with perfect understanding. He is the last of the Crichel four with whom I so often stayed, enjoying their hospitality, good food, talk and fun.[29]

The vicar at the memorial service at St Martin-in-the-Fields the following March allowed it to be entirely non-religious. Pat organised service sheets showing photographs of Desmond at various ages of his life and giving extracts from his reviews. The principal address was given by Lord Harewood. He was followed by Frances, who was too small to reach the microphone, so she remained inaudible, while Dadie, aged ninety-three, positively boomed.

After Desmond's death, Derek invited Sir Edward Heath, who lived in Salisbury, to Long Crichel. It was a twenty-five-minute drive. Derek had painted Heath a couple of times, and they were on friendly terms. Heath had also been for lunch before, which had meant having police all over both house and garden. He phoned beforehand to ask if there would be any 'pomposos', a word perhaps of his own invention which he probably intended to mean important – or self-important – people. On both occasions he was half an hour late but did not apologise. On his arrival he went straight into the drawing room, scarcely acknowledging Pat, his host, and in thirty minutes he stuffed two sacks full of Desmond's collection of music tapes to take away with him. Although in Desmond's opinion musically Heath was better than an amateur, he could not bear him personally. He found Heath physically distasteful. It was Desmond's habit to avoid the unattractive and self-important whenever possible. The former prime minister was as far from the 'warm sweet-natured, slightly vain, and *not* too intellectual, college boy' or 'the leather-and-levi kind' of Desmond's dreams as could possibly be imagined. (Jim, who was also present, described Heath's appearance as 'a beer barrel aboard deck poised on two inadequate supports'.[30]) Derek finally departed, taking Heath, who had made a very bad impression for his greedy, graceless behaviour, back to Salisbury. When Derek returned, he said, 'That didn't go very well, did it?' The other residents of the house were of the opinion that the disposal of Desmond's possessions was none of Derek's business and he should not have invited Heath to the house to take them in the first place. Not long afterwards the story of Heath's Long Crichel raid found its way into *Private Eye*.

Fifty years after Mrs Watkins had asked him where he intended to be buried, Desmond's ashes were interred close to the fence in the churchyard adjoining Long Crichel House.

17

Facing a Row of Books

After Eardley died in 1991, Mattei, who lived another eighteen years, inherited nearly the whole of his estate, including all of his pictures. Mattei's business thrived, and he had sixteen assistants working under him, always following his mantra, 'Remember that gold doesn't necessarily suit everything.' The workshop had a convivial atmosphere. Princess Michael of Kent, whom Mattei had known as Mrs Troubridge, an interior decorator, before her marriage to the prince, was a regular customer and frequently stayed for lunch or dinner. He only discovered her change of identity when he saw her wedding reported on television. Afterwards, she set about refurbishing her husband's collection of pictures and photographs, commissioning Mattei to do the framing. Commissions also came from The Queen's Gallery, but when he was offered a Royal Warrant, he politely refused in case the honour discouraged clients of more modest means.

Eventually, Mattei retired. The Slade was sold back to its original owners for considerably more than its original price. His Fitzrovia property became his home again. It was where he lived with the theatrical designer Norman Coates, with whom he entered a civil partnership in 2006. The pictures which he had inherited from Eardley, or acquired for himself, were now hung on the walls or stacked on the floor, with Graham Sutherland's large 'Pembrokeshire' picture taking pride of place over the kitchen table. Over the years the paintings had already been in West Halkin Street, Long Crichel and The Slade. Some of the pictures which Eardley inherited from Eddy Sackville-West must also have been in the Gate House at Knole.

The collection as a whole reflected the differing tastes of Eddy and Eardley. Despite being so profoundly conservative in many of his tastes and attitudes, in art Eddy was the more modern and exploratory of the two. In 1938 he had been a patron of the *First Exhibition of Twentieth Century German Art*, held at the New Burlington Gardens. The exhibition had been arranged in riposte to Hitler, who had dubbed such pictures as '*entartete*', or 'degenerate', and banished them from German collections. Other patrons included Clive Bell, Kenneth Clark, Le Corbusier, Pablo Picasso, Jean Renoir, H.G. Wells and Virginia Woolf. In a speech Hitler made at the time he, perhaps surprisingly, referred to the relatively modest exhibition in London as the work of 'Moscow and the Jews'. Eardley's preference was for French painting, but, once Eardley and Eddy's collections had been added together, there was a wide selection from British and Continental schools.

The pictures Mattei now owned included a Roderic O'Conor Pont Aven landscape, an unfinished sketch of Chaim Soutine by Amadeo Modigliani, and, unusually, for both Eddy and Eardley preferred representational art, an abstract picture by the Russian Expressionist Alexej von Jawlensky, which must have attracted Eardley by the brilliance of its colour. There were also paintings by Alfred Wallis, Lucien Pissaro, Ben and Winifred Nicholson, Vanessa Bell and Duncan Grant, Frances Hodgkins, John Piper, Edward Le Bas (a significant collector himself), Ivon Hitchens, Graham Sutherland, Matthew Smith, and Robert Medley. A painting by Keith Vaughan given to Mattei by E.M. Forster had originally been a present to Forster from Christopher Isherwood. John Banting's painting of the naked torso of Stephen Tomlin, one of Eddy's former lovers, was strikingly bold and untypical in its homoeroticism: Eardley was sometimes surprisingly priggish. Duncan Grant's portrait of Eardley was painted in his studio at Long Crichel. There were three pictures of Eardley's former lover Frank Coombs: a small, colourful abstract painting; a brightly coloured oil of the Hospital St Louis at La Rochelle; and another very draughtsman-like oil titled 'Chapel des Relgieuses de Notre Dame (Chartres)', in which the colour is much more subdued – the picture is unpeopled and silent and has a haunted, tragic air.

Following Mattei's death, a selection of 'The Radev Collection', as his collection was now to be known, was exhibited in a number of art galleries around England accompanied by a short explanatory film. Starting at Pallant House, Chichester, it was also shown at Abbot Hall, Kendal, the Victoria Art Gallery, Bath, and The Collection, Lincoln. In London it was shown at the Redfern Gallery in Cork Street, the gallery which Napier Alington had helped open with his loan of £500 eighty years earlier. After Duncan Grant's death, his erotic sketches were bequeathed to Edward Le Bas, who, in turn, left them to Eardley. Subsequently they were inherited by Mattei. They have now been given to the Charleston Trust.

Raymond and Desmond came for drinks with Frances bringing Monroe Wheeler and Glenway Wescott. 'Both were voluble, friendly, liking to talk about themselves and about money,' she wrote. 'They both treated me with a sort of deferential respect – as what? A dodo? On leaving, Monroe Wheeler took me aside and said, 'Raymond told me just now you were the woman of greatest intellect he knew. But don't tell him I told you,' and he squeezed my arm, and said he would like to come and see me in London,' but of course he won't.[1] Wescott died of a stroke on 22 February 1987 aged eighty-five. He was acclaimed as one of the last major expatriate American writers who had lived in France in the 1920s and '30s. Andy Warhol died on the same day. Wescott's final novel was also his most commercially successful. But it had been published in 1945. His obituary in *The Times* said:

> After this Wescott slipped into inactivity. The late Henry Yorke (the novelist, Henry Green) described his own recreation in *Who's Who*

as 'romancing over a bottle to a good band'. In Wescott's case the good band was missing; but the conversation ranging over the many strange things this elegant and rather tragic writer had seen and over those famous authors he had known was excellent. He did enough to be remembered so long as fiction is read and may, perhaps, be complimented on choosing silence (except for two trifling non-fiction books) when he had no more to say. He was unmarried.[2]

In his will Wescott left everything to Monroe Wheeler. Wheeler too had had a stroke. He was addicted to painkillers for his sciatica, was in a wheelchair and had limited vision. Book dealers and others took advantage of his incapacity, and there were thefts from his New York apartment. A number of major libraries now vied for Wescott's papers, and only two days after a memorial for Wescott, Wheeler had a visitor from a university library bringing a document for him to sign. Wheeler asked his visitor to leave it behind. Arriving the next day, a friend and protégé – all his life Wheeler had protégés – saw that it was a one-paragraph contract that would have turned all Wescott and Wheeler's papers over to the library, with terms to be decided later. Wheeler turned to the wall and wept at the heartlessness of it all. Despite having turned eighty-nine and his physical frailty, in late July 1988 he made a last visit to England with the MoMA International Council. He told several people, 'I want to see London again, to see a certain painting, and to visit a certain friend.'[3] Shortly after his return to New York, Monroe Wheeler – 'Monie' as Eardley had called him – died in his apartment. The *New York Times* obituary recalled his early acquaintance with Picasso, Renoir and Chagall, and his efforts in bringing their work to America. It cited his supervision of more than 350 books on the visual arts and his curating of dozens of exhibitions.

The Glenway Wescott and Monroe Wheeler archives were purchased by the Beinecke Library at Yale University.

* * *

In 1972 Elizabeth Bowen, who had smoked sixty cigarettes a day for most of her adult life, developed lung cancer. She died in February 1973 in University College Hospital, London, and was buried in her husband's grave in St Colman's Church in Farahy in County Cork. In December that year Charles Ritchie recorded in his diary:

> Each night for the last three nights I have dreamed of E. Each dream has been a variation of the same theme, alienation. Either in my dream I have in some way neglected or angered her or she has retreated from me, so that last [night] I dreamt that I stood facing a row of books saying, 'Perhaps I can find her here since she eludes me and I elude her.' . . .
>
> I need to know again from her that I was her life. I would give anything I have to talk to her again, just for an hour. If she ever thought she loved me more than I loved her, she is revenged.[4]

Rosamond Lehmann wrote Elizabeth's obituary for the *New Statesman*. Their friendship had lasted. Its great trial had been the party at Bowen's Court when she had spent the night with Goronwy Rees, whom Elizabeth had wanted. The following morning, he was ordered from the house. Isaiah Berlin, who was present, said Elizabeth was mad with jealousy. The recurring theme of Rosamond's own books had been women wronged in love, a story she too knew well. Tall and exotically beautiful as a young woman, as she aged Rosamond stayed as vain as ever. She coloured her hair and grew fat, and Maurice Bowra cruelly called her 'a meringue-utan'. But she was warm-hearted and welcoming. Jim's lasting memory of 'Ros' was of dining in her pretty flat in Eaton Square behind windows looking down on tree tops. Three was her favourite number if her two guests were congenial to one another:

> Talk would range over every subject under, and one might say, behind the sun. Slowly and deliberately, after much forethought, and between short gusts of rather stifled laughter as though seeking

our approval, Rosamond would give rein, in clear and earnest tones remarkable for their sincerity, to her views while reclining on the sofa, enveloped in a kaftan, her noble head always in profile, gazing, seldom at her interlocutor, but into space, and pulling at a cigarette in a long, elegant holder.[5]

Rosamond died at her London home in March 1990.

In 1975 Jim and Alvilde moved to Essex House, a pretty Queen Anne house at the gates of Badminton House. It was lime-washed the colour of pale blood oranges. Before long the house was decorated by Alvilde in an elegant Anglo-French style, and they entertained there almost every weekend, all meals being eaten in the kitchen. While Jim was earning a modest income from his books, Alvilde, somewhat unexpectedly, produced several bestselling books of her own. At the suggestion of Sebastian Walker when he was still at Chatto, she and a fellow gardener Rosemary Verey compiled a lavishly illustrated volume entitled *The Englishwoman's Garden*. Forty, mostly upper-class, women wrote about the gardens they had created. This was followed by *The Englishman's Garden*, *The Englishwoman's House* and *The Englishman's Room* (which included an essay by Jim). She also designed gardens for the Queen of Jordan, Valéry Giscard d'Estaing, the French president and Mick Jagger at his *manoir* at Amboise on the Loire. After forty years of marriage, during which it was always her husband who received every attention, Alvilde was acknowledged in her own right. In August 1989 she celebrated her eightieth birthday with a large party. Jim prepared the invitations, writing in the corner of each one that there were to be no presents. Alvilde opened every envelope and crossed out what he had just written.

Jim was asked if he would accept a CBE, but he was not interested. He could not be bothered with the fuss. He admitted that he would have accepted a knighthood, because that was an honour he could have shared with Alvilde, but otherwise he saw little point to it all. In 1988 he was visited by Roy Strong, who was making a programme about the National Trust for a Radio 4 series called *Pillars of Society*. Strong recorded in his own diaries that James Lees-Milne was 'vintage material' and, until he got tired, had given 'a great performance'.[6] He had succeeded in getting out of him what he had thought he would not, that Jim knew perfectly well that he was taking the Trust in a different direction with his scheme for rescuing beleaguered country houses, despite the fact that a lot of members of the Committee, who remembered the aims and context of 1895, objected. That was something which would go into the BBC archives.

As a former director of both the National Portrait Gallery and the Victoria and Albert Museum, and an Establishment figure himself, Strong reflected on how fascinating it was to analyse such a great cultural institution. He concluded that the rise of the National Trust, along with the cult of heritage, coincided with the decline of the place once occupied by the Church of England in the mental mythology of the middle classes. The worship of God had been replaced by one of heritage. The voluntary stewards, guides and housekeepers were like churchwardens, sidesmen and congregation ministering to a building, formerly the church but now the country house, which was a shrine of past national glory and repository of a lost golden life of refined cultured gentility: 'On the whole the National Trust emerged out of it very well, in spite of its sanitized vision of England and a version of history in which all conflict is removed.'[7]

Jim's account of his meeting with Roy Strong was more self-effacing: 'Don't know if I was any good. Roy is charming, gentle and modest. Brought four copies of my diaries to sign; said my *Tudor Renaissance* [1951] first inspired his interest in Tudor art. I am bewildered at times when clever people tell me what I have done for the cause. He asked me if I thought I had had insufficient recognition. Of course I deprecated that notion.'[8]

Yet Jim was undeniably responsible for beguiling dozens of owners – reluctant, suspicious, eager or desperate alike – to hand over their houses, contents and estates into the hands of the National Trust and rescue them from being either turned into institutional use or from the wrecking ball.

Alvilde died suddenly in March 1994. Jim was filled with remorse, but at the same time it was a liberation of sorts. He also decided that he both preferred the society of women and to disapprove of homosexuality: 'The male persona has little allure. I suppose that, by a tilt of the scales, a nudge from the tip of an angel's wing, I would have been "normal" from adolescence onwards. Perhaps it is just as well that this was not the case, as I would probably have been a nasty, intolerant, anti-queer young fogey.'[9] He continued to write, but much of his time was spent with friends and family.

On a visit to Diana Mosley, an old love, at Orsay in France, Jim fell ill. On his return to England he was taken as a patient to the Royal United Hospital, Bath. He wrote in his diary: 'Debo phoned at 6.35. Walked away elated by my talk with her and went into the wrong ward. Approached what corresponded with my bed by the window & was about to get into it when a terrified lady gave a yelp of horror. My handwriting is very shakey [sic]. Damn it.'[10]

This was the last entry Jim ever made. His final diary was a marbled notebook headed simply 'November 1997'. Very frail after a major operation for cancer, the doctors were unable to do much more for him. At the end of November Jim was transferred from Bath to Tetbury Cottage Hospital, where he died in the early hours of Sunday, 28 December 1997.

When Derek Hill was invited to accept a CBE in the Queen's Birthday Honours list of 1996 he was deeply hurt. It was, he believed, another slight after a lifetime of lack of recognition by the country of his birth. He told a friend that he would rather have the Order of Merit. Derek said that the CBE was something that went to

Women's Institute stalwarts, and other parish worthies up and down the country. It had to be explained to him that there were only sixty-five Companions of Honour and, at best, two or three painters and sculptors might expect to be included. The Order of Merit was even more exclusive. Jim said that he would not be satisfied with anything less than the Order of the Garter.

After Derek's death at the end of July 2000, the critic Brian Sewell wrote a long and generous tribute in the *Evening Standard*, and his foreword to Bruce Arnold's biography of Derek was both apologetic and enthusiastic. He began with the apology – he had known Derek for only the last five years of his life, never having been interested in him before: 'He seemed very much of the old establishment, the ubiquitous and often noisy presence at the lordly dinner . . . I damned him as a roving painter to nabobs, nobs and snobs, [and] paid little attention to his canvases.'[11] However, they met properly in 1995 and became friends after which Sewell began to look at his work with greater appreciation: he thought his little landscapes would hang comfortably with Corot and the minor Impressionists. Then, three years later, after having flown to see Derek's fourth retrospective at the Royal Hibernian Academy in Dublin in 1998, Sewell realised that he was more than the dilettante many thought him; in fact, he was 'a consummate professional who had continued to develop, broaden and refine through his career as was demanded of him'. In the afternoon before the opening, Mary Robinson, the former President of the Republic of Ireland, arrived. Annoyed by the 'bletherings' of one of her 'posse', Sewell marched over and grabbed her elbow and told her he was taking her away 'from all this nonsense' and he 'talked to her of the sounds and fury of the wind and sea, the salt spatterings on the canvas, the grains of sand caught in the paint, the light and atmosphere, and showed her the meaning of a brush stroke'. It was an act of homage to an artist whose talents he had just seen for himself.

When they last had lunch together Derek ate, as usual, a double helping of foie gras, although he suffered from what might once have been diagnosed as dropsy (fluid retention). He tested on Sewell episodes he thought he might include in his autobiography: 'Affections for young men were the reasons for not settling down . . . His best drawings often embodied the wishful anguish of a man who looks but feels he cannot touch.' Everyone knew this of course, although he continued to claim that there had been three women in his life he might have married had he asked them. But the admission that he had known little sexual contact was very likely the truth. 'Poor Derek – a seriously under-rated painter,' Sewell wrote.[12]

Seamus and Marie Heaney had known Derek and were fond of him, and Seamus Heaney went to St Columb's to have his portrait painted. In a poem called 'The Sitting' he quoted Derek's frequently made words about portraiture: the mouth is not a physical feature – 'it is an expression.'[13] Not long before Derek died, he went to see Heaney again, and afterwards Heaney wrote for him an eight-stanza poem, 'The Baler', about an evening after a summer's day spent baling a hayfield. In the poem Heaney recalls how Derek sat at the Heaneys' table as the sun went down until he could not longer bear to watch it and asked to be put with his back to the window.

Derek's funeral was held at the parish church of East Wellow in Hampshire, where other members of his family were buried. Florence Nightingale was buried in the same churchyard. His ashes were divided between Hampshire, the garden by the shore of Lough Garten at St Columb's in Donegal and around his hut on Tory Island.

By the time of his death, Derek had already departed from Long Crichel House, taking his paintings and valuables and the Wemyss ware items he kept on the shelves in Eardley's old studio. He bequeathed his Wemyss ware to the Prince of Wales.

The 40,000 letters and documents in his archive – Derek was a hoarder – were accepted by the Northern Ireland Records Office. Derek and his brothers owned a cottage in Hollybush Hill in Hampstead, where Derek always kept his own, very untidy, room.

A picture of the room was included in Alvilde Lees-Milne's book *The Englishman's Room*. Derek contributed a brief essay:

> Hating to get rid of things probably represents some Freudian twist in me, and my wish to own something belonging to friends who have died is romantic and sentimental. Syrie Maugham's daughter gave me a rock crystal parrot that always stood on her mother's desk and reminds me that Syrie gave a luncheon party for my first exhibition when I was eighteen – a day when half the sophisticated world of Paris could be invited because of their being in London to view Princess Marina's wedding presents . . .[14]

A small brown plaque has recently been fixed to the wall of the Hampstead house: 'Derek Hill (1916–2000) Painter lived here (1947–2000)'. Mostly, in fact, Derek lived somewhere else entirely.

Frances Partridge became something of a celebrity in her own right. In March 1994, at the age of ninety-three, she was invited to be interviewed about her life by Sue Lawley, and to choose eight records, for *Desert Island Discs* on Radio 4. Frances said that she regarded the greatest success of her life was to have known the most interesting people of her time. Maynard Keynes was the most brilliant person she had ever met – and, although she recalled his blue eyes, due to the passing of time, she could no longer bring to mind Dora Carrington's voice. Her music choices were mostly classical, but, because as a young woman she had loved dancing so much, among the discs she chose 'Ain't Misbehavin'' by Fats Waller. The book she would want to take with her was the *Memoirs of the Duc de Saint-Simon*, and her luxury was a flower press: along with all her other interests Frances had also been a semi-professional botanist. She died in February 2004, a few weeks before her 104th birthday.

Pat Trevor-Roper was always interested in the young, and he was popular with them. He had an endless sense of fun. By popular acclaim he was chairman or president of many medical-student clubs, and he also founded Westminster Hospital's arts festival. He continued to campaign for the lowering of the age of consent for men to sixteen, which he had recommended in the Wolfenden Report. In 1994 the age of consent was lowered to eighteen, then finally to sixteen in the Sexual Offences (Amendment) Act of 2000. In 2003 Pat was diagnosed with Alzheimer's disease. The following year he developed cancer in his neck, and he died in April 2004 at the age of eighty-seven. In his unassuming self-written obituary for the *British Medical Journal* he claimed that 'he was a diffident bachelor of modest erudition and talent but enjoyed tilting at social prejudices within his reach'.[15] Which was, of course, to vastly underestimate his achievements. His funeral service was held in St Marylebone parish church and a buffet was set up in the churchyard afterwards. It was provided by the Chinese restaurant where he was a frequent patron. The friendly waiters had helped bring Pat pleasure and satisfaction in the last years of his life. Pat was buried beside Desmond in the Long Crichel churchyard and only yards away from his home of nearly forty years.

In March 1972 Jim was dining with his niece and her husband at their home near Cirencester and found himself sitting next to Napier Alington's daughter Mary Anna Marten. Napier had been dead for more than thirty years, and Mary Anna was forty-two.

'She has some strong appeal,' he wrote. 'I don't know that she is strictly beautiful although her head is very splendid: piles of raven-black hair, and she carries herself and moves like a queen. Has a whimsical smile, is earnest, intense and intelligent. She talks with uncompromising politeness which is always a little disconcerting. Puts one in one's place. I am intrigued.'[16]

Jim was attracted by women who both charmed and intimidated. Seventeen years had passed since the Crichel Down Affair. Since then there had been also a dispute with the Ramblers Association about the closing or realigning of footpaths. Deeply private, Mary Anna hated having her property overlooked.

With their six children, five girls and a boy called Napier, the growing Marten family needed greater space. In 1962 the girls' school tenancy – which Mary Anna had hated – was terminated, and Toby and Mary Anna Marten and their children moved into Crichel House. They embarked upon an ambitious programme of repair, restoration and reduction. The Victorian north wings were pulled down, the roof repaired and the water supply improved. An elegant upstairs salon which had been divided into three bedrooms was opened up again. This was where they mostly lived, while the state rooms downstairs were reserved for special occasions. The rooms were also extensively redecorated. John Fowler in Brook Street being closed for lunch, Mary Anna turned to Malletts instead for their advice and workmanship. In the Crichel cellars they found dozens of boxes full of objects which her father had sent home from his overseas travels but had never opened.

Mary Anna also had an interest in art and antiques. As her children grew up, she became actively involved with the British Museum, taking a particular interest in the Romano-British department and its staff. She became a trustee and chaired the Buildings and Development Committee for the Great Court, which was completed for the Millennium. On the retirement of the director she presented the museum with a lost 'Coburg Eagle' brooch which she had identified; it was one of twelve designed by Prince Albert and given by Queen Victoria to her train-bearers after her wedding.

She was also an equally enthusiastic trustee of the Royal Collections, going on one of its courses for curators. She travelled to Russia more than thirty times, visiting the Hermitage in St Petersburg. Her interest in Persian culture and archaeology came about when Tim, her brother-in-law, was head of chancery at the embassy in Tehran. She returned many times, and, in memory of the orientalist Vladimir Lukonin, she set up the Ancient Persia Fund at the British Academy with the aim of promoting the study of Iran and the surrounding areas in pre-Islamic times. Many other charities interested her. She was a member of the appeals committee for the spire of Salisbury Cathedral, and she was also a trustee of the Charles Sturt Museum in South Australia.* Sturt's journal of the River Murray expedition was offered for sale, but the Australian state and federal authorities were insufficiently interested, and it was bought by the British Library instead.

Appointed Deputy Lieutenant of Dorset and OBE in 1979, and High Sheriff from 1989 to 1990, in 2008 Mary Anna published *As It Was*, the story of her life. Her husband Toby having predeceased her in 1997, Mary Anna Marten survived him by thirteen years and died in January 2010. Her eldest daughter Victoria attended the funeral as High Sheriff; she was wearing the dress and hat which her mother had worn when she had held the office.

Over the course of her lifetime she had collected jade, rare books (Cecil Beaton designed her book plate) and Chinese works of art, as well as Persian artefacts. After her death, Crichel House and its 5,000-acre estate – which included four villages, a church, a school and a cricket pitch – as well as many of her possessions, were put up for sale in order to provide for her six children and other beneficiaries. In 2013 the house, together with its furniture and pictures, the park, 1,500 acres of land, and fifty houses and cottages, were bought by Richard L. Chilton, an American billionaire, the CEO of an investment company. Much of the rest of the estate was purchased by Lord Phillimore, a neighbour who was known to farm along traditional lines and would be a sympathetic owner.

According to the *Bournemouth Echo*, 'Mr Chilton's spokesperson told a national newspaper: "In purchasing Crichel House, Mr Chilton, who has a rich history of preserving and restoring some of the finest houses in the United States, is excited to restore and preserve its architectural integrity."'[17]

---

* Captain Charles Sturt (1795–1865), a British explorer of Australia. He had a passionate belief that there was an inland sea at the centre of the continent.

For four years, Crichel House and the church beside it turned into a conservation project. Ceilings were uncovered, doors put back into place, the scagliola columns replaced in the Venetian window at the south end of the drawing room, and the walls and woodwork repainted in original colours. Items from the Chiltons' own collection were added to original items sold along with the house. When it was finished, *Country Life* published a long feature on the conservation of Crichel House project. The black-and-white photographs from the 1925 *Country Life* articles had provided useful evidence.

Edward Montagu, Lord Montagu of Beaulieu, died in 2015. As well as having a role in the history and advancement of gay rights, he was one of the founders in 1973 of the Historic Houses Association, which exists to help the owners of historic homes maintain and conserve the nation's heritage. Fewer houses get pulled down these days.

In 1955, at the height of the destruction, two country houses were destroyed each week. It was the greatest loss to British architecture since the dissolution of the monasteries, and, in aesthetic value, greater than the losses caused by the Blitz. For the most part, the amenity societies which then existed were too weak and meek to do anything about it. The National Trust, however, was a lifeline and saved more country houses than any other organisation in the world – Jim Lees-Milne alone probably saved about fifty. In 1974, during Roy Strong's period as director, an exhibition at the Victoria and Albert Museum organised by Marcus Binney and John Harris called *The Destruction of the Country House* was a watershed. The whole exhibition was designed as a ruin, with photographs of demolished houses pasted on to cubes of rubble. It was a magical kingdom of ruins. In its wake Marcus Binney and others, including Pat Trevor-Roper, founded SAVE Britain's Heritage, and in the decades since then the national mood has changed and become more sympathetic to the conservation cause.

In 2001, according to the census, Long Crichel had a population of eighty-one, less than a quarter of what it had been seventy years earlier. Inevitably the church congregation was also much smaller and in 2003, the parish church, which had been designated as Grade II listed, was declared redundant. In 2010 St Mary's was vested with the Friends of Friendless Churches and a few years later the Friends' annual meeting and church service took place at Long Crichel. Afterwards members were served afternoon tea in the former rectory, Long Crichel House.

After the war St Giles House in Wimborne St Giles – which Jim had described as 'magnificent' and added, 'pray God, let the contents never be dispersed' – was left empty and deserted for decades. A tree grew through the roof. However, in 2005 the house was inherited by the twenty-five-year-old great-grandson of the ninth Earl and the 'g-clippin'' Countess, 'Nick AC', a disc-jockey in Manhattan. The *Daily Telegraph* called the new earl 'a tattooed young raver'. The tattooed young raver and his wife, a veterinary surgeon, have since returned to St Giles House and set about restoring the house as their family home.

In 1936, while negotiations were underway to pass Knole into the inalienable possession of the National Trust, Jim stayed with Eddy in the Gate House Tower. He recalled how during the lengthy negotiations 'Eddy's obstructive unborn children became a sick joke'.[18] The discussions were put on hold throughout the Second World War and not finally concluded until 1946: the last signatures written in Eddy's visitors' book were those of Raymond, Desmond and Eardley.

Despite the length of time Knole had been in the National Trust's ownership, it had not enjoyed the level of attention and investment which had been given to other properties of similar significance. In 2010, however, serious plans were made for giving the house an extensive investigation and overhaul. For several years afterwards, the house became a building site, underneath scaffolding and a tin roof with polythene sheeting in front of the windows. Beneath all this Knole was restored, preserved and explored, and yet more of its history revealed. As panelling was taken down, roof tiles raised and floorboards lifted, past decorative schemes, buttons, messages in bottles and graffiti scratches were discovered. Then, when the work was finished in 2016, new rooms were opened to the public for the first time as part of the Knole tour. These included Eddy's quarters – 'Mr Edward's Rooms' – in the Gate House painted in the vivid Bloomsbury colours which Vita had once found 'decadent, theatrical and cheap'.[19] Eddy's books, photographs and visitors' book were put on display. And, appropriately, in his sitting room, over everything and moved from the Armoury where it had hung before, looms Graham Sutherland's magnificent portrait of Eddy, of which, on its completion in 1955, Eddy had written with gratitude to Sutherland:

> I must say I think it's absolutely masterly (so does Raymond). It is the face I see when I look in the glass, but the expression is very different. I always expected you to find me out & of course you have. The picture is the portrait of a very frightened man – almost a ghost, for nothing is solid except the face and hands. All my life I have been afraid of things – other people, loud noises, what may be going to happen next – of life in fact. This is what you have shown . . . I am profoundly impressed. I am quite sure it is a work of genius, which will continue to interest people long after I have been forgotten.[20]

Ben Nicholson thought it a 'magnificent image of controlled distress'.[21] Vita put it even more succinctly: 'It's Eddy to the death.'[22]

When Jim visited Long Crichel after Desmond's death, exactly half a century had passed. 'Still the same beautiful deep-rose damask pattern in the drawing room. House inevitably a little gone to seed,' he wrote in his diary, but he praised Mrs Best's cooking. Only Derek and Pat were left. Derek was not interested in books, but he looked in the indexes of memoirs and biographies to see if either he or his portraits were mentioned and how often. He used to read the obituaries in *The Times* after breakfast and invariably say, 'Another friend gone,' then get up and leave the room. A guest once remarked to Pat that there could not be many days when there was not an obituary of one of Derek's friends. Pat replied waspishly, 'Yes, and what's more, it's always "one of my best and oldest friends".' In the end Mrs Best also left, and with her went 'the boys', her two large and loud Alsatians.

In his unfinished autobiography *A Little Learning*, Evelyn Waugh describes his father as 'a Man of Letters', something which belongs to a 'category, like the maiden aunt's, that is now almost extinct'.[23] The literary salon created by Eddy, Desmond and Raymond, together with Eardley and later Pat and Derek, along with its creature comforts of books, music and excellent conversation, wonderful food and plentiful drink, was made possible by the staff who looked after both hosts and visitors. For a few years this 'prose factory' accommodated younger guests like Julian Jebb from the world of television or Sebastian Walker from children's publishing, but eventually, its purpose served, Long Crichel's days as a literary salon faded away. By the end the very idea of such a thing might have seemed as quaint and elitist as the oil lamps and candles which Eardley encountered when he first came to the house at the end of the war. People don't live like that anymore, any longer than they do at Crichel House, and so the literary salon has been snuffed out, and become almost extinct like the maiden aunt and the man of letters.

The twenty-first century world of modern media and messaging which now exists was utterly inconceivable in Long Crichel's golden, gossipy years. Now, when every village has its own book club, every town its own book festival, literary conversation has been everywhere democratised. Discussions which took place around the Crichel dining table – when Nancy Mitford, Graham Greene or Somerset Maugham were visiting – are just as likely now to take place 'on line' (a phrase incomprehensible to all three writers) or in front of an actual audience. Should any Jim Lees-Milne or Frances Partridge be keeping diaries as rich and pithy as their literary forebears, their thoughts will probably not be written in marbled notebooks but on a laptop. And the letters penned by the Crichel Boys and their friends, Frank Coombs, Rose Macaulay, Rosamond Lehmann and others, which have made this book possible, will, in all likelihood, not be written at all – or sent by email.

By the beginning of the twenty-first century Long Crichel House had new owners. Desmond and Pat's portions were bought in turn by Jamie Campbell and Rose Jackson. Both were architects. Jamie came from Canada to England to study at the Architectural Association. He had an introduction to Paul Hyslop, who became a close friend, and through Paul he first started visiting Long Crichel. In the early 1980s he became a regular visitor: Desmond, Pat and Derek enjoyed his company and became reliant on his youthful energy. Rose was the daughter of Janetta Parladé.* She had known Desmond and Frances all her life but had never been to Long Crichel until February 1993. Rose and Jamie's two young children were brought up in the house, the first since the days of the dreadful Mrs Seivewright during the war. They also set up Campbell Jackson Architects in Eardley's old studio, a practice which has a particular interest in projects involving old buildings. In 2001 they renovated the eighteenth-century stable block; inside they built a 9 sq. metre brick oven and started an artisanal bakery. Jamie spent many months learning the craft of master baker in Tours in France. Rose would translate for Jamie and the English bakers, and also for the French bakers when they came to Long Crichel. It was a cultural exchange of rather a different nature to Raymond's literary one but at the same time probably as alien to Long Crichel inhabitants as the Crichel Boys must have seemed in the first place. Inside, Long Crichel House remains much the same as it was when it was first bought by Eddy, Eardley and Desmond – although pictures and furniture have been moved around from time to time. There is a new bathroom upstairs,

---

* Janetta Jackson had married Jaime Parladé, Marquis de Apezteguia.

and underfloor central heating has been installed. A dividing wall has been pulled down in the kitchen and there are new cookers and kitchen gadgets but the old press used for glasses and crockery has been there since the beginning. Meanwhile, outside, the kitchen garden, the rector's glebe land, has been completely replanted.

On 11 May 2007 the writer Alan Bennett came down to Long Crichel to view the house with his partner Rupert Thomas, the editor of the *World of Interiors*. In his diary Bennett remarked that the prime minister Tony Blair – of whom he strongly disapproved – had gone up to Sedgefield, his constituency in County Durham, to resign. 'Note how in the south-west even the humblest hamlet nowadays seems to boast a business park.' On leaving Long Crichel the following day they drove through rain-soaked Dorset to view the church in Puddletown 'which is full of fixtures and character: a chantry chapel with alabaster tombs and the remains of what looks like its own reredos; there are good pews and lovely Laudian altar rails.'[24] An article about Long Crichel by Jane Hill with photographs by Thomas appeared in the magazine shortly afterwards.

In 1985, when Desmond was the only member of the original household of four still alive and living in the house, Frances wrote: 'A house can't of course be thought of apart from those who live in it, and over the years the cast of Long Crichel has been altered by two much-lamented deaths and one departure . . . yet as a household it has still astonishingly and persistently retained its delightful atmosphere.'[25]

And the croquet hoops are still fixed on the lawn, awaiting the arrival of summer.

Endnotes

Principal Characters

1 Beaton, Cecil, *The Years Between: Diaries 1939–44* (Weidenfeld and Nicolson, 1965), p71

2 Leavis, QD, quoted in entry on Rose Macaulay by Constance Babington Smith, revised by Katherine Mullin, in ODNB

3 Partridge, Frances, *Ups and Downs* (Weidenfeld and Nicolson, 2001), p284

1: Two Houses

1 *Western Gazette*, 1 August 1930

2 De-la-Noy, Michael, *Eddy: The Life of Edward Sackville-West* (Bodley Head, 1988), p184

3 Bankhead, Tallulah, *Tallulah: My Autobiography* (Gollancz, 1952), p121

4 Ibid., p122

5 Carrington, Dora, *Letters and Extracts from Her Diaries*, ed. David Garnett (Cape, 1970), pp417–18

6 Nicolson, Harold, *Diaries and Letters, 1930–1964*, ed. Stanley Olsen (Penguin, 1980), p139

7 Beaton, Cecil, *The Years Between: Diaries 1939–1944*, pp72–3

2: Love and Melancholy: The National Trust and War

1 Bedford, Sybille, *Aldous Huxley: A Biography*, vol. 1, *The Apparent Stability* (Quartet, 1973), p89

2   Boyd, Julia, *Travellers in the Third Reich* (Elliott & Thompson, 2018), p52

3   Ibid., p55

4   Edward Sackville-West (ESW) to E.M. Forster, 7 January 1928 (King's College, Cambridge (KCC))

5   Spalding, Frances, *Duncan Grant: A Biography* (Chatto & Windus, 1997) p267

6   James Lees-Milne (JLM) to ESW, 16 July 1941 (Beinecke Library, Yale)

7   ESW to JLM, 20 August 1941 (Yale)

8   Bloch, Michael, *James Lees-Milne: The Life* (John Murray, 2009), p97

9   ESW to JLM, 20 July 1941 (Yale)

10 Mitford, Nancy, *The Letters of Nancy Mitford*, ed. by Charlotte Mosley (Sceptre, 1994), p151

11 Lees-Milne, James, *Ancestral Voices* (Faber & Faber, 1975), p18

12 Ibid., p29

13 De-la-Noy, Michael, *Eddy: The Life of Edward Sackville-West* (Bodley Head, 1988), p182

14 Desmond Shawe-Taylor (DST) to ESW, 27 February 1941 (Lilly Library, Indiana University (LLI))

15 Stourton, Edward, *Auntie's War: The BBC during the Second World War* (Doubleday, 2017), p311

16 ESW to JLM, 23 August 1941 (Yale)

17 Ibid., p7

18 Nicolson, Harold, *Diaries and Letters 1930–1964*, p225

19 Ibid., p259

20 Bedford, Sybille, *Aldous Huxley: A Biography*, vol. 2, *The Turning Points* (Quartet, 1979), p15

21 Lees-Milne, James, *Prophesying Peace: Diaries 1944–1945* (Chatto & Windus, 1977), p187–8

3: The Bruderhof

1   DST to Eric Falk, 9 July 1935 (British Library (BL))

2   DST to ESW, 8 September 1939 (BL)

3   DST to ESW, no date (nd) (BL)

4   DST to ESW, 15 August 1941 (LLI)

5   Lee, Hermione, *Virginia Woolf* (Chatto & Windus, 1996), p472

6   Martin, Kingsley, *Editor: Autobiography*, vol. 2 (Hutchinson, 1968), p7

7   Raymond Mortimer (RM) to Frances Partridge (FP), nd [October/ November 1940] (KCC)

8   Lees-Milne, James, *Midway on the Waves: Diaries 1948–1949* (Clockwork Paperbacks, 2005), p17

9   Ibid., p55

10 Lees-Milne, James, *Caves of Ice: Diaries 1946–1947* (Chatto & Windus, 1983), p172

11 Nicolson, Harold, *Comments 1944–1948* (Constable & Co, 1948), p250

12 Lees-Milne, James, *Caves of Ice*, p94

13 Ibid., p165

14 Ibid., p255

15 Partridge, Frances, *Memories* (Gollancz, 1981), p92

16 Interview with Sue Lawley, *Desert Island Discs*, February 1994

17 Partridge, Frances, *Everything to Lose: Diaries 1945–1960* (Gollancz, 1985), p98

4: Peculiar Friends

1   Partridge, Frances, *Everything to Lose*, p99

2   Ibid., p100

3   Lees-Milne, James, *Caves of Ice*, p136

4   Ibid., p126

5   RM to FP, 29 December 1949 (KCC)

6   RM to Eardley Knollys (EK), nd (Yale)

7   EK to Monroe Wheeler, 26 January 1925 (Yale)

8   Note by EK (collection of Norman Coates)

9   Knollys, Eardley, 'The Storran Gallery', *Burlington Magazine*, March 1989, p203

10 Frank Coombs to EK, nd (Yale)

11 EK to ESW, nd (BL)

12 EK to RM, nd (BL)

13 EK to Frank Coombs, 8 August [1940] (Yale)

14 EK to Frank Coombs, 10 January [1941] (Yale)

15 EK to Monroe Wheeler, 9 June 1941 (Yale)

16 EK to Frank Coombs, 26 January [1941] (Yale)

17 EK to Frank Coombs, 30 March 1941 (Yale)

18 Frank Coombs to EK, 7 February 1941 (Yale)

19 Frank Coombs to EK, 2 April 1941 (Yale)

20 EK to Frank Coombs, 12 April 1941 (Yale)

21 EK to Monroe Wheeler, 9 June 1941 (Yale)

22 EK to Frank Coombs, 22 April 1941 (Yale)

5: The Sackville Glove

1 Lehmann, Rosamond to EK, RM, DST, ESW, 23 December 1949 (Yale)

2 Partridge, Frances, *Everything to Lose*, p131

3 Mitford, Nancy, *The Pursuit of Love* (The Reprint Society, 1947), p82

4 Hastings, Selina, *Nancy Mitford: A Biography* (Chatto & Windus, 2002), p369

5 Ibid., p370

6 DST to EK and ESW, 2 June 1948 (LLI)

7 De-la-Noy, Michael, *Eddy: The Life of Edward Sackville-West*, p245

8 *Times Literary Supplement*, 19 October 1951

9 *Observer*, 19 August 1951

10 DST to EK and ESW, 2 June 1948 (LLI)

11 Hill, Lionel, *Lonely Waters: The Diary of a Friendship with E.J. Moeran* (Thames Publishing, 1985), p70

12 Carpenter, Humphrey, *Benjamin Britten: A Biography* (Faber & Faber, 1992), p186

13 De-la-Noy, Michael, p166

14 Ibid., pp206–7

15 Ibid., p208

16 Oliver, Michael, *Benjamin Britten* (Phaidon, 1996), p107

17 De-la-Noy, Michael, p216

18 Carpenter, Humphrey, *Benjamin Britten*, p187

19 ESW to Patrick Leigh Fermor, 2 November 1950 (National Library of Scotland (NLS))

20 Cooper, Artemis, *Patrick Leigh Fermor: An Adventure* (John Murray, 2012), p264

21 RM to Patrick Leigh Fermor, 28 November 1958 (NLS)

22 Leigh Fermor, Patrick, *Dashing for the Post: The Letters of Patrick Leigh Fermor*, ed. by Adam Sisman (John Murray, 2016), p309

23 Partridge, Frances, *Other People: Diaries 1963–1966* (HarperCollins, 1993), p245

24 Devonshire, Deborah and Leigh Fermor, Patrick, *In Tearing Haste: Letters Between*, ed. by Charlotte Mosley (John Murray, 2009), pp323–5

25 DST, draft obituary, 'Raymond Mortimer: A Partial Portrait', published *Sunday Times*, 13 January 1980 (private collection)

6: Perfect Life

1 ESW, 'A Fragment of Autobiography', nd (private collection)

2 Ibid.

3 De-la-Noy, Michael, p231

4 Ibid., p231

5 Ibid., p237

6 Partridge, Frances, *Hanging On: Diaries 1960–1963* (Collins, 1990), p146

7 Ibid., p250

8 H.G. Wells, quoted in entry on Gerald O'Donovan by Adrian Frazier and John F. Ryan in *Oxford Dictionary of National Biography* (*ODNB*)

9 Lee, Hermione, *Virginia Woolf*, p689

10 Macaulay, Rose, *The World My Wilderness* (Collins, 1950), p65

11 Ibid., p128–9

12 Lefanu, Sarah, *Rose Macaulay* (Virago, 2003), p261

13 Emery, Jane, *Rose Macaulay: A Writer's Life* (John Murray, 1961), p297

14 Lees-Milne, James, *Midway on the Waves*, p143

15 Macaulay, Rose, *Last Letters to a Friend 1952–1958*, vol. 2 (Collins, 1962), p114

16 Macaulay, Rose to RM, 22 July [1958] (Princeton)

17 Macaulay, Rose, *The Towers of Trebizond* (The Reprint Society, 1959), p200–201

18 EK to Monroe Wheeler, 9 June 1941 (Yale)

19 Lees-Milne, James, *Midway on the Waves*, p198

20 Lees-Milne, James, *Fourteen Friends* (John Murray, 1996), p195

21 Ibid., p196

22 Ibid., p198

23   Mitfords, the, *Letters Between Six Sisters*, ed. by Charlotte Mosley (Harper Perennial, 2008), p243

24   Bloch, Michael, p204

25   Ibid., p205

26   DST to JLM, 21 November 1951 (Yale)

27   Bloch, Michael, p211

7: The Ecliptophiles

1   EK to FP, 3 July 1954 (KCC)

2   EK to John Piper, nd [1946/1947] (Tate Gallery)

3   Huxley, Aldous, *The Doors of Perception* (Granada Publishing Ltd, 1980), p15

4   Bedford, Sybille, *Aldous Huxley: A Biography*, vol. 1 (Quartet, 1973), p44

5   Mortimer, Raymond, *Sunday Times*, 14 August 1955

6   Hastings, Selina, *Rosamond Lehmann* (Chatto & Windus, 2002), p331

7   Hastings, Selina, *Rosamond Lehmann*, p331

8   Ibid., p356

9   ESW diary (BL)

10 Bedford, Sybille, *Aldous Huxley: A Biography*, vol. 2 (Quartet, 1979), p55

11 Bowen, Elizabeth, to RM, 4 August 1953 (private collection)

12 De-la-Noy, Michael, pp273–4

13 Bowen, Elizabeth and Ritchie, Charles, *Love's Civil War: Letters and Diaries*, ed. by Victoria Glendinning with Judith Robertson (Simon & Schuster, 2009), pp221–2

14 Ibid., pp225–6

15 Ibid., p225

16 Bowen, Elizabeth and Ritchie, Charles, p284

17 ESW, diary, 13 June 1956 (BL)

18 Ibid., 22 June 1956

19 Partridge, Frances, *Everything to Lose*, p259

20 Ibid., p260

21 Ibid., p259

22 Ibid., p260

23　Ibid.

24　Bowen, Elizabeth and Ritchie, Charles, p247

25　ESW, diary, 13 June 1956 (BL)

26　Bowen, Elizabeth, *A World of Love*, p7

27　Jebb, Julian, to FP, 3 May 1969 (KCC)

8: The Crichel Down Affair

1　Lees-Milne, James, *Midway on the Waves,* p64

2　Ibid., p64

3　Ibid., p65

4　Carrington, Peter, Baron, *Reflect on Things Past* (Collins, 1988), p90

5　Brown, R. Douglas, *The Battle of Crichel Down* (Bodley Head, 1955), p73

6　Lee, Christopher, *Carrington: An Honourable Man* (Viking, 2018), pp126–7

7　Brown, R. Douglas, p78

8　Ibid. pp78–9

9　Ibid., pp92–5

10　Ibid., p121

11　Ibid., p109

9: The Montagu Trial

1　DST to EK, RM and ESW, 5 October 1953 (LLI)

2　Hansard 5C, 251.1298, 3 Dec.1953

3　Gathorne-Hardy, *Alfred C. Kinsey: Sex: The Measure of All Things: A Biography*, (Chatto & Windus, 1998), p422

4　Partridge, Frances, *Everything to Lose*, p198

5　Ibid., pp198–9

6　Kynaston, David, *Family Britain 1951–57* (Bloomsbury, 2009), p373

7　Mars-Jones, Adam, 'The Wildeblood Scandal: The Trial that Rocked 1950s Britain' (*Guardian*, 4 July 2017)

8　Montagu, Edward, *Wheels within Wheels* (Weidenfeld & Nicolson, 2000), pp117–18

9　Wolfenden, John FW, Baron, *Turning Points* (Bodley Head, 1976), p130

10　Higgins, Patrick, *Heterosexual Dictatorship* (Fourth Estate, 1996), p5

11 Wolfenden, John FW, p129

12 Ibid., p133

13 Ibid., p134

14 Higgins, Patrick, *Heterosexual Dictatorship*, p40-41

15 Lees-Milne, James, *A Mingled Measure: Diaries 1953–1972* (John Murray, 1994), p45

16 Ibid., p43

17 Carl Winter, obituary, *The Times*, 23 May 1966

18 Sisman, Adam, *Hugh Trevor-Roper: The Biography* (Weidenfeld & Nicolson), p105

19 Ibid., p44

20 Wolfenden, p139

21 Wolfenden, p141

22 Wolfenden, p141

23 Higgins, Patrick, *Heterosexual Dictatorship* (Fourth Estate, 1996)

24 Wolfenden, p141

25 Higgins, Patrick, p117

26 Wolfenden, p140

27 Faulks, Sebastian, *The Fatal Englishman* (Hutchinson, 1996), p237

28 Ibid., p241

29 Ibid., p294

30 Wolfenden, John FW, p146

10: The Buggery House at Crichel

1 Lewis, Jeremy, *Cyril Connolly: A Life* (Jonathan Cape, 1997), p454

2 Gathorne-Hardy, Jonathan, *Half an Arch: A Memoir* (Timewell Press, 2004), p164

3 H.R. Coates to DST, 9 September 1943 (LLI)

4 F. Selwyn-Keith to DST (LLI)

5 John E. Jarvis to DST (LLI)

6 H.R. Coates to DST, 30 July 1954 (LLI)

7 DST to EK, RM and ESW, 5 October 1953 (LLI)

8 Ibid.

9 DST to Glenway Wescott, 3 October 1953 (Yale)

10 Rosco, Jerry, *Glenway Wescott Personally* (University of Wisconsin Press, 2002), p63

11 Ibid., p60

12 Ibid., pp75–6

13 Rosco, Jerry, *Glenway Wescott Personally* (Wisconsin, 2002), p89

14 nyrb.com/products/the-pilgrim-hawk-a-love-story-1?variant=1094932433

15 DST to EK, RM and ESW, 2 December 1953 (LLI)

16 Ibid.

17 Ibid.

18 Ibid.

19 Wildeblood, Peter, *A Way of Life* (Weidenfeld & Nicolson, 1956), p80

20 Boyd, Julia, pp193–4

21 Partridge, Frances, *Everything to Lose*, pp342–3

22 Partridge, Frances, *Other People*, p186

11: Other People's Complexities

1   Lees-Milne, James, *Midway on the Waves*, p192

2   EK to JLM, 21 December 1958 (Yale)

3   Ibid.

4   EK to JLM, 28 January 1958 (Yale)

5   JLM to EK, 18 August 1959 (Yale)

6   JLM to EK, 9 September 1959 (Yale)

7   Ibid.

8   EK to JLM, 27 August 1959 (Yale)

9   Bloch, Michael, p247

10 RM to FP, 21 July 1961 (KCC)

11 EK to JLM, 26 July 1965 (Yale)

12 Partridge, Frances, *Life Regained* (Weidenfeld & Nicolson, 1999), p174

13 Partridge, Frances, *Hanging On*, p9

14 Ibid., p7

15 Ibid., p81

16 Partridge, Frances, *Other People*, p1

17 Ibid., p1

18 Ibid., pp13–14

19 Partridge, Frances, *Hanging On*, p62

20 Partridge, Frances, *Other People*, p21

21 Ibid., p21

22 Powell, Tristram and Georgina (eds), *A Dedicated Fan* (Peralta Press, 1993), p27

23 Ibid., p43

24 Powell, Tristram and Georgina (eds), p11

25 Julian Jebb to Rosamond Lehmann, 25 September 1953 (KCC)

26 Julian Jebb to Rosamond Lehmann, nd (KCC)

27 Rosamond Lehmann to Frances Partridge, nd (KCC)

28 Ibid., p52–53

29 Powell, Tristram and Georgina (eds), p93

30 Julian Jebb to FP, 1 August 1968 (KCC)

31 Ibid., p101

12: Far, Far Away from Reality

1 EK to JLM, 28 January 1959 (Yale)

2 Ibid.

3 EK to JLM, 28 January 1959 (Yale)

4 EK to JLM, 12 February 1959 (Yale)

5 EK to JLM, 12 February 1959 (Yale)

6 Ibid.

7 EK to JLM, August 1959 (Yale)

8 JLM to EK, 9 September 1959 (Yale)

9 EK to JLM, 7 March 1959 (Yale)

10 RM to Michael Adeane, draft letter, 26 March 1960

11 J.R. Ackerley, quoted in article on E.M. Forster in *ODNB*

12 Forster, E.M., 'What I believe', *Two Cheers for Democracy* (Penguin, 1974), p76

13 Partridge, Frances, *Everything to Lose*, pp228–9

14 Mattei Radev to E.M. Forster, 13 September 1964 (KCC)

15 Mattei Radev to E.M. Forster, 20 March 1965 (KCC)

16 Mattei Radev to E.M. Forster, 24 June 1965 (KCC)

17 De-la-Noy, Michael, p308

18 Partridge, Frances, *Other People*, p141

19 Ibid., p142

20 Ibid., p148

21 Ibid., p92

22 EK to JLM, 26 July 1965 (Yale)

23 Ibid., p147

24 Ibid., p148

25 Ibid., p158

26 Ibid., p158

27 Ibid., p158

28 Ibid., p219

13: Pat's Room

1   Trevor-Roper, Hugh, Letters from Oxford (Weidenfeld and Nicolson, 2006), p256

2   Ibid., p257

3   Shakespeare, Nicholas, *Bruce Chatwin* (Vintage, 2000), pp158–9

4   Ibid., p159

5   Fleming, Ann, *The Letters of*, ed. by Mark Amory (Collins Harvill, 1985), p424

6   Partridge, Frances, *Good Company: Diaries 1967–1970* (Harper Collins, 1994), p8

7   Yorke-Long, Alan, *Music at Court: Four Eighteenth Century Studies* (Weidenfeld and Nicolson, 1956), p1

8   Trevor-Roper, Patrick, *The World Through Blunted Sight* (Allen Lane, 1988), p13

9   Ibid., p62

10 Ibid., p184

11 Partridge, Frances, *Good Company*, p206

12 Ibid., p251

13 Ibid., p66

14 Partridge, Frances, *Ups and Downs*, p28

15 Ibid., p29

16 De-la-Noy, p274

17 Ibid., p276

18 W.W. Deverell to RM, nd (private collection)

19 DST to FP, 22 December 1955 (KCC)

20 De-la-Noy, p286

21 JLM to EK, 28 June 1961 (Yale)

22 RM to 'Dadie' Rylands (DR), 18 October 1967 (KCC)

14: Through a Vodka Glass Darkly

1 RM to Kenneth Clark, 19 March 1952 (Tate Archives)
2 Partridge, Frances, *Other People*, p163
3 Partridge, Frances, *Life Regained*, p228
4 RM to DR, 6 July 1971 (KCC)
5 Partridge, Frances, *Life Regained*, p172
6 Ibid., p208
7 Ibid., p209–11
8 FP to DR, 7 October 1977 (KCC)
9 RM to DR, 9 November 1978 (KCC)
10 RM to DR, 26 October 1979 (KCC)
11 Lees-Milne, James, *Deep Romantic Chasm: Diaries 1979–1981* (John Murray, 2003), p65
12 Ibid., p70
13 Ibid., p78
14 DST, proof copy (private collection)
15 Ibid.
16 RM to DR, 13 October 1972
17 RM to DR, 6 January 1980
18 Powell, Tristram and Georgina (eds), p110
19 Powell, Tristram and Georgina (eds), p114
20 Powell, Tristram and Georgina (eds), p164
21 Julian Jebb to DST, 22 March 1979 (LLI)
22 JJ to DST, 22 March 1979 (LLI)
23 Plante, David, *Becoming a Londoner: A Diary* (Bloomsbury, 2013), p370
24 Powell, Tristram and Georgina (eds), p168
25 Powell, Tristram and Georgina (eds), p164
26 Ibid., p15
27 DST to FP, nd (KCC)
28 Powell, Tristram and Georgina (eds), p164
29 Partridge, Frances, *Other People*, p21

15: Loves and Muddles

1 Arnold, Bruce, *Derek Hill* (Quartet, 2010), p19
2 Shentalinsky, Vitaly, *The KGB's Literary Archive* (Collins Harvill, 1995), p35

3   Arnold, Bruce, p79

4   Ibid., p98

5   Derek Hill to EK [postmark 25 March 1946] (Yale)

6   Lees-Milne, James, *A Mingled Measure*, p107

7   Ibid.

8   Ibid., p108

9   RM to DR, 8 August 1974

10 Arnold, Bruce, p117

11 Gowrie, Grey, *Derek Hill: An Appreciation* (Quartet, 1987) p114

12 Arnold, Bruce, p360

13 Lees-Milne, James, *A Mingled Measure*, p187

14 Ibid., p190

15 Quinton, Anthony, *Listener*, 4 December 1975

16 DST to JLM, 26 June 1976 (Yale)

17 Bloch, Michael, p284

18 EK to JLM, nd (Yale)

19 JLM to Rosamond Lehmann, 5 August 1976 (KCC)

20 Lees-Milne, James, *Deep Romantic Chasm*, p10

21 JLM to Rosamond Lehmann, 23 August 1980 (KCC)

22 JLM to Rosamond Lehmann, 12 April 1979 (KCC)

23 Bloch, Michael, p312

24 JLM to Rosamond Lehmann, 30 April 1979 (KCC)

25 Bloch, Michael, p312

26 Bloch, Michael, p313

27 JLM to Rosamond Lehmann, 17 March 1984 (KCC)

28 Lees-Milne, James, *Ceaseless Turmoil: Diaries 1988–1992* (John Murray, 2004), p252

29 Ibid., p254

30 Ibid., p258

16: Olive Green Leaves on Ivory Skin

1   Lees-Milne, James, *Beneath a Waning Moon: Diaries 1985–1987* (John Murray, 2003), p151

2   Lees-Milne, James, *The Milk of Paradise: Diaries 1993–1997* (John Murray, 2005), p54

3   Ibid., p128

4   Quip usually attributed to Dorothy Parker

5   Partridge, Frances, *Life Regained*, p82

6   Tatham, Michael, *Dora Carrington: Fact into Fiction* (Cecil Woolf, 2004), p11

7   Ibid., p14

8   Ibid., p14

9   FP to DR, nd (April 1973) (KCC)

10 Partridge, Frances, *Ups and Downs: Diaries 1973–1975* (Weidenfeld & Nicolson, 2001), p70

11 Ibid., p300

12 Ibid., p300

13 Ibid., p300

14 RM to DR, 14 July 1974 (KCC)

15 Ibid., p314

16 DST to Patrick Leigh Fermor (PLF), 6 June 1987 (NLS)

17 PLF to Michael De-la-Noy, 2 April 1988 (BL)

18 John Bayley, *London Review of Books*, 5 January 1989

19 FP to DST, Patrick Trevor-Roper (PTR) and RM, nd (1970s) (LLI)

20 www.gaysinthe80s.com/2013/01/1984-85-media-aids-and-the-british-press

21 www.academic.oup.com/hmj/article/83/1/51/3093555

22 legislation.gov.ukpga.1988/9/section/28/enacted

23 Cecil, Mirabel, *Sebastian Walker: A Kind of Prospero* (Walker Books, 1995), p41

24 Lees-Milne, James, *Through Wood and Dale: Diaries 1953–1972* (John Murray, 1998), p167

25 Shakespeare, Nicholas, *Bruce Chatwin*, pp342–3

26 Lees-Milne, James, *Beneath a Waning Moon*, p157

27 Lees-Milne, James, *Ceaseless Turmoil: Diaries 1988–1992*, (John Murray, 2004), pp89–90

28 PTR to PLF, 16 November 1995 (NLS)

29 Lees-Milne, James, *The Milk of Paradise*, p194

30 Ibid., p199

17: Facing a Row of Books

1   Partridge, Frances, *Ups and Downs: Diaries 1972–1975* (Weidenfeld and Nicolson, 2001), p.6

2   Glenway Wescott, obituary, *The Times*, 27 February 1987

3   Rosco, Jerry, p265

4   Bowen, Elizabeth and Ritchie, Charles, p475

5   Lees-Milne, James, *Fourteen Friends*, p87

6   Strong, Roy, *Scenes and Apparitions: The Roy Strong Diaries 1988–2003* (Weidenfeld & Nicolson, 2016), p8

7   Ibid., p8

8   Lees-Milne, James, *Ceaseless Turmoil*, p31

9   Lees-Milne, James, *The Milk of Paradise*, p70

10   Ibid., p303

11   Arnold, Bruce, p ix

12   Ibid., p xi

13   Ibid., p402

14   Lees-Milne, Alvilde, *The Englishman's Room* (Viking, 1986), p77

15   Patrick Trevor-Roper, quoted in entry in *ODNB* by Stephen Lock

16   Lees-Milne, James, *A Mingled Measure*, p215

17   *Bournemouth Echo*, 24 July 2013

18   Slocombe, Emma, 'The Reluctant Heir' in *National Trust Historic Houses and Collections Annual, 2016*, p25

19   Ibid., p22

20   Ibid., p25

21   De-la-Noy, Michael, p272

22   De-la-Noy, Michael, p271–2

23   Waugh, Evelyn, quoted in Gross, John, *The Rise and Fall of the Man of Letters* (Pelican, 1973)

24   Bennett, Alan, 'What I Didn't Do in 2007', *London Review of Books*, 3 January 2008

25   Partridge, Frances, *Everything to Lose*, p99

Principal Archival Sources

Beinecke Library, Yale
Eardley Knollys
James Lees-Milne
Glenway Wescott
Monroe Wheeler

British Library
Edward Sackville-West

Kings College, Cambridge
Rosamond Lehmann
Frances Partridge
George 'Dadie' Rylands

Lilly Library, University of Indiana
Desmond Shawe-Taylor

National Library of Scotland
Patrick Leigh Fermor

Princeton University Library, New York
Raymond Mortimer

Tate Gallery
Kenneth Clark
John Piper

Select Bibliography

Books

Alison, Jane, and Malissard, Coralie, *Modern Couples: Art, Intimacy and the Avant-Garde (*Prestel, 2018)

Arnold, Bruce, *Derek Hill* (Quartet, 2010)

Bankhead, *Tallulah: My Autobiography* (Gollancz, 1952)

Beaton, Cecil, *The Years Between: Diaries 1939–44* (Weidenfeld & Nicolson, 1965)

Bedford, Sybille, *Aldous Huxley: A Biography*, vol. 1, *The Apparent Stability* (Quartet, 1973)

Bedford, Sybille, *Aldous Huxley: A Biography*, vol. 2, *The Turning Points* (Quartet, 1979)

Bell, Vanessa, *Selected Letters*, ed. by Regina Marler (Bloomsbury paperback edn., 1994)

Benedick, Adam, and Newman, Sydney, Obituary of Peter Luke, *Independent*, 26 January 1995

Bloch, Michael, *James Lees-Milne: The Life* (John Murray, 2009)

Bowen, Elizabeth and Ritchie, Charles, *Love's Civil War: Letters and Diaries from the Love Affair of a Lifetime*, ed. by Victoria Glendinning with Judith Robertson (Simon & Schuster, 2009)

Boyd, Julia, *Travellers in the Third Reich: The Rise of Fascism Through the Eyes of Everyday People* (Elliott & Thompson, 2018)

Brown, R. Douglas, *The Battle of Crichel Down* (Bodley Head, 1955)

Butterfield, David, *10,000 Not Out: The History of the Spectator 1828–2020* (Unicorn, 2020)

Carpenter, Humphrey, *Benjamin Britten: A Biography* (Faber & Faber, 1992)

Carrington, Dora, *Letters and Extracts from Her Diaries*, ed. David Garnett (Cape, 1970)

Carrington, Peter, Baron, *Reflect on Things Past: The Memoirs of Lord Carrington* (Collins, 1988)

Cecil, Mirabel, *Sebastian Walker: A Kind of Prospero* (Walker Books, 1995)

Chisholm, Anne, *Frances Partridge: The Biography* (Weidenfeld & Nicolson, 2009)

Cooper, Artemis, *Patrick Leigh Fermor: An Adventure* (John Murray, 2012)

De-la-Noy, Michael, *Eddy: The Life of Edward Sackville-West* (Bodley Head, 1988)

Devonshire, Deborah and Leigh Fermor, Patrick, *In Tearing Haste: Letters Between*, ed. by Charlotte Mosley (John Murray, paperback edn., 2009)

Emery, Jane, *Rose Macaulay: A Writer's Life* (John Murray, 1961)

Faulks, Sebastian, *The Fatal Englishman: Three Short Lives* (Hutchinson, 1996)

Fleming, Ann, *The Letters of*, ed. by Mark Amory (Collins Harvill, 1985)

Forster, E.M., *The Journals and Diaries of*, vol. 2, ed. by Philip Gardner (Pickering & Chatto, 2011),

Gathorne-Hardy, Jonathan, *Alfred C Kinsey: Sex, the Measure of All Things: A Biography* (Chatto & Windus, 1998)

Gathorne-Hardy, Jonathan, *Half an Arch: A Memoir* (Timewell Press, 2004)

Gay, Peter, *Weimar Culture* (Penguin, paperback edn., 1974)

Glendinning, Victoria, *Elizabeth Bowen: Portrait of a Writer* (Weidenfeld & Nicolson, 1977)

Gowrie, Grey, *Derek Hill: An Appreciation* (Quartet, 1987)

Gowrie, Grey, Obituary of Derek Hill (*Guardian*, 10 August 2000)

Griffiths, Richard, *Fellow Travellers of the Right: British Enthusiasts for Nazi Germany, 1933–9* (Constable, 1980)

Gross, John, *The Rise and Fall of the Man of Letters: English Literary Life since 1800* (Penguin, 1969)

Harris, John, *No Voices from the Hall: Early Memories of a Country House Snooper* (John Murray, 1998)

Harris, John, *Echoing Voices: More Memories of a Country House Snooper* (John Murray, 2002)

Hastings, Selina, *Nancy Mitford: A Biography* (Hamish Hamilton, 1985)

Hastings, Selina, *Rosamond Lehmann* (Chatto & Windus, 2002)

Headley, Gwyn, and Meulenkamp, Wim, *Follies: A National Trust Guide* (Jonathan Cape, 1986)

Higgins, Patrick, *Heterosexual Dictatorship: Male Homosexuality in Postwar Britain* (Fourth Estate, 1996)

Huxley, Aldous, *The Doors of Perception* (Granada, 1980)

Jarman, Derek, *At Your Own Risk: A Saint's Testament* (Vintage, 1993)

King, Francis, *E.M. Forster and his World* (Thames & Hudson, 1978)

Kynaston, David, *Family Britain 1951–57* (Bloomsbury, 2009)

Lander, J.R., Obituary of Paul Hyslop (*Independent*, 16 November 1988)

Lee, Christopher, *Carrington: An Honourable Man* (Viking, 2018)

Lee, Hermione, *Virginia Woolf* (Chatto & Windus, 1996)

Lees-Milne, Alvilde and Moore, Derek, *The Englishman's Room* (Viking, 1986)

Lees-Milne, James, *Ancestral Voices: Diaries 1942–1943* (Faber & Faber, paperback edn., 1984)

Lees-Milne, James, *Prophesying Peace: Diaries 1944–1945* (Chatto & Windus, 1977)

Lees-Milne, James, *Caves of Ice: Diaries 1946–1947* (Chatto & Windus, 1983)

Lees-Milne, James, *Midway on the Waves: Diaries 1948–1949* (Clockwork Paperback edn., 2005)

Lees-Milne, James, *A Mingled Measure: Diaries 1953–1972* (John Murray, 1994)

Lees-Milne, James, *Through Wood and Dale: Diaries 1975–1978* (John Murray, 1998)

Lees-Milne, James, *Deep Romantic Chasm: Diaries 1979–1981* (John Murray, paperback edn., 2003)

Lees-Milne, James, *Holy Dread: Diaries 1982–1984* (John Murray, paperback edn., 2003)

Lees-Milne, James, *Beneath a Waning Moon: Diaries 1985–1987* (John Murray, paperback edn., 2003)

Lees-Milne, James, *Ceaseless Turmoil: Diaries 1988–1992* (John Murray, 2004)

Lees-Milne, James, *Milk of Paradise: Diaries 1993–1997* (John Murray, 2005)

Lees-Milne, *Fourteen Friends* (John Murray, 1996)

Lefanu, Sarah, *Rose Macaulay* (Virago, 2003)

Leigh Fermor, Patrick, *Dashing for the Post: The Letters of Patrick Leigh Fermor*, ed. by Adam Sisman (John Murray, 2016)

Macaulay, Rose, *Letters to a Friend, 1950–1952*, ed. by Constance Babington Smith (Collins, 1961)

Macaulay, Rose, *The Towers of Trebizond* (The Reprint Society, 1959)

Macaulay, Rose, *Last Letters to a Friend, 1952–1958*, ed. by Constance Babington Smith (Collins, 1962)

Macaulay, Rose, *The World My Wilderness* (Collins, 1950)

Macdonnell, Randal, *The Lost Houses of Ireland* (Weidenfeld & Nicolson, 2002)

Machin, Julian, 'Mattei Radev: Mainstay of Bloomsbury artistic society' (*Independent* obituary, 14 October 2009)

Mars-Jones, Adam, 'The Wildeblood Scandal' (*Guardian*, 14 July 2017)

Maclaren-Ross, Julian, *Selected Letters*, ed. by Paul Willetts (Black Spring Press, 2008)

Martin, Kingsley, *Editor: Autobiography,* vol. 2 (Hutchinson, 1968)

Martin, Simon, Vanessa Bell, *Flowers in a Vase, Long Crichel House, c1951* (*Insight* No. XVI)

Maxwell, Ian, *Ernest John Moeran: His Life and Music* (Boydell & Brewer, 2021)

Mitford, Nancy, *The Letters of*, ed. by Charlotte Mosley (Sceptre, 2004)

Mitford, Nancy, *The Pursuit of Love* (The Reprint Society, 1947)

Mitfords, the, *Letters Between Six Sisters*, ed. by Charlotte Mosley (Harper Perennial, 2008)

Montagu, Edward, *Wheels within Wheels* (Weidenfeld & Nicolson, 2000)

Moore, Charles, *Margaret Thatcher: The Authorized Biography*, vol 3: *Herself Alone* (Allen Lane, 2019)

Muir, Robin, Cecil Beaton's *Bright Young Things* (National Portrait Gallery, 2020)

Nicolson, Harold, *Comments 1944–1948* (Constable & Co, 1948)

Nicolson, Harold, *Diaries and Letters 1930–1964*, ed. and condensed by Stanley Olson (Penguin, 1980)

Nicolson, Nigel, *Long Life* (Weidenfeld & Nicolson, 1997)

Partridge, Frances, *Memories* (Gollancz, 1981)

Partridge, Frances, *Everything to Lose: Diaries 1945–1960* (Gollancz, 1985)

Partridge, Frances, *Hanging On: Diaries 1960–1963* (Collins, 1990)

Partridge, Frances, *Other People: Diaries 1963–1966* (HarperCollins, 1993)

Partridge, Frances, *Good Company: Diaries 1969–1970* (HarperCollins, 1994)

Partridge, Frances, *Life Regained: Diaries 1970–1972* (Weidenfeld & Nicolson, 1999)

Partridge, Frances, *Ups and Downs: Diaries 1973–1975* (Weidenfeld & Nicolson, 2001)

Plante, David, *Difficult Women: A Memory of Three* (Gollancz, 1983)

Plante, David, *Becoming a Londoner: A Diary* (Bloomsbury, 2013)

Potter, Julian, *Stephen Potter at the BBC* (Orford Books, 2004)

Powell, Tristram and Georgina (eds), *A Dedicated Fan: Julian Jebb 1934–1984* (Peralta Press, 1993)

Pryce-Jones, David, *Unity Mitford: A Quest* (Weidenfeld & Nicolson, 1976)

Quennell, Peter, (ed.), *Genius in the Drawing-Room: The Literary Salon in the Nineteenth and Twentieth Centuries* (Weidenfeld & Nicolson, 1980)

Rosco, Jerry, *Glenway Wescott Personally* (University of Wisconsin Press, 2002)

Scotland, Tony, *Joy Ride to a Reunion at Kardamyli* (Shelf Lives, 2018)

Shakespeare, Nicholas, *Bruce Chatwin* (Vintage, 2000)

Shentalinsky, Vitaly, *The KGB's Literary Archive* (Collins Harvill, 1995)

Sisman, Adam, *Hugh Trevor-Roper: The Biography* (Weidenfeld & Nicolson, 2010)

Spalding, Frances, *Duncan Grant: A Biography* (Chatto & Windus, 1997)

Spender, Stephen, *Journals 1939–1983* (Faber & Faber, paperback edn., 1992)

Spurling, Hilary, *The Girl from the Fiction Department: A Portrait of Sonia Orwell* (Hamish Hamilton, 2002)

Tatham, Michael, *Dora Carrington: Fact into Fiction* (Cecil Woolf, 2004)

Tiniswood, Adrian, *A History of Country House Visiting* (Basil Blackwell and the National Trust, 1989)

Trevor-Roper, Hugh, *Letters from Oxford: Hugh Trevor-Roper to Bernard Berenson* ed. by R.P.T. Davenport-Hines (Weidenfeld & Nicolson, 2006)

Trevor-Roper, Patrick, *The World Through Blunted Sight: An Inquiry into the Influence of Defective Vision on Art and Character* (Allen Lane, 1988)

Tunney, Kieran, *Tallulah: Darling of the Gods* (Secker & Warburg, 1972)

Waugh, Evelyn, *The Diaries of*, ed. by Michael Davie (Weidenfeld & Nicolson, 1976)

Wildeblood, Peter, *A Way of Life* (Weidenfeld & Nicolson, 1956)

Wolfenden of Wescott, John Frederick Wolfenden, Baron, *Turning Points: The Memoirs of Lord Wolfenden* (Bodley Head, 1976)

Woodward, Christopher, *In Ruins* (Chatto & Windus, 2001)

Yorke-Long, Alan, *Music at Court: Four Eighteenth Century Studies*, preface by Patrick Trevor-Roper, introduction by Professor Edward Dent (Weidenfeld & Nicolson, 1954)

Television

Being Gay in the Thirties, London Weekend Television: player.bfi.org.uk/free/film/watch-being-gay-in-the-thirties-1981-online

Gay Life, London Weekend Television: player.bfi.org.uk/free/film/watch-male-sexuality-1981-online

Index